Medical Treatment and the Law

The high profile cases of Charlie Gard, Alfie Evans, and Tafida Raqeeb raised the questions as to why the state intrudes into the exercise of parental responsibility concerning the medical treatment of children and why parents may not be permitted to decide what is in the best interests of their child. This book answers these questions. It argues for a reframing of the law concerned with the medical treatment of children to one which better protects the welfare of the individual child, within the context of family relationships recognising the duties which professionals have to care for the child and that the welfare of children is a matter of public interest, protected through the intervention of the state.

This book undertakes a rigorous critical analysis of the case law concerned with the provision of medical treatment to children since the first reported cases over forty years ago. It argues that understanding of the cases only as disputes over the best interests of the child, and judicial resolution thereof, fails to recognise professional duties and public responsibilities for the welfare and protection of children that exist alongside parental responsibilities and which justify public, or state, intervention into family life and parental decision-making. Whilst the principles and approach of the court established in the early cases endure, the nature and balance of these responsibilities to children in their care need to be understood in the changing social, legal, and political context in which they are exercised and enforced by the court.

The book will be a valuable resource for academics, students, and practitioners of Medical Law, Healthcare Law, Family Law, Social Work, Medicine, Nursing, and Bioethics.

Jo Bridgeman is Professor of Healthcare Law and Feminist Ethics at the University of Sussex, UK.

Biomedical Law and Ethics Library

Scientific and clinical advances, social and political developments, and the impact of healthcare on our lives raise profound ethical and legal questions. Medical law and ethics have become central to our understanding of these problems and are important tools for the analysis and resolution of problems – real or imagined.

In this series, scholars at the forefront of biomedical law and ethics contribute to the debates in this area, with accessible, thought-provoking, and sometimes controversial, ideas. Each book in the series develops an independent hypothesis and argues cogently for a particular position. One of the major contributions of this series is the extent to which both law and ethics are utilised in the content of the books, and the shape of the series itself.

The books in this series are analytical, with a key target audience of lawyers, doctors, nurses, and the intelligent lay public.

Series Editor: Sheila A. M. McLean
Professor Sheila A.M. McLean is Professor Emerita of Law and Ethics in Medicine, School of Law at the University of Glasgow, UK.

Available titles:

Islam and Biomedical Research Ethics
Mehrunisha Suleman

Medical Treatment of Children and the Law
Beyond Parental Responsibilities
Jo Bridgeman

For more information about this series, please visit: www.routledge.com/Biomedical-Law-and-Ethics-Library/book-series/CAV5

Medical Treatment of Children and the Law
Beyond Parental Responsibilities

Jo Bridgeman

Routledge
Taylor & Francis Group
LONDON AND NEW YORK

First published 2021
by Routledge
2 Park Square, Milton Park, Abingdon, Oxon OX14 4RN

and by Routledge
52 Vanderbilt Avenue, New York, NY 10017

Routledge is an imprint of the Taylor & Francis Group, an informa business

© 2021 Jo Bridgeman

The right of Jo Bridgeman to be identified as author of this work has been asserted by them in accordance with sections 77 and 78 of the Copyright, Designs and Patents Act 1988.

All rights reserved. No part of this book may be reprinted or reproduced or utilised in any form or by any electronic, mechanical, or other means, now known or hereafter invented, including photocopying and recording, or in any information storage or retrieval system, without permission in writing from the publishers.

Trademark notice: Product or corporate names may be trademarks or registered trademarks and are used only for identification and explanation without intent to infringe.

British Library Cataloguing-in-Publication Data
A catalogue record for this book is available from the British Library

Library of Congress Cataloging-in-Publication Data

Names: Bridgeman, Jo, author.
Title: Medical treatment of children and the law: beyond parental responsibilities/Jo Bridgeman.
Description: Milton Park, Abingdon, Oxon; New York, NY: Routledge, 2021. |Includes bibliographical references and index.
Identifiers: LCCN 2020023759 (print) | LCCN 2020023760 (ebook) | ISBN 9780367200022 (hardback) | ISBN 9780429244636 (ebook)
Subjects: LCSH: Child health services--Law and legislation--Great Britain. | Child welfare--Great Britain. | Children--Legal status, laws, etc.--Great Britain. | Parent and child (Law)--Great Britain. | Great Britain. Children Act 1989.
Classification: LCC KD3405.C48 B75 2021 (print) | LCC KD3405.C48 (ebook) | DDC 344.4104/1083--dc23
LC record available at https://lccn.loc.gov/2020023759
LC ebook record available at https://lccn.loc.gov/2020023760

ISBN: 978-0-367-20002-2 (hbk)
ISBN: 978-0-429-24463-6 (ebk)

Typeset in Galliard
By Deanta Global Publishing Services, Chennai, India

Contents

Preface/Acknowledgements	vi
Abbreviations	viii
1 The Changing Context for Children's Medical Treatment Cases	1
2 The Children Act 1989 and Responsibilities for Children's Medical Treatment	26
3 The Development of the Legal Framework for Children's Medical Treatment Cases	46
4 The Legal Duties of Doctors to Children in Their Care	73
5 Protecting the Interests and Welfare of Vulnerable Children	93
6 Professional Duties and Public Responsibilities in Limitation of Life-Sustaining Treatment Cases	116
7 At the Frontiers of Medicine	148
8 Professional Duties, Public Responsibilities, and State Intervention into Family Life	167
Appendix: Reported Cases Concerning the Medical Treatment of Children (up to 30/4/20)	183
Bibliography	230
Cases index	241
Index	244

Preface/Acknowledgements

The argument advanced in this book has been formed over some period of time – my last book on children's medical treatment, *Parental Responsibility, Children and Healthcare Law,* was published in 2007. The focus of that book was parental responsibilities. My aim then was to develop a theoretical framework of relational responsibilities, including the relationship of dependency of parents upon doctors treating their child and the interdependency of parents and the state.

The focus of this book is the duties which doctors have to children in their care and public responsibilities in relation to the medical treatment of children. Over the last few years there has been much public interest in the high-profile cases concerning the medical treatment of a child, such as Charlie Gard and Alfie Evans. It seemed to me that these cases were not only interesting to the public, that was undoubtedly so, but that there is a public interest in decisions that are made about the medical treatment of a child. The parents in these cases considered the Trust's application to the court for a judge to make the decision about their child's future medical treatment, specifically the decision not to continue treatment which would result in the death of the child, to be an infringement of their parental responsibilities or rights. If, as the law, professional guidance and academic analysis claims, the only issue is the best interests of the child then the parents had a valid point, given that they had a claim to know best what was in the interests of their child. However, this established characterisation seemed to me to fail to capture what was really at issue in these cases. What could not be articulated was how the child's doctors felt about continuing to treat the child. As Lady Hale recorded in the Supreme Court in the case of Charlie Gard, his doctors felt that to continue to treat him was professionally wrong. This raised questions about the duties of doctors, which brought in public responsibilities for the care of children, through their duty to refer the case to court and for the court to decide it. In that view, the legal framework is one which brings together and determines the balance of the responsibilities between parents, doctors, the courts and also, given the Children Act 1989 and the role of local authorities in the early cases and in those cases today concerning children in care, the public responsibilities for the welfare and protection of children from harm. This also required a review of the body of case law, recognising that the duties which the law balances are determined within the particular social, legal, and political context.

Thanks to Isabelle Le Gallez who did some initial research for me on the role of local authorities in cases concerned with the withdrawal and withholding of life-sustaining treatment which has fed into chapters five and six. Thanks also to the students on the Perspectives on Healthcare Law module in the Sussex Law School with whom, over the years, I have been developing these ideas and with whom I have discussed the cases analysed in this book. I have had the privilege of discussing the cases, laws, and ideas in this book with colleagues in the community of healthcare law and in the Sussex Law School. This book has not been written alone, so most of all, thanks to my family who have accompanied me on this journey, for listening and encouraging, for the interest and the love.

30 April 2020

Abbreviations

BMA	British Medical Association
ECtHR	European Court of Human Rights
EPO	Emergency Protection Order
GMC	General Medical Council
GOSH	Great Ormond Street Hospital for Sick Children
GP	General Practitioner
ICO	Interim Care Order
NHS	National Health Service
NICE	National Institute for Health and Care Excellence
PSO	Prohibited Steps Order
RCPCH	Royal College of Paediatrics and Child Health
SIO	Specific Issue Order
UNCRC	United Nations Convention on the Rights of the Child

1 The Changing Context for Children's Medical Treatment Cases

Introduction

This chapter situates the case law concerned with the provision of medical treatment to children within its social, political, and legal context. First, academic critique of the law governing medical practice is explained, to demonstrate the importance of positioning the law in its context if the balance of responsibilities between parents, doctors, public authorities, and the state in children's medical treatment cases is to be understood. The context mapped out includes developments in medical science and technology affecting the medical treatment of children in consistently underfunded services and alongside changes in the legal regulation of the adult patient/doctor relationship; the social and legal construction of the parent/child relationship; and the responsibilities of the state for the protection of the welfare of children.

The Nature of Medical Law

The question of the appropriate balance of responsibilities in medical decision-making between individual patients and their families, doctors, society, and the state was raised by Ian Kennedy, in his 1981 Reith Lectures, *The Unmasking of Medicine*,[1] at a time when the body of medical law was very limited. Diagnosis, identification of treatment options, and selection of the treatment option which is clinically optimal are, he argued, 'technical-medical' and properly within the competence of doctors.[2] However, many decisions being made by doctors, Ian Kennedy argued, were not within the exclusive expertise of doctors, as they also involved social, moral, political, economic, and legal issues upon which doctors

---

1 Ian Kennedy, *The Unmasking of Medicine* (Granada, 1981, revised 1983).
2 Ian Kennedy, 'What is a Medical Decision?' in Ian Kennedy, *Treat Me Rights: Essays in Medical Law and Ethics* (Clarendon Press, 1988), 19–31. These ideas had been aired in his Astor Lecture at Middlesex Hospital Medical School in July 1979 and published in the School's journal. Other examples given in that essay were about informing patients of a diagnosis of a serious illness, the provision of AID to same sex couples, and conscientious objection to abortion.

had no specific knowledge, training, or particular expertise.[3] Arising within medical practice, these decisions were left to doctors by default because others had not taken the responsibility for establishing the parameters within which they should be made.

The primary example concerned with the medical treatment of children, given by Ian Kennedy, were decisions about the treatment of babies with spina bifida, based on judgements about their quality of life.[4] Whilst recognising the social and political context for the delivery of medical treatment and care, Ian Kennedy focused upon the moral, or ethical, issues raised by such cases. He argued that decisions, such as whether medical treatment should be withheld from a baby with spina bifida, involved moral issues and consequently should not be left to doctors, nor were they private matters to be determined by doctors and parents according to their own values. In contrast with 'medical-technical' decisions, properly made within the sphere of medical competence, decisions about 'medical-moral and medical-legal'[5] issues needed to be made, he argued, with 'reference to socially established and institutionalised principles' which conform to the ethical standards of society.

Ian Kennedy emphasised that doctors were already subject to legal rules from criminal and civil law, as demonstrated by the cases of *R v Arthur*[6] and *Re B*,[7] but in its application to medical practice the law should 'reflect and promote', and guide doctors to act in ways that accord with good medical ethics, that is, with consideration of respect for autonomy, truth telling, respect for dignity and justice, or equity.[8] He observed that cases were being brought before the courts due to lack of clarity whether conduct was legally and ethically justified, the need for guidance, and as a consequence of greater visibility of the ethical issues raised by medical practice. But, he suggested, guidance to doctors was not best secured in criminal prosecutions or civil hearings or even in declaratory hearings which, although they have the advantage of being determined before action is taken, are still confined to a specific set of facts.[9]

In his subsequent essay, 'Emerging Problems of Medicine, Technology, and the Law', Ian Kennedy suggested that to leave issues of medical practice to be determined by the courts through existing legal categories would preclude the

---

3 Kennedy (n 2).
4 Kennedy (n 1) 86–8. Other examples given were whether to tell a patient the diagnosis of a fatal condition, issues of reproduction, and decisions at the end of life.
5 Ian Kennedy, 'Emerging Problems of Medicine, Technology, and the Law' in Ian Kennedy, *Treat Me Right: Essays in Medical Law and Ethics* (Clarendon Press, 1988), 1–18, 16 delivered to the Canadian Institute for Advanced Legal Studies, Cambridge, 1983 and first published in *The Cambridge Lectures* (Butterworths, 1985).
6 [1981] 12 BMLR 1, considered further in chapter three.
7 [1981] 1 WLR 1421, considered further in chapter three. Ian Kennedy also considered *R v Reed* [1982] Crim LR 819.
8 Kennedy (n 1) 121–6.
9 Kennedy (n 1) 125–7.

development of a 'body of doctrine which has coherence and some internal consistency'.[10] Instead, he argued for recognition of medical law as a discrete legal discipline through which 'ethical precepts' ran, referring to philosophical ethics, rather than professional ethics.[11] Expecting legislation to deal only with 'major issues of social policy', Ian Kennedy argued for the appointment of a Permanent Standing Advisory Committee to draw up a comprehensive code governing the ethics of medical practice and to respond to developments in medicine.[12] A Code of Practice could provide a guide for doctors as to the applicable principles, provide the analytical tools by which to identify the range of choices that are ethically and socially acceptable, and establish the boundaries within which doctors could be expected to exercise their discretion.[13] Compliance with the Code would ensure that the conduct of doctors was ethical and lawful; a doctor who did not comply would have to justify their actions. A Code of Practice would thus serve to guide doctors, provide a basis from which to explain their actions to patients, and for the patient and community to judge the actions of doctors. The alternative, Ian Kennedy later proposed, was for a Code of Practice or guidance to be drawn up by professionals and others from relevant constituencies, compliance with which would be prima facie evidence of lawfulness, but if a court subsequently decided that guidance in the code was not lawful, a doctor who complied with it would not be subject to sanction.[14]

These arguments were subjected to much critical comment in the popular press and medical journals.[15] Yet, Ian Kennedy, as well as others researching and publishing in the developing discipline of medical law including Sheila McLean and Ken Mason,[16] shaped the discipline as one in which the law governing medical

---

10 Kennedy (n 5) 3.
11 Kennedy (n 5) 3.
12 Kennedy (n 1) 126–9.
13 Kennedy (n 1). Michael Freeman in *The Rights and Wrongs of Children* (Frances Pinter, 1983) 262 argued for a 'code of principles', drawn up through consultation, which could be tested and refined in application by the courts undertaking 'independent principled review' of children's healthcare decisions.
14 Kennedy (n 5) 18.
15 In 'Response to the Critics', Ian Kennedy wrote that he had been 'taken aback somewhat by the vehemence of the attacks' which included that his views were 'patently absurd, untenable, clearly unoriginal, and riddled with inaccuracies and/or misperceptions' (1981) 7 Journal of Medical Ethics 202–211, the volume contained a number of responses to the lectures.
16 The work of Sheila McLean celebrated in Pamela R Ferguson and Graeme T Laurie (eds), *Inspiring a Medico-Legal Revolution: Essays in Honour of Sheila McLean* (Routledge, 2015); and that of Ken Mason honoured in Sheila McLean (ed), *First Do No Harm: Law, Ethics and Healthcare* (Ashgate: 2006). As Stephen W Smith has commented, the ethical approach of Margot Brazier, one of the other pioneers of the discipline, is harder to capture. The essays in the Festschrift in her honour emphasise an approach based in care, humanity, responsibility, and relationships, and one in which ethics is understood to supplement law rather than underpin it. Stephen W Smith, 'Catherine Stanton, Sarah Devaney, Anne-Maree Farrell, Alexandra Mullock (eds), *Pioneering Healthcare Law: Essays in Honour of Margaret Brazier*,

practice is understood to be underpinned by ethical principles.[17] Academic analysis at the birth of the subject of medical law consequently provides relevant context for the development of 'modern'[18] children's medical law, considered in chapter three. As demonstrated there, the approach Ian Kennedy argued for dominates the law, and academic analysis, governing the provision of medical treatment to children, focused upon consideration of the best interests of the child. The analysis of the cases in chapter three demonstrates that there is now an established body of law concerned with children's medical treatment with coherent principles and internal consistency, influenced not only by professional and philosophical ethical principles but by the social context in which the legal framework was established. The lack of legal regulation, the dominance of medical paternalism, and the turn to the courts for guidance thus provides an important part of the context for the particular form the case law took and the principles upon which it is based.

Jonathan Montgomery argued, in 2000, twenty years after Ian Kennedy's Reith Lectures, by which time there was a body of case law, that a paradigm shift was required in the conceptualisation of medical law. The framework adopted in early academic analysis, he argued, did not represent the reality of medical law as it had developed and consequently failed to understand or explain the law and outcomes of cases concerning the provision of medicine.[19] The examples through which he advanced his thesis were the then reach of *Bolam*;[20] failure of the law to protect patient rights in access to healthcare; consent and confidentiality; the failure of the court to 'establish rules for ethical practice' in the caesarean section cases; and the regulation of 'medical ethics through the filter of peer review' in the withdrawal of treatment cases, including some concerned with the treatment of children.[21] Rather than seeing standards for medical practice as set by the law underpinned by ethical principles, Jonathan Montgomery argued for 'a paradigm

---

and Pamela R Ferguson, Graeme T Laurie (eds), *Inspiring a Medico-Legal Revolution: Essays in Honour of Sheila McLean*' (2017) 25 *Medical Law Review* 165.

17 And concerned to protect human rights. Sheila McLean in *Old Law, New Medicine: Medical Ethics and Human Rights* (Pandora, 1999) xiii, 3, argued that deference to medicine, a reluctance to challenge medical decision-making or to question whether the decision was a medical one resulted in medicalisation and erosion of human rights.

18 Margaret Brazier and Jonathan Montgomery in 'Whence and Whither "modern medical law"' (2019) 70 *Northern Ireland Legal Quarterly* 5 demonstrated the long history of medical law offering as examples: questions of how to regulate medical practice; breach of contract and counterclaims for negligence; use of human material; public health; and, legislation, case law and academic writing earlier in the twentieth century. Although as with the literature generally, their focus was upon the adult patient rather than issues concerning the medical treatment of children.

19 Jonathan Montgomery, 'Time for a Paradigm Shift? Medical Law in Transition' (2000) 53 *Current Legal Problems* 363–4.

20 Montgomery (n 19) 372 applied to information disclosure, treatment of incapacitated adults and withholding or withdrawal of life-sustaining treatment.

21 Montgomery (n 19).

based on the development of values within the health care communities'.[22] He argued that more attention needed to be given to the values of the health professions and to the public nature of the healthcare system, to 'organizational and professional norms' and its 'institutional context'.[23] Focused upon children's medical treatment, it is argued in this book that the law has to be understood within the social, political, economic, and cultural context in which the balance of responsibilities amongst those caring for the child is reached. Trust in the medical profession; rights, welfare, and protection of children; public responsibilities and state intervention into family life; and choices in medical care all influence the balance of responsibilities.

Kenneth Veitch has argued that an approach to medical law which focuses solely upon analysis of the ethical strengths and weaknesses underpinning the law is inadequate, in that it offers no explanation of the 'institutional exigencies' or their consequences.[24] One example he considered is the case of the conjoined twins, *Re A*,[25] arguing that 'features of legal reasoning', such as the need to discover the relevant legal principles in the existing body of law and the duty of the court to decide cases brought before them, meant that the court failed to address the issues at the heart of the difference of opinion between the parents and doctors.[26] Beyond questions of ethics in medical law, Kenneth Veitch argued, it was necessary to question how the courts asserted jurisdiction over issues arising in medical practice, such as decisions about the medical treatment of a child and the 'institutional apparatus that structures' the functioning of the courts.[27] The focus upon the ethical justifications for the resolution of issues of medical law, in this context upon the determination of a child's best interests, has resulted in a failure to consider the best interests analysis within the wider context in which it is determined. As Kenneth Veitch argued in his analysis of *Re A*, the consequence of the exclusive focus on the moral conflict was that,

> it is not merely the reality of the original conflict of values that finds no place within the common law; what could be called the broader social or

---

22 Montgomery (n 19) 364.
23 Montgomery (n 19) 408.
24 Kenneth Veitch, *The Jurisdiction of Medical Law* (Ashgate, 2007). More recently, *Ethical Judgments* sought to examine the extent to which medical law is underpinned by ethical principles. Recognising that many of the cases raise ethical issues, the editors observed that judgments may lack 'rigour or consistency', may lack 'regard for the nuances' or fail to resolve 'clashes between principles'. Stephen W Smith, John Coggon, Clark Hobson, Richard Huxtable, Sheelagh McGuiness, José Miola, Mary Neal (eds), *Ethical Judgments: Re-Writing Medical Law* (Hart 2017) 2–3. However, their re-writing of judgments from nine cases from an ethical perspective led to the conclusion that a 'court of morals' would not necessarily achieve outcomes that were different or any more palatable than those arrived at by courts of law', 259.
25 [2001] Fam 147.
26 Veitch (n 24) 4.
27 Veitch (n 24) 5.

political conflicts of which it is a microcosm also fail to be played out in the courtroom.[28]

Questions about the nature of parenthood, state interference in private life, and the extent to which personal values should be respected, are not addressed in judgments focused upon ethical issues. But, of course, without being acknowledged, those broader conflicts are determined. However, in order to understand the issue which the court is deciding in any specific case and the influences upon the judge in reaching a decision, these broader factors have to be recognised. The key argument of this book is that decisions made by parents in partnership with doctors about a child's medical treatment and the body of cases which comprise the jurisprudence concerning the medical treatment of children, have to be understood within the changing social, political, economic, legal, and cultural context.

As the approach taken, and the principles by which current cases are determined, originate in the very first cases in the last decades of the twentieth century, the context for the issues in those cases and the decisions reached have to be understood in order to appreciate the balance of responsibilities between parents, doctors, public authorities, and the state, for seriously ill children. It is also necessary to consider how those influences have changed over the decades and the different context for cases being brought today. In this introductory chapter, I set out the context in which the initial cases were decided, consider key changes over time and the particular context for cases being decided now. The first concerns advances in medical science and technology within the context of consistently underfunded children's healthcare services.

Children's Healthcare Services

Developments in medical science, equipment, technology, diagnostic techniques, and treatments have brought radical change to preventative medicine, children's medical treatment, and to the ability to sustain the life of children with complex conditions, over the decades in which questions about children's medical treatment have been before the courts. The cases concern the treatment of children within the National Health Service (NHS), created by the National Health Service Act 1946, publicly funded and publicly delivered, and free at the point of delivery. As Ian Kennedy observed, 'as a value-driven politically sensitive enterprise', the NHS is constantly subject to 'tinkering', to reflect changing views about the role of the private and public sectors in the provision of services and the levels of general taxation to provide for the latter.[29] As a comprehensive health

---

28 Veitch (n 24) 140.
29 Ian Kennedy (Chair), *Report of the Public Inquiry into Children's Heart Surgery at the Bristol Royal Infirmary 1984–1995: Learning from Bristol*, CM5207(I), July 2001, http://web

service, the NHS has faced constant demands for the provision of the expanding range of therapeutic medicines and technologies.

The Report of the Public Inquiry into the quality of care provided to children undergoing cardiac surgery at the Bristol Royal Infirmary between 1984 and 1995 (the Bristol Inquiry, chaired by Ian Kennedy and which reported in 2001) concluded, from the statistical and other evidence, that the standard of care for children undergoing open-heart surgery in Bristol was 'less than adequate'.[30] However, this was not a conclusion which was clearly confined to one hospital or specialism. The conclusion of the Inquiry was that it was 'not possible to say, categorically, that events similar to those which happened in Bristol could not happen again in the UK; indeed, are not happening at this moment'.[31] There were many reasons for this conclusion but, significantly, despite children making substantial use of acute healthcare services, children's services were given low priority. The Report noted the repeated emphasis of independent reviews over the preceding four decades that the needs of children had to be placed at the centre of their care; recommendations that had consistently not been implemented.[32] Furthermore, the Report considered that the specific failings in the treatment of children with heart conditions in Bristol had occurred within the context of a neglect of children's healthcare services generally within an underfunded NHS. The NHS was underfunded in that Governments had repeatedly failed to make the necessary funds available to the NHS to meet the claims they made for it.[33] The conclusions of a briefing paper published by the Nuffield Trust in 2016 on the state of child health and quality of care in the UK, would suggest that lessons were not learned from the Bristol Inquiry. It concluded that the failure to implement recommendations of previous reviews of children's health services and quality standards had resulted in a variation in the quality of healthcare services for children and young people across the UK.[34]

Parental trust in the medical profession was adversely affected by the circumstances which required the establishment of the Bristol Inquiry[35] and the

---

archive.nationalarchives.gov.uk/20090811143745/http://www.bristol-inquiry.org.uk accessed 26 March 2020, ch 4, para 2.

30 *Bristol Inquiry Report* (n 29) section one, conclusions, para 6.
31 *Bristol Inquiry Report* (n 29) summary, para 49.
32 *Bristol Inquiry Report* (n 29) ch 29, para 8.
33 *Bristol Inquiry Report* (n 29) ch 4, para 31.
34 L Kossarova, D Devakumar and N Edwards, *The future of child health services: new models of care* (Nuffield Trust, 2016) 6–7. A further review into the safety and quality of children's cardiac services in Bristol was established in 2014 and reported in 2016, https://www.thebristolreview.co.uk/ accessed 26 March 2020.
35 An independent inquiry into paediatric cardiac services at the Royal Brompton and Harefield Hospitals, established in response to concerns of parents about their child's treatment, found that some doctors offered parents a biased view of the treatment options resulting in less favourable treatment because of their child's Down's Syndrome, and demonstrated a comparable appreciation of the context for the delivery of healthcare services, R Evans (Chair), *Report of the Independent Inquiries into Paediatric Cardiac Services at the Royal Brompton*

subsequent revelations at that Inquiry about the widespread practice of the retention of organs following post-mortem. Whilst the practice of retaining organs following post-mortems was nationwide and not confined to children, the enormous outcry about the practice with respect to children revealed to the Bristol Inquiry[36] and in particularly scandalous circumstances at Alder Hey[37] emphasised differences between professional and parental perspectives and priorities with respect to the care of children.[38] For practitioners, the practice of retaining human material removed at post-mortem was commonplace and considered to be legally, and ethically, justified. The law then contained in the Human Tissue Act 1961 was unclear and consequently, practice proceeded on the basis of folklore and a paternalistic attitude in which the failure to respect the feelings of parents was masked by a pretence of sensitivity. For parents, the removal and retention of organs from the bodies of their children demonstrated a failure to respect them as persons. The parents felt betrayed by the professionals to whom they had entrusted the care of their children and who, they felt, had treated their children as medical specimens.

In contrast to the failures in the quality of care identified by the Bristol Inquiry, many of the cases which are brought before the court involve children with rare or complex conditions who have received care of the highest possible standard, something that parents are able to recognise even though they are now in an irreconcilable dispute with the doctors upon whom they depend to care for their child. However, because of their rare or complex conditions, the children in question are often being cared for by specialist multi-disciplinary teams. Research by Liz Forbat et al on conflict between parents and doctors about the future medical treatment of a child identified that parental concerns are most likely to arise when there is 'poor prognosis, complex multidisciplinary approaches and high levels of uncertainty'[39] as in the treatment of rare and complex conditions. They found that the most common cause of conflict is communication breakdown.[40] In particular, when the child's condition requires the expertise of multidisciplinary teams of professionals, parents can feel they are being provided with

---

Hospital and Harefield Hospital (April 2001), Zosia Kmietowicz, 'Down's children received "less favourable" hospital treatment' (2001) 322 *British Medical Journal* 815.

36. The Bristol Royal Infirmary Interim Report, *Removal and Retention of Human Material*, (May 2000).
37. M Redfern (Chair), *The Royal Liverpool Children's Inquiry: Report* (January 2001).
38. Jo Bridgeman, 'When Systems Fail: Parents, Children and the Quality of Healthcare' in Jane Holder and Colm O'Cinneide (eds), (2005) 58 *Current Legal Problems* (OUP 2006) 183–213.
39. Liz Forbat and Others, 'Conflict in a paediatric hospital: a prospective mixed-method study' (2016) 101 *Archives of Disease in Childhood* 23.
40. At 22%, disagreements about treatment, 13% and unrealistic expectations, 11%, Forbat (n 39).

inconsistent advice about their child's treatment, undermining their trust in the professionals upon whom they depend.[41]

Research on conflict between parents and professionals about a child's treatment has shown that parental concern may arise from fears, justified or otherwise, about the quality of care provided[42] or that treatment is being limited due to scarcity of resources.[43] Whilst the cases considered in this book do not involve compensation claims for failings in the standard of medical care, parental concerns that decisions about their child's treatment are driven by the allocation of limited NHS resources has been a consistent issue across the body of case law. Whilst the 1995 case of Jaymee Bowen directly addressed the decision of Cambridge Health Authority not to fund an extra-contractual referral for experimental treatment for acute myeloid leukaemia,[44] in other cases concerns about the allocation of resources form part of the background to the conflict over the child's future medical treatment. For example, Parker J noted, and rejected, the suspicions of the father which compounded his opposition to the withdrawal of ventilation from nine-month-old OT, born with a mitochondrial condition of genetic origin, who had spent all but the first three weeks of his life in hospital, that,

> From July 2008 there have been suggestions that the hospital has been negligent in failing to identify and treat OT's incredibly rare condition. The case has been overtly put to the treating clinicians that the hospital's position as to limitation and withdrawal of treatment is based upon the availability of resources and that he is seen by them as a 'bed-blocker'.[45]

Doctors stress that decisions about a child's medical treatment are reached according to their professional judgement of which of the treatment options is in the child's best interests and not with consideration of resources, and judges likewise emphasise that the allocation of resources is not relevant to their determination of the best interests of the child.

Whilst doctors use professional judgement to identify the treatment options and which they consider to be clinically best for the child, parents will undertake their own research into their child's condition which may reveal potential therapeutic options not being offered by the treating doctors. The father of Jaymee Bowen researched her condition and its treatment in the library of the Royal College where studies published in the medical journals are subject to research ethics committee approval and peer review. It is no longer necessary to consult the latest editions of medical journals in the halls of learning, parents can access

---

41 Liz Forbat, Bea Teuten, Sarah Barclay, 'Conflict escalation in paediatric services: findings from a qualitative study' (2015) 100 *Archives of Disease in Childhood* 769.
42 Forbat (n 41), 770.
43 Simon Meller and Sarah Barclay, 'Mediation: an Approach to Intractable Disputes Between Parents and Paediatricians' (2011) 96 *Archives of Disease in Childhood* 619, 619.
44 *R v Cambridge District Health Authority, ex parte B* [1995] 1 FLR 1055.
45 *Re OT* [2009] EWHC 633, [12].

a wealth of information, of varying degrees of veracity, via the internet. When parents have located alternative therapy which their child's treating doctors cannot provide because it requires equipment not available in the UK as in the case of Ashya King,[46] or because in their professional judgement it would be futile as in the case of Charlie Gard,[47] for the parents the issue has become securing the funds to pay for private treatment abroad. Although, as Francis J stated in relation to the dispute over the provision of innovative therapy to Charlie Gard, NHS resourcing was not an issue, as his doctors would have administered nucleoside therapy to him had they considered it clinically beneficial. Yet, because his parents had raised in excess of a million pounds for his treatment in the United States, there was much debate in the media and social media in both countries about the limits of a 'socialised' medical system.[48] Charities offering funds for treatment abroad, media stories of parents raising funds by selling or mortgaging property,[49] and crowdfunding[50] for treatment abroad are now part of the context for cases about the future medical treatment of children. The hope offered by therapies, which are often unproven or not yet approved, not being offered within the NHS fuels mistrust in the child's treating doctors whilst trust is placed in the offer of hope from practitioners subject to different regulatory regimes or values.[51] Services which fail to place the child at the centre of care, inquiries prompted by concerns about the quality of care, questions about resource allocation, loss of trust, and access to a range of information offering hope, have all served to challenge the view that the doctor 'knows best', changes that have occurred alongside changes to the parent/child relationship.

Changes in the Parent/Child Relationship

The Law Commission in its *Review of Child Law: Guardianship and Custody*, referenced the case of *Gillick* in support of the view that the term *parental rights* was inaccurate and misleading, and that any rights parents had were to enable them to

---

46 *In the Matter of Ashya King* [2014] EWHC 2964, considered further in chapter seven.
47 *Gosh v Yates & Gard* [2017] EWHC 972, the Appendix provides details of the appeals in this case which is considered in chapters six, seven and eight.
48 Ranjana Das, 'Populist discourse on a British social media patient-support community: The case of the Charlie Gard support campaign on Facebook' (2018) 24 *Discourse, Context & Media* 76.
49 Ashya King's parents had taken him to Spain where they intended to sell their property there in order to raise funds for his treatment in Prague.
50 Gabrielle Dressler and Sarah Kelly, 'Ethical implications of medical crowdfunding: the case of Charlie Gard' (2018) 44 *Journal of Medical Ethics* 453.
51 Sara Fovargue, 'Preserving the Therapeutic Alliance: Court Intervention and Experimental Treatment Requests' in Imogen Goold, Jonathan Herring and Cressida Auckland (eds), *Parental Rights, Best Interests and Significant Harms: Medical Decision-Making on Behalf of Children Post-Great Ormond Street Hospital v Gard*, (Hart, 2019) 153–176.

fulfil their duties to their children.[52] The Children Act 1989 replaced notions of parental authority or rights over their children, evident in the cases of *R v Arthur* and *Re B*[53] in 1981, with parental responsibility, which means both responsibility *to* their children and primary responsibility *for* the care and upbringing of children. As Brenda Hoggett explained,

> Parents owe their children a duty to look after and bring them up: they can be sued by their children and prosecuted by the authorities if they do not do so. From this duty arises their right to decide, within certain broad limits, how to go about it. Their rights are the product of their duties rather than the other way about. Bringing up children is a never-ending responsibility – getting them fed, clothed, housed, across the road, to school, to the doctor. The compensations are enormous, among them the right to choose how to do it, but the duty to care comes before the choice of how to do so. Parents also owe the rest of us a duty to look after and bring up their children: we have various ways of punishing them if they do not. That duty also gives them rights, not the sort which the courts must invariably enforce, but the sort which acknowledge a claim not to be interfered with by outsiders without due process and good cause. In either case, it is because both children and the rest of society expect parents to bring up their own children that parents are given the rights they have. Whether the law calls this 'parental responsibility' or 'parental responsibilities and rights' may not matter much. But it is meant to reflect both the jurisprudential truth and the practical reality.[54]

Notably, as Brenda Hoggett identified in this quote, the duties of parents to fulfil their responsibilities to care for their children are owed first to the child but then to the 'rest of us', that is, the public and the state. The public interest in cases concerning the medical treatment of children lies in the interests of society, in ensuring that children get the medical treatment that they require but also that children are treated with dignity and not subjected to interventions which offer no prospect of benefit, at the request of their parents, or which are not socially acceptable. As MacDonald J observed in the recent case concerning whether ventilation should be withdrawn from Tafida Raqeeb, or whether she should be

---

[52] Law Commission, *Review of Child Law: Guardianship and Custody* (Law Com No 172, 1988) para 2.4.
[53] *R v Arthur* (n 6); *Re B* (n 7).
[54] Brenda Hoggett, 'Joint Parenting Systems: The English Experiment' (1994) 6 *Tolley's Journal of Child Law* 8, 9. Professor Brenda Hoggett was the Law Commissioner for the Family Law team which developed the private law provisions of the Children Act 1989 and worked with a team of DHSS officials on the public law provisions. Professor Hoggett was subsequently appointed to the judiciary and was Lady Hale, President of the Supreme Court 2017–2020.

transferred to Italy where doctors were prepared to give her more time to determine whether home ventilation might be possible, such cases,

> touching as they do on the very nature, purpose, and value of human life, raise emotive, complex, and contentious issues that generate strong feelings on both sides of the litigation and in the wider public and professional sphere.[55]

Furthermore, as Brenda Hoggett explained, the state gives parents substantial freedom to care for and raise their children as they consider best, according to their values, preferences, and abilities. Minimum standards of parenting are set by the criminal law and laws of child protection. Although many parents will have no need for any knowledge of either, given that their decisions will be motivated by the concern to do their best for their children within the limits imposed upon them by, for example, finances, working obligations, the needs of others to whom they have caring responsibilities, or their own health. Yet, there is a role for the law when parental concern to do the very best for the child, to pursue further or continued treatment, presents the risk of, with the very best of motives, acting contrary to the interests of their child.

As well as influencing the shape of parental duties to their children, *Gillick* was received as recognising a growing commitment in the 1980s to children as individuals entitled to rights. As Michael Freeman identified, the speeches of their Lordships in *Gillick* appeared to many to 'usher in a new age' in which the personality, integrity, and autonomy of children was recognised.[56] Roger Smith has argued that in the 1980s there was an increasing commitment to children's rights and protection of their welfare, reflected in the Short Report on child care policy, *Gillick*, the Cleveland Inquiry Report, and the Children Act 1989.[57] The consequence, he argued, was a linking of the provision of support services for children, children's welfare and the protection of children from harm, to children's rights and specifically the right of children to be heard, to have their wishes and feelings taken seriously, and for consideration to be given to their ethnic, linguistic, and religious background.[58] The dominance of the welfare principle upon children's medical treatment decision-making and limited direct engage-

---

55 *Tafida Raqeeb v Barts NHS Foundation Trust* [2019] EWHC 2531 (Admin); *Barts NHS Foundation Trust v Shalina Begum and Muhhamed Raqeeb & Tafida Raqeeb* [2019] EWHC 2530 (Fam), [2].
56 Michael Freeman, 'Removing Rights from Adolescents' in Michael Freeman, *The Moral Status of Children: Essays on the Rights of the Child* (Martinus Nijhoff Publishers, 1997) 345–356, 345.
57 Roger Smith, 'Child Care: Welfare, Protection or Rights?' (1991) 13 *Journal of Social Welfare & Family Law* 469, 469; House of Commons Social Services Committee, *Children in Care* (HC 360, 1984); Butler-Sloss LJ, *Report of the Inquiry into Child Abuse in Cleveland* (Cm 412, 1988).
58 Smith (n 57) 469.

ment with children's rights by judges in cases concerned with children's medical treatment is examined in detail in chapter three. However, these cases occurred in a social and legal context in which the child was recognised as a legal subject not an object,[59] an independent being rather than the property of his or her parents,[60] which influenced understanding of the parent/child relationship and the role of the law in protection of the individual interests of the child. As Silber J observed in the 2006 case of *Axon,* in the years since *Gillick,* there had been a 'change in the landscape of family matters', which included a 'keener appreciation of the autonomy of the child and the child's consequential right to participate in decision-making processes that fundamentally affect his family life', as a result of the Human Rights Act 1998 and the United Nations Convention on the Rights of the Child.[61]

Cressida Auckland and Imogen Goold have argued that media attention and public debate around the cases of Charlie Gard, Isaiah Haastrup and Alfie Evans[62] demonstrated a 'disjunction' between the law and what people thought it should be. They suggested that the prevailing opinion was that parents should have the authority to make decisions about their child's medical treatment.[63] They argued that these cases demonstrated that the law gives judges the power to determine the best interests of a child on any matter referred to court and expressed the view that this amounts to a significant 'intrusion by the state into the private decisions of parents'.[64] Whilst recognising that there was a lot of misreporting and misunderstanding around these cases, they argued that the public response demonstrated objection to the power of the court to intervene and override the parental assessment of the best interests of the child. But, as examined in detail in this book, understanding of the facts and the circumstances, which are referred to court as a matter of practice, are central to the balance of responsibilities between those caring for the child.

On the second occasion that the Court of Appeal considered the future care of Alfie Evans, in an appeal by his parents against the decision of Hayden J not to make an order for a writ of habeas corpus, the judgment directly addressed the underlying claims of parental rights. It was emphasised that parental views or rights did not take precedence nor did his parents have an '"unfettered right"

---

59 Michael Freeman, 'Taking Children's Rights More Seriously' (1992) 6 *International Journal of Law, Policy and the Family* 52, 54.
60 Jonathan Montgomery, 'Children as Property?' (1988) 51 *Modern Law Review* 323.
61 *R (on the application of Axon) v Secretary of State for Health & Another* [2006] EWHC 37, quoting Thorpe LJ in *Mabon v Mabon* [2005] 3 WLR 460, [76], [80].
62 All concerned with applications by the Trust for declarations that it was lawful to withdraw ventilation from, and provide palliative care to, Charlie Gard in 2017 and Isaiah Haastrup and Alfie Evans in 2018, considered in chapters six, seven and eight.
63 Cressida Auckland and Imogen Goold, 'Parental Rights, Best Interests and Significant Harms: Who should have the final say over a child's medical care?' (2019) 78 *Cambridge Law Journal* 287, 290.
64 Auckland and Goold (n 63) 293.

to make choices and exercise rights on behalf of Alfie'. If the rights of the child are inconsistent with the rights of the parents, the rights of the child prevail.[65] Recognising that it has not always been the case, the judgement stressed that the courts 'are vigilant guardians and promoters of the rights and interests of children', given effect in cases of the medical treatment of children by a determination of the best interests of the child.[66] To allow a child to be treated in a way which is 'irreconcilable' with his best interests, even if that is a choice parents are seeking to make for the very best of motives, would be a serious breach of the rights of the child.

As John Eekelaar has pointed out, the law rarely gets involved in functioning families, although it does prohibit the infliction of certain invasions upon the body of a child, such as female circumcision or tattooing. The common law has placed limits upon some interventions which involve registered medical practitioners, which were previously considered to be private matters to be decided between parents and doctors, such as the requirement to get approval of the court for non-therapeutic sterilisation.[67] When questions about a child's upbringing are before the court, as explained in chapter three, the court undertakes a best-interest analysis. Although within the context of a decision about children's education rather than medical treatment, Sir James Munby P explained that in acting as a judicial reasonable parent, the judge must ensure that the application of the law 'reflect[s] and adopt[s] the changing views, as the years go by, of reasonable men and women, the parents of children, on the proper treatment and methods of bringing up children'.[68] Conceptions of welfare change with regard to the ever changing nature of the world, technology, social standards, and social attitudes.[69] However, the best interests of the child have to be,

> assessed by reference to general community standards, making due allowance for the entitlement of people, within the limits of what is permissible in accordance with those standards, to entertain very divergent views about the religious, moral, social, and secular objectives they wish to pursue for themselves and for their children.[70]

There are parenting fashions, plenty of parenting books and now, websites and discussion forums on aspects of parenting for parents to consult. And whilst all parents will at some point rely upon the help of family and friends, childcare providers, and professionals such as teachers and General Practitioners (GP), the care of a seriously ill child is unique in parenting, as parents have to rely upon

---

65 *Evans v Alder Hey Children's NHS Foundation Trust* [2018] EWCA Civ 805, [51].
66 *Evans* (n 65) [52].
67 Considered in chapter five.
68 *Re G* [2012] EWCA Civ 1233, [32], referring back to Lord Upjohn in *J v C* [1970] AC 668.
69 *Re G* (n 68) [33].
70 *Re G* (n 68) [39].

the expertise of doctors to diagnose, identify the treatment options, and provide treatment to their child. A parent who is not satisfied with their childcare provider can find another. A parent who considers the standard of education inadequate can move their child to a different school or home school their child if there are no places available. A parent can apply to register their child with a different GP. Whilst the NHS Constitution gives patients the right to choose where to have treatment and to be provided with information upon which to make the choice, when a child is seriously ill the needs of the child, perhaps dependent upon medical equipment or upon expertise in rare and complex conditions, can have the practical effect that there is no alternative to choose. Childcare providers and teachers, like doctors and other health professionals, have legal duties to children in their care to fulfil the professional standard of care and report to the local authority any concerns about child protection. In the cases considered in chapter five concerning children in the care of the state, it is the responsibility for the welfare and protection of the child which results in referral to court. One feature that marks out cases concerned with disagreements between parents and doctors about the future medical treatment of a child as distinct, is that they involve a parental challenge to the expertise of the professionals upon whom they depend to provide their child with the best possible care. Whilst doctors will respect parental choices on the grounds that they know their child best and are best placed to choose from the available treatment options, the majority of these cases now come before the courts because doctors, exercising their professional judgement, cannot accept parental decisions. Fulfilment of their legal duties to protect the welfare of the child requires that questions about the child's medical treatment are referred to court. Professional duties to the child require an independent judgement in order to ensure that the interests of the child are protected.

The Role of the State in Protecting the Welfare of Children

John Eekelaar and Mavis Maclean have suggested that the increased reach of the law into the family can be explained by two factors: first, the increased sensitivity to the different interests of individual family members; and second, the need to legitimate state intrusion in families.[71] The state has a supervisory role, delegated to public authorities, over the parental care of children. The Children Act 1989 provides for the state, through local authorities, to support parents to fulfil their responsibility and provides compulsory powers, and intervention where necessary, through the courts when parents are unable to care.[72] Inevitably, political decisions about the duties imposed upon and funding of public services determine the services provided by local authorities and the NHS. Nigel Parton has argued that since the Coalition Government in 2010 committed to reduce public

---

[71] John Eekelaar and Mavis Maclean (eds), *A Reader on Family Law* (OUP, 1994) 19–22.
[72] R Dingwall, JM Eekelaar and T Murray, 'Childhood as a Social Problem: A Survey of the History of Legal Regulation' (1984) 11 *Journal of Law and Society* 207.

services and brought in austerity measures, there has been a reduction in universal and preventative services with an increased role for the private sector, and a focus on child protection rather than broader concerns about the welfare of all children.[73]

Many of the cases early in the jurisprudence and a steady number over the years since the courts have been asked to determine questions about the future medical treatment of children, have been brought to court by the local authority with respect to children in the care of the state, where independent review of major decisions affecting that child's life are made in the public forum of a court, and where decision-makers can be held to account. Although NHS Trusts are public institutions and as such subject to judicial review and required to comply with the Human Rights Act 1998, as Lord Hoffman stated in *Gorringe*,

> A hospital trust provides medical treatment pursuant to the public law duty in the National Health Service Act 1977, but the existence of its common law duty is based simply upon its acceptance of a professional relationship with the patient no different from that which would be accepted by a doctor in private practice.[74]

Health professionals have legal duties to children in their care, creating a tripartite relationship between child, doctor, and the holder of parental responsibility. In addition to the common law professional duties of care and good medical practice,[75] the Children Act 1989 and 2004 place duties upon Trusts and their employees to work together with local authorities to support them to fulfil their duties and to discharge their duties with consideration to the protection and welfare of children.[76] Therefore, an important context for the law governing the provision of medical treatment to children and the individual cases to determine the treatment of specific children are the professional duties of doctors with respect to the welfare and protection of children in their care. In the cases concerned with treatment decisions in relation to specific children, focused upon determination of the best interests of a child seriously ill with a rare or complex condition, whether the treatment proposed is in the best interests of the child or harmful to the child is inevitably not clear cut. The goal of recovery or improvement in health justifies invasions of the child's body through medical or surgical intervention; however the use of medical equipment causing pain and side effects, absent the prospect of consequential improvement, would undoubtedly be considered harmful. When the benefits weighed against the harms are uncertain or assessed

---

73 Nigel Parton, 'The Changing Politics and Practice of Child Protection and Safeguarding in England' in Stephen Wagg and Jane Pilcher (eds), *Thatcher's Grandchildren?* (Palgrave Macmillan, 2014).
74 *Gorringe v Calderdale Metropolitan Borough Council* [2004] UKHL 15, [38].
75 Considered in chapter four.
76 Considered in chapters two and five.

differently by those with primary responsibility, i.e. parents and doctors, state intervention through an independent judiciary is justified to ensure the protection of the welfare of the child.[77]

Whilst decisions concerning a child's future medical treatment are considered matters of private law, the cases considered throughout this book, including the recent judicial review of the decision of St Bart's with regard to the future treatment of Tafida Raqeeb, demonstrate that public law also has a function. In the case of Tafida Raqeeb, MacDonald J identified the public policy requirement to bring a dispute between parents and doctors about a child's medical treatment before the court as being in the public interest. The public interest was in ensuring the best interests of the child in the context of medical treatment as 'one of the fundamental interests of society', which should be decided by the courts, not the treating doctors. Furthermore, there was a public interest in ensuring that doctors had a 'legally certain route' by which to determine their legal obligations, that the child had an independent voice, and that children were treated equally.[78] Many of the cases involve children in the care of the state; consequently, the statutory responsibilities of public authorities to children and the state's responsibility to protect the interests of the vulnerable are also an important part of the legal framework.[79] Over forty years after the first reported case concerning a proposed medical intervention upon a child, the purpose of this book is to reflect upon the allocation of responsibilities between parents, professionals, public authorities, and the courts.

Best Interests and Responsibilities for Children's Medical Treatment

Writing in 1981, Ian Kennedy pointed to the lack of guidance for doctors which, he argued, should be provided by the law through a framework which reflected good medical practice. The Standing Advisory Committee which Ian Kennedy argued for was not established. There has been no comprehensive review or Code of Practice developed to guide practitioners and give confidence to patients. The legal and ethical issues of specific aspects of medical practice concerning children have been examined by the Nuffield Council on Bioethics since it was established in 1991. Following review, the Council has made recommendations on critical care decisions in fetal and neonatal medicine[80] and children and medical research,[81] and published a policy paper on conflict in children's medical decision-

---

77 The summary of cases in the Appendix identifies which cases were concerned with the medical treatment of children in the care of the state and which were disagreements between parents and doctors over a child's medical treatment.
78 *Tafida Raqeeb* (n 55) [151].
79 Considered in chapters two and five.
80 Nuffield Council on Bioethics, *Critical care decisions in fetal and neonatal medicine: ethical issues* (2006).
81 Nuffield Council on Bioethics, *Children and Clinical Research: Ethical Issues* (2014).

making,[82] which have contributed to informed debate but have not resulted in any legislative or policy change.

Consequently, the applicable principles of law have been left to be developed through the case law in response to questions about the medical treatment of often seriously ill children. The courts have been asked to respond to historic events in criminal trials[83] and negligence actions,[84] to review the decisions of public bodies,[85] and to clarify legal obligations in declaratory proceedings.[86] Through rulings on specific issues concerning the treatment and care of children and applying the existing legal frameworks in place at the time, the applicable legal principles and the dominance of the best interests principle were soon established.[87] As the Appendix demonstrates, an increasing number of cases are being brought before the courts. This could be attributed to what Waite LJ observed in *Re T* that whilst the paramouncty of the welfare of the child is an easy principle to state, the difficulty arises when applying the welfare principle to a decision with respect to a seriously ill child.[88] As the examination of the case law demonstrates, it is not the case that Trusts are more willing to bring issues about a child's medical treatment before the court than health authorities were earlier in the case law. As argued in chapter three, the early cases were not only about the best interests of the child, they were also fundamentally about the allocation of responsibilities between parents, doctors, public authorities, and the state, through an independent judiciary. The argument presented in this book is that we need to understand these cases as raising issues beyond the best interests of the child, that is, the balance of responsibilities which alter in the changing social and political context.

From Paternalism to Consumerism

In comparison with the wealth of academic literature reflecting upon changes in the doctor/adult patient relationship and its legal regulation, the nature of the parent/professional relationship has been rarely addressed in judicial determination of a child's medical treatment and consequently, has not received the same attention in academic literature.[89] Writing in 2000, Montgomery explained that the failure of the courts to take a more interventionist approach in medical malpractice was due to the view amongst the judiciary that doctors are altruistic and work under pressure in the public interest, and due to a concern amongst

---

82 Nuffield Council on Bioethics, *Bioethics Briefing Note: Disagreements in the Care of Critically Ill Children* (2019).
83 For example, *R v Arthur* (n 6).
84 For example, *Bolitho v City & Hackney HA* [1998] AC 232.
85 Considered in chapter three.
86 *Gillick v West Norfolk and Wisbech AHA* [1986] AC 112.
87 As detailed in chapter three.
88 [1997] 1 WLR 242, 253.
89 Which has focused upon best interests and alternative 'tests' such as significant harm as well as alternative dispute resolution.

the judiciary about their own ability to comprehend technical-medical detail.[90] In his Reith Lectures, Ian Kennedy argued for an understanding of the patient as a consumer seeking to assert his or her interests in self-determined, responsible participation in decisions about his or her life, which was then undermined by medical paternalism.[91] Jonathan Montgomery characterised this approach as 'highly rational ethical consumerism'.[92] Yet, in the decades since, there has been a shift in the approach of the law governing the medical treatment of adults, from medical paternalism to greater respect for patient autonomy,[93] both generally on the provision of information about treatment options[94] and specifically in relation to decisions about adults who lack capacity, both of which are no longer determined by clinical judgement.[95] As Jonathan Montgomery has suggested, the decision of the Supreme Court in *Montgomery* confines *Bolam* to those aspects of medical treatment that are 'solely clinical',[96] dividing professional judgement in the way the House of Lords had declined to do in *Sidaway*.

Although in the context of the care of children generally, and not children's medical treatment where choices are limited by the available treatment options, Brenda Hoggett, in the quote above, linked choice and responsibility, concepts that were, some 20 years later, linked in the context of adult treatment by the Supreme Court in *Montgomery*.[97] Academic analysis has considered *Chester* and *Montgomery* to be a continuation of the trajectory in which the law has been travelling, towards greater respect for patient autonomy.[98] The changed context

---

90 Montgomery (n 19) 378.
91 Kennedy (n 1) 162.
92 Montgomery (n 19), 363.
93 As acknowledged by the Supreme Court Justices in *Montgomery v Lanarkshire Health Board* [2015] UKSC 11 [81] and Lord Steyn in *Chester v Afshar* [2004] UKHL 41 [16]–[19]. Writing in 2006, Jonathan Montgomery argued that the requirement to disclose information about treatment options was a way of reducing the power of the medical profession, 'a negative justification' in 'limiting undesirable paternalism' which had the effect of increasing scope for the exercise of autonomy, 'Law and the Demoralisation of Medicine' (2006) 26 *Legal Studies* 185, 187.
94 *Montgomery* (n 93).
95 From *Re F* [1990] 2 AC 1 to *Re A* [2000] 1 FLR 549 and *Re S* [2000] 2 FLR 389; and from *Airedale NHS Trust v Bland* [1993] 2 WLR 316 to the Mental Capacity Act 2005 in which assessments of best interests are no longer based upon *Bolam*.
96 Jonathan Montgomery, 'Patient No longer? What Next in Healthcare Law?' (2017) 70 *Current Legal Problems* 73, 88.
97 *Montgomery* (n 93).
98 Rob Heywood and José Miola, 'The changing face of pre-operative medical disclosure: placing the patient at the heart of the matter' (2017) 133 *Law Quarterly Review* 296; Judy Laing, 'Delivering informed consent post-Montgomery: Implications for medical practice and professionalism' (2017) 2 *Professional Negligence* 128. Although Jonathan Montgomery and Elsa Montgomery argued that the principle of respect for patient autonomy was only upheld by failing to respect the choices and characteristics of the patient, 'Montgomery on informed consent: an inexpert decision' (2016) 42 *Journal of Medical Ethics* 89–94.

in which the Supreme Court determined the standard for information disclosure was identified in the speech of Lord Kerr and Lord Reid in *Montgomery*:

> Since *Sidaway*, however, it has become increasingly clear that the paradigm of the doctor-patient relationship implicit in the speeches in that case has ceased to reflect the reality and complexity of the way in which healthcare services are provided, or the way in which the providers and recipients of such services view their relationship. One development which is particularly significant in the present context is that patients are now widely regarded as persons holding rights, rather than as the passive recipients of the care of the medical profession. They are also widely treated as consumers exercising choices: a viewpoint which has underpinned some of the developments in the provision of healthcare services. In addition, a wider range of healthcare professionals now provide treatment and advice of one kind or another to members of the public, either as individuals, or as members of a team drawn from different professional backgrounds.[99]

Furthermore, their Justices observed that 'bureaucratic decisions as to such matters as resource allocation, cost-containment, and hospital administration' taken by non-medical professionals means that clinical judgement is exercised within a 'framework of institutional rather than personal responsibilities' subject to public rather than private law.[100] Patients, it was noted, are able to secure information about symptoms, investigations, treatment options, risks, and side-effects via the internet and from patient support groups; other sources of information include patient and pharmaceutical information sheets. These changes mean that the doctor/adult patient relationship can no longer be viewed as one in which medical paternalism prevails but rather one in which the law perceives patients as 'adults who are capable of understanding that medical treatment is uncertain of success and may involve risks, accepting responsibility for the taking of risks affecting their own lives, and living with the consequences of their choices'.[101] As Kenneth Veitch observed, judicial and academic focus in medical law has been upon patient empowerment through respect for autonomy and the human rights of the patient and upon the ethical justification for legal decisions. In his critical examination of medical law's context, Kenneth Veitch argued that accompanying the focus upon autonomy is a construction of the patient as consumer. Although, as Jonathan Montgomery has observed, there is no necessary connection between autonomy and choice. Where autonomy involves living according to one's own system of values, the pursuit of choice can result in indiscriminate exercise of choice not informed by those values.[102] Making choices does not necessarily involve the

99 *Montgomery* (n 93) [75].
100 *Montgomery* (n 93) [75].
101 *Montgomery* (n 93) [81].
102 Jonathan Montgomery (n 93) 186.

exercise of autonomy, if having and making choices becomes the focus and where the choice seems to offer hope, the danger is that the necessary information is not sufficiently considered. Six years later, Jonathan Montgomery developed his critique observing that whilst the law was not informed by (philosophical) ethical principles, it had permitted (professional) ethical principles to set high standards. However, the persuasiveness of market- rather than morality-based arguments and the dominance of choice was, he argued, threatening the 'demoralisation of medicine'.[103] Recent high-profile cases support Jonathan Montgomery's view that it is the dominance of choice in a global market that is threatening the partnership between parents and professionals in the care of children.

If patients are regarded not as passive recipients of care but as rights-holders and increasingly 'consumers exercising choices'[104] in the context of the care of children who depend upon both professionals and their parents, it is parents who are claiming rights and making choices. However, there are fundamental differences between the adult patient and parents making decisions about their child's medical treatment. As Brenda Hoggett stated in the quote above, whilst discharge of parental duties will not be interfered with without good cause or due process, doctors treating children have professional duties and public authorities have responsibilities to protect the interests and welfare of children.

The consequence of promises of choice offered by consumerism, Kenneth Veitch predicted, would be a rise in litigation founded on lack of choice, a prediction borne out in the more recent case law considered in the chapters which follow. Further, he argued, respect for autonomy may result in respect for individual rights but also in responsibility for the self and the choices made. This responsibility plays out in a particular way in respect of parental decisions about the medical treatment provided to seriously ill children, that is, a responsibility upon parents to do everything that they possibly can to secure treatment for their seriously ill child. Whilst individual parents will reach different conclusions about where the limits lie, parents may push at those limits, seeking to introduce new treatment options, or challenging not only professional judgement but also judicial decisions. Drawing upon the work of Ulrich Beck, Kenneth Veitch observed that

> [C]itizens, armed with their newly acquired rights, no longer view their role as obedient observers of the dictates of the executive and parliament. Rather, by deploying those rights as a means by which to challenge and monitor decisions of the state and its public bodies, a new mode of political participation emerges in the form of citizens' interest groups and new social movements created by particular issues. And rather than challenges and rights claims being pursued solely through centralized political channels, the law

---

103 Jonathan Montgomery (n 93) 207.
104 *Montgomery* (n 93) [75].

also becomes a vehicle for attempts to secure various interests, thereby ensuring that the courts become sites of sub-politics.[105]

Parental use of the media to tell their story and garner support for their position is evident throughout the case law. The father of Jaymee Bowen, who challenged the decision of Cambridge Health Authority not to fund further treatment for leukaemia, asked for the order he had previously requested to protect her anonymity to be discharged to enable him to use the media to raise money should Jaymee require further treatment, and to permit broadcast of the Panorama documentary, *The Story of Child B*.[106] The families of David Glass, Charlotte Wyatt and the mother of Neon Roberts shared their views on blogs.[107] The family of Ashya King, responding to initial criticism of their actions, presented their side of the story on YouTube[108] and interviews with his parents appeared on television and in newspapers.[109] A social movement grew in support of the parents of Charlie Gard[110] and Alfie Evans[111] with Twitter, Facebook, and Instagram all used to 'mobilise support' and 'create public awareness' of their child's condition and the dispute concerning their care. By uploading footage, photographs, and updates, the parents were able to take 'direct control' of the 'narrative'.[112] Others then used social media to comment 'regardless of whether they possessed all the

---

105 Veitch (n 24) 48.
106 Sarah Barclay, *Jaymee; The Story of Child B* (Viking, 1996); *R v Cambridge District Health Authority ex p B (No 2)* [1996] 1 FLR 375. Her initial treatment had been funded by an anonymous donor following the publicity given in the press to her case.
107 David Glass: *R v Portsmouth Hospitals NHS Trust, ex parte Glass* 50 BMLR 269; *R v Portsmouth Hospitals NHS Trust, ex parte Glass* [1999] 2 FLR 905; *Glass v UK* [2004] EHRR 15, http://www.angelfire.com/ex/davidglass1/ accessed 19 April 2020. Charlotte Wyatt, http://charlottewyatt.blogspot.com [no longer available]. Neon Roberts: *An NHS Trust v SR* [2012] EWHC 3842; *Against All Odds: The Sally Roberts Story*, https://sallyrobertsourstory.wordpress.com/sally-roberts-story/ accessed 19 April 2020. Neon Roberts' mother, Sally Roberts, initially participated in the documentary *You're Killing My Son: The Mum who went on the Run*, Channel 4 (2013) but withdrew when she felt that her position was being negatively portrayed. She described the documentary as 'a travesty of half-truths, misrepresentation and subtle mainstream bias', Alliance for Natural Health International, 'Sally Roberts in her own Words' (2013) https://www.anhinternational.org/2013/08/21/anh-exclusive-sally-roberts-in-her-own-words/ accessed 19 April 2020.
108 Naveed King, 'Real Story of Ashya King', https://www.youtube.com/watch?v=F93RjILFOXk, posted 30 August 2014, accessed 19 April 2020.
109 They declined to participate in the documentary *Ashya – The Untold Story*, BBC 1, which consequently focused upon the perspectives of his doctors and nurses.
110 Website: www.charliesfight.org; Facebook: Charlie Gard public group; Twitter: @Fight4Charlie; Instagram: #charliesfight. Analysed by Ranjana Das, 'Populist discourse on a British social media patient-support community: The case of the Charlie Gard support campaign on Facebook' (2018) 24 *Discourse, Context and Media* 76.
111 Website: http://www.savealfieevans.com/; Facebook: https://www.facebook.com/groups/alfiesarmy/; Twitter: @Alfiesarmy16; Instagram: alfiesarmy16.
112 Nuffield Council on Bioethics, *Disagreements in the care of critically ill children: emerging issues in a changing landscape* (2018) [12], [15].

relevant facts, subject matter, knowledge, or expertise'. Comment was dominated by emotive language and rhetoric rather than the views of experts, including comment from abroad which failed to understand the context and by those who used it as an opportunity to pursue their own cause. The result was public protest and abuse of those caring for the child.[113] Crowdfunding enabled the parents of Charlie Gard to raise the funds to enable them to pay for untested therapy which was not supported by any of the doctors who had examined Charlie.[114] Although in order to secure the attention and concern for his plight necessary to raise the money, his parents had to disclose personal and medical information. Put alongside parental wishes to access innovative treatment abroad, Neera Bhatia has suggested that we have entered a 'new era of medical science, technology and communication' which has 'reshap[ed] the social landscape in which the care and treatment of critically ill children are taking place'.[115]

The decisions of the courts at all levels in support of the conclusions of the children's doctors rather than parents could, at first sight, seem a failure to respond to 'transformations in the wider world and to consumer expectations of the public'.[116] However, the supporters were a small and vocal minority giving one impression of the nature of those transformations and expectations. Balanced against the claims to autonomy, self-determination, choice, exercise of rights, and fulfilment of responsibilities of parents are professional duties to the child and public responsibilities for the protection of child welfare.

Examining the Balance of Responsibilities

Academic analysis of medical and healthcare law has largely focused upon developments in the law concerned with the medical treatment of adults. This book is concerned with the law concerning children's medical treatment where the issues are different due to parental responsibilities, professional duties, and public responsibilities for the welfare and well-being of children. My argument is that alongside the focus upon best interests, there needs to be recognition of, not only parental responsibilities, but also professional duties and public responsibilities in the case law, in professional guidance, and in academic analysis. Furthermore, there needs to be appreciation that the understanding of parental responsibilities, professional duties, and public responsibilities reflects the legal, social, historical, and political context in which they are fulfilled and therefore changes with changes in the context in which they are determined. This argument will be advanced through a detailed analysis of over forty years of jurisprudence concerning the medical treatment of children.

---

113 Nuffield Council on Bioethics (n 112) [17].
114 Gabrielle Dressler and Sarah A Kelly, 'Ethical implications of medical crowdfunding: the case of Charlie Gard' (2018) 44 *Journal of Medical Ethics* 453, 455.
115 Nuffield Council on Bioethics (n 112) [56].
116 Veitch (n 24) 80.

Chapter two explains the legal framework provided by the Children Act 1989. This places the provision of medical treatment to children and professional duties to children in their care within the context of the balance that legislation sought to strike between parental and public responsibilities for the care, welfare, and protection of children. Chapter three provides an account of the initial case law in which the approach of the court in determination of cases concerning children's medical treatment, focused upon the best interests principle, was established. The law is positioned within the prevailing context of the time, which had a determinative effect upon the principles and approach of the courts which endures today. Chapter four examines the neglected issue of the legal duties of doctors to children in their care, which, in certain circumstances, requires referral of questions about children's medical treatment to court and, consequently, requires state intervention in family life.

Chapter five examines the range of issues which have been brought to court by local authorities with respect to children in care within the social and political context in which they occurred. As will be apparent, many of these, decided early in the jurisprudence, became leading cases and had a profound influence upon the approach of the courts in all cases involving children and also upon the balance struck between the responsibilities of those caring for the child.

Chapter six examines professional duties in the context of the body of case law concerned with decisions to withhold or withdraw life-sustaining treatment from children with life-limiting conditions. As the list of cases set out in the Appendix shows, these cases are becoming more frequent, and recent cases such as those concerning the treatment of Charlie Gard and Alfie Evans have been emotionally debated amongst the public and across media and social media. Presenting the issue to the court exclusively in terms of the best interests of the child raises the valid question as to why parents are not best placed or permitted to determine their child's best interests. The answer is that decisions about life-sustaining treatment of children are not only made in the exercise of parental responsibility but also in fulfilment of professional duties to children in their care which, as noted above, can require state intervention through the courts.

Chapter seven considers parental attempts to secure innovative or experimental treatment of children. It is argued in the conclusion that the legislative reform which has been proposed in response to individual cases is reactive and reactionary and, unlike the common law, would not adapt to accommodate social norms in the care of children. Rather, judicial reasoning, good practice guidance, and academic analysis need to recognise professional duties and public responsibilities, alongside the best interests of the child and parental responsibilities, in respect of children's medical treatment.

As will be apparent, the focus of this book is reported cases, the exercise of parental responsibility, the content of professional duties, and the nature of state intervention in family life cases concerning children's medical treatment. It should be emphasised that the critique is not of day-to-day practice in the treatment and care of seriously ill children, it is of the understanding of the law in the resolution of issues surrounding their care. This is important, not only for the children, their parents, and doctors involved in such cases, but for the understanding of the partnership of care in which a child receives medical treatment. Whilst all involved in the care of the child are seeking to achieve what they consider to be best for the child, understanding of best interests has to be situated within the nest of responsibilities and duties of parents, professionals, public authorities, and the court. My aim is a reframing of the law concerned with the medical treatment of children to one which better protects the welfare of the individual child within the context of family relationships, recognising the duties that professionals have in order to care for the child, and that the welfare of children is a matter of public interest, protected through the intervention of the state.

2 The Children Act 1989 and Responsibilities for Children's Medical Treatment

The Care, Upbringing and Protection of Children: Private and Public Responsibilities

This chapter examines the Children Act 1989 (hereafter 'the Children Act') which establishes the legal framework for the determination of the balance of responsibilities between parents, professionals, public authorities, and the courts for the provision of medical treatment to children. It introduces the Children Act and explains the relevance of key concepts of parental responsibility and welfare and the legal basis for intervention into parental decision-making. Consideration of the case law in chapter three demonstrates the impact of the balance of responsibilities framed by the Children Act, which mean that health professionals, in the fulfilment of their duties to children in their care, have to refer the issue of a child's medical treatment to the courts in certain circumstances.

The Children Act 1989

The Children Act was the product of careful review and consultation. In response to the Short Report,[1] which had concluded in 1984 that a thorough review of child law was required, the Department for Health and Social Security established an interdepartmental working party to review the public law governing the childcare responsibilities of local authorities. The majority of the recommendations in its working paper, *Review of Child Care Law*,[2] were accepted in the White Paper, *The Law on Child Care and Family Services*[3] and informed the public law provisions of the Children Act. At the same time, the Law Commission had been reviewing child law,[4] and the recommendations in its final report on

---

1 House of Commons Social Services Committee, *Children in Care* (HC 360, 1984).
2 Department of Health and Social Security, *Review of Child Care Law. Report to Ministers of an Interdepartmental Working Party* (HMSO, 1985).
3 White Paper, *The Law on Child Care and Family Services* (Cm 62, 1987).
4 There were four working papers from the Law Commission: *Review of Child Law: Guardianship* (Law Com No 91, 1985); *Review of Child Law: Custody* (Law Com No 96, 1986);

Guardianship and Custody[5] provide the policy basis for the private law provisions of the Children Act. The resultant Bill was described in the Commons by the then Leader of the House, Sir Geoffrey Howe, as 'a comprehensive and integrated statutory framework to ensure the welfare of children'.[6] Introducing the second reading of the then Children Bill, the Lord Chancellor, Lord Mackay, explained that it brought 'together the public and private law concerning the care, protection and upbringing of children, and the provision of services to them and their families'[7] with a set of remedies for child law consistent across both public and private law.[8] The Children Act created a comprehensive, single, statutory framework bringing together the public and private law relating to children in a comprehensive set of rules with a coherent set of legal concepts and principles.[9] It provides for private law orders to settle disputes over the upbringing of children between parents, holders of parental responsibility, or persons who are involved in the day-to-day care and upbringing of children. It sets out the duties upon local authorities to provide services to help parents with children in need. It provides compulsory powers for intervention when parental care places the child at least at risk of significant harm, specifying the role of the local authority and of the court when proceedings are commenced to intervene in family life through public law orders, and ultimately taking a child into the care of the local authority. Whilst providing the statutory basis for intervention by public authorities and the courts into family life in the interests of child protection, the Act imposes clear and principled limits upon the exercise of those powers. The Act does not explicitly address the medical treatment of children but provides the framework rules for the balance of responsibilities between parents, the local authority, and the courts in the care of children and the professional duties of healthcare professionals in relation to children's medical treatment.

The political context for the Act was, as Jean Packman and Bill Jordan explained, one in which a 'radical, market-minded government had restructured almost all of the public services, in an endeavour to "roll back the frontiers of the state" and introduce commercial principles in the provision of social welfare'.[10] Jean Packman and Bill Jordan contrasted the concepts of the Children Act with

---

Review of Child Law: Care, Supervision and Interim Orders in Custody Proceedings (Law Com No 100, 1987); *Review of Child Law: Wards of Court* (Law Com No 101, 1987).

5 Law Commission, *Review of Child Law: Guardianship and Custody* (Law Com No 172, 1988). Law Commissioner, Professor Brenda Hoggett was also member of the DHSS working party, which was supported by a joint team of DHSS officials and lawyers from the family law team at the Law Commission, para 1.3. Professor Hoggett subsequently was appointed to the judiciary and went on to become Lady Hale, President of the Supreme Court.
6 HC Deb 26 October 1989, vol 158, col 1075.
7 HL Deb 6 December 1988, vol 502, col 488.
8 Law Commission (n 5) para 1.5.
9 Brenda Hoggett, *Parents and Children: The Law of Parental Responsibility* (Sweet & Maxwell, 1993) 9. The Bill was passed in 1989 and came into force in October 1991.
10 Jean Packman and Bill Jordan, 'The Children Act: Looking Forward, Looking Back' (1991) 21 *British Journal of Social Work* 315, 315.

those of the Community Care legislation of the same time, which was premised upon 'privatization' and individual 'packages of care'.[11] In contrast, the Children Act, which provided for state support for parents to fulfil their primary responsibility, had a 'communitarian or collectivist' ethos, which they attributed to the influence upon its terms of the 'themes, issues, developments, and conflicts' that had emerged in the 1970s and continued into the 1980s.[12] Gillian Douglas argued that rather than representing a distinctive family policy of the conservative government of Margaret Thatcher, the Children Act was shaped by other developments of the time affecting family law, such as changes in family structure that had already taken place, as well as the need to comply with the European Convention on Human Rights.[13] Nigel Parton, writing in 1991, argued that the Bill presented to Parliament had been shaped by the reviews noted above, but as it proceeded through Parliament, the inquiries which resulted from the Cleveland Child Abuse scandal[14] and the deaths of Jasmine Beckford,[15] Tyra Henry,[16] and Kimberley Carlile,[17] meant that it was the child protection clauses rather than those concerned with the provision of services to support children that dominated the debate.[18]

Inevitably, whilst the Children Act provides the legal framework of respective responsibilities, how those are discharged are affected by shifting policies and political priorities. Nigel Parton has explained that the focus of public authorities in the early 1990s was upon protecting a small number of 'high risk' children from abuse in dangerous and dysfunctional families.[19] State intervention was not required into the majority of families where parents discharged their responsibilities for the upbringing of their children. Policy changes in the mid-1990s to late 2000s resulted in a wider focus upon safeguarding and promoting the welfare of children,[20] as the New Labour's *Every Child Matters* agenda, directed at improving outcomes for all children, broadened the frame to services to support the families, and wellbeing, of all children. The austerity measures introduced by the

---

11 Packman and Jordan (n 10) 315. The National Health Service and Community Care Act 1990 which was before Parliament at the time did not apply to children.
12 Packman and Jordan (n 10) 315.
13 Gillian Douglas, 'Family Law under the Thatcher Government' (1990) 17 *Journal of Law and Society* 411, 422.
14 Butler-Sloss LJ, *Report of the Inquiry into Child Abuse in Cleveland* (Cm 412, 1988).
15 London Borough of Brent, *A Child in Trust* (1985).
16 London Borough of Lambeth, *Whose Child?* (1987).
17 London Borough of Greenwich, *A Child in Mind* (1987).
18 Nigel Parton, *Governing the Family: Child Care, Child Protection and the State* (Macmillan, 1991) 191.
19 Nigel Parton, "The Changing Politics and Practice of Child Protection and Safeguarding in England' in Stephen Wagg and Jane Pilcher (eds), *Thatcher's Grandchildren? Politics and Childhood in the Twenty-First Century* (Palgrave Macmillan, 2014) 45-68, 46.
20 Parton (n 19) 46-52.

Coalition government in 2010 led to a re-focus upon child protection, with the state 'residualised', but when it intervened, more 'authoritarian'.[21]

The underpinning premise of the legislation, as explained by the Law Commission, is that children are best raised by their parents, that public authorities should support parents to take responsibility for their children and only intervene compulsorily when the child is 'placed at unacceptable risk'.[22] The limits set by the Children Act upon compulsory state intervention in family life were identified by Lord Mackay in a lecture on the Children Bill, in which he explained that: 'unless there is evidence that a child is being or is likely to be positively harmed because of a failure in the family, the state, whether in the guise of a local authority or a court, should not interfere'.[23] As Baker J observed in his judgment in the high-profile case of Ashya King, with respect to the response of the local authority which had applied for Ashya to be made a ward of court when informed that his parents had removed him from specialist care when he urgently required post-operative treatment, the law is premised upon the understanding that parents are best placed to make decisions about a child[24] and parents are given considerable freedom to take responsibility for their child's upbringing and welfare. The duty of the state, through public services and intervention of the courts, is 'to help rather than to interfere'[25] with the fulfilment of parental responsibility. The legislation is premised on the view that parental care is generally the most effective way of ensuring the needs of the child are met but that limits to parental authority and autonomy are set by the interests of the child as generally understood. Where parental decisions are considered to be contrary to these, there is a professional duty, and a public responsibility, to intervene. Parents in a dispute about their child's medical treatment might protest that their rights have been infringed,[26] but whilst the courts have recognised that the responsibility to make decisions about their child's medical treatment is the exercise of a right, it is one that is limited, not by countervailing rights of others to decide, but by the welfare of the child.[27] As the Law Commission explained, parents have a prior claim against third parties to care for their child but one that can be displaced

---

21 Parton (n 19) 62.
22 Law Commission (n 5) para 2.1, an approach which the Report explained was equally valid in both public and private law.
23 Lord Mackay, 'Joseph Jackson Memorial Lecture – Perceptions of the Children Bill and beyond' (1989) 139 *New Law Journal* 505.
24 *In the Matter of Ashya King (A Child)* [2014] EWHC 2964, [31]
25 Brenda Hoggett, 'The Children Bill: The Aim' (1989) *Family Law* 217, 217.
26 For example, the GOSH position statement in the case of Charlie Gard stated: 'Charlie's parents fundamentally believe that they alone have the right to decide what treatment Charlie has and does not have. ... They believe that only they can and should speak for Charlie and they have said many times that they feel they have been stripped of their rights as parents.' GOSH's position statement of the 13th July 2017, [7], https://www.serjeantsinn.com/news/charlie-gard-position-statements/ accessed 29 February 2020.
27 *Gillick v West Norfolk and Wisbech Area Health Authority and another* [1986] AC 112, 184 (Lord Scarman).

in the interests of the child.[28] And, in the context of the medical treatment of a seriously ill child, doctors have expertise upon the welfare of the child, which justifies intervention through the courts into family life. *In the Matter of E*, the local authority applied for leave under s.100(3) of the Children Act 1989 for the court to exercise its inherent jurisdiction in relation to questions about two-year-old E's medical treatment.[29] The question was whether E, who was in foster care, should undergo a craniotomy. The evidence was that this decision was usually left to the child's parents or carer as there were risks in carrying out the procedure, and the advantages were primarily cosmetic and psychological and were to facilitate interaction, rather than having any effect upon neurological function. Sir James Munby P concluded that as the decision about the craniotomy could be left until decisions had been made about E's future care, it was 'inappropriate' for the judge 'to be arrogating to myself a decision which ought to be left to E's long term carers'.[30] The approach adopted by the court reflects the principles of the Children Act, that ordinarily carers rather than the court are best placed to make decisions about a child's best interests and that courts should not make unnecessary orders. The application of the Children Act to the provision of medical treatment to children is considered further below. First it is necessary to explain the concepts introduced by the Act.

The Concepts and Principles of the Children Act

Parental Responsibility

Brenda Hoggett, who was the Law Commissioner responsible for the review of child law, which resulted in the Children Act, described parental responsibility as 'the fundamental *concept* of the Children Act 1989 and one of its most important underlying *principles*'.[31] Reflecting *Gillick*, the Law Commission had expressed the view that the concept of parental rights was misleading as the paramountcy of the welfare of the child imposed a duty upon parents and justified interference by the state to promote child welfare.[32] Equally applicable to public and private law, parental responsibility is defined in s.3(1) of the Children Act as 'all the rights, duties, powers, responsibilities, and authority which by law a parent of a child has in relation to the child and his property', located in various statutory provisions and the common law.[33] Whilst notably, this definition retains the concept of parental rights and places these first in the bundle of responsibilities,

---

28 Law Commission (n 5) para 2.4.
29 *In the Matter of E* [2016] EWHC 2267.
30 *In the Matter of E* [2016] EWHC 2267, [35].
31 Hoggett (n 9) 9, emphasis in the original.
32 Law Commission, *Family Law, Review of Child Law: Guardianship* (Law Com No 91, 1985) para 1.11. Published in July 1985, after submissions to the House of Lords in *Gillick* but before their Lordships' decision.
33 Hoggett (n 25) 217.

the concept encapsulates both that parents have responsibilities *to* their children rather than rights over them and that children are primarily the responsibility *of* their parents, not the state. John Eekelaar observed that as the proposals for child law were developed through the consultation and review process, the emphasis shifted from parental responsibility in the sense that parents must behave responsibly *towards* their children to parental responsibility in the sense of the primary responsibility *for* children resting with their parents rather than the state.[34] The consequence of this, he argued, was greater freedom for parents in bringing up their children and a weakening of the supervision of the state over the parent-child relationship. He gave as examples the 'tenacity' of parental responsibility, which cannot be surrendered or transferred;[35] when a child is taken into care, this responsibility is shared with the local authority rather than passed to the authority;[36] and the principle that the court should not make an order under the Act unless doing so would be better for the child than making no order – the no unnecessary order principle.[37]

Parental responsibility for the child rests with those who care for a child, initially the child's parents, but it can be acquired by others,[38] including the local authority as a result of public law proceedings. The Law Commission declined to list responsibilities to children on the grounds that, and with reference to *Gillick*, they change according to needs and circumstances and the age and maturity of the child.[39] The duty to seek medical advice for a sick child comes from the Children and Young Persons Act 1933 and is imposed upon parents and other persons legally liable to maintain a child or young person not just upon holders of parental responsibility.[40] Failure to do so, deliberately, recklessly, or due to a lack of care whether assistance is required can amount to the criminal offence

---

34 John Eekelaar, 'Parental responsibility: State of nature or nature of the state?' (1991) 13 *Journal of Social Welfare and Family Law* 37 from the sense as used for example in Law Commission, *Family Law: Illegitimacy* (Law Com No 118, 1982) or by Lord Fraser in *Gillick* (n 27), 170. In later analysis, John Eekelaar argued that this balance reflected both a lack of confidence in the state and an emphasis upon individual responsibility and choice, *Family Law and Personal Life* (OUP 2007) 16.
35 CA 1989 s 2(9).
36 CA 1989 s 33(3)(a).
37 CA 1989 s 1(5).
38 For the detail surrounding acquiring parental responsibility for a child see e.g. Jonathan Herring, *Family Law* (Pearson, 2019) 396-409. Whilst it is crucial for health professionals to ensure that the decision-maker has parental responsibility for the child, this is not an issue in the case law where the parents are in agreement about the treatment they want for their child.
39 Law Commission (n 5) para 2.6.
40 Children and Young Persons Act 1933 s 1(2), failure by the child's parent, legal guardian, or other person 'legally liable to maintain a child' to provide, or to take steps to procure medical aid, amounts to the offence of child neglect in s 1(1). This section also makes it an offence for a person over the age of 16 with responsibility for the child to wilfully assault, ill-treat, neglect, abandon, or expose in a manner likely to cause unnecessary suffering or injury to health.

of child neglect and, if the child dies, to murder or manslaughter. It is, however, in the exercise of parental responsibility that day-to-day decisions are made about a child's upbringing, including issues that affect their health and also major decisions which will have an impact upon their child's future such as religious upbringing, education, and their medical treatment. The Children Act placed primary responsibility for the welfare of children with their parents, including the responsibility to make decisions about the medical treatment their child will receive from the options available,[41] according to their judgement of the best interests of the child.[42] Doctors cannot treat a child, who is too young to give consent on their own behalf, without the consent of the child's parents or where agreement cannot be reached between parents and the child's doctors, a decision of the court.

The Welfare Principle

Holders of parental responsibility are required to adopt a 'child-centred approach to their responsibilities in meeting the child's welfare'.[43] The 'prior claim' of parents to responsibility for the care of their child can be interfered with in the interests of the child's welfare,[44] although compulsory intervention is limited to circumstances where parental care places the child at an unacceptable risk of harm. Section 1(1) of the Children Act provides that the welfare of the child is the paramount consideration when a court determines any question with respect to the upbringing of the child or the administration of the child's property or income arising from it. When parental care is challenged, whether in private disputes or public proceedings, the welfare principle applies to any court determination of a child's future medical treatment, irrespective of the procedure by which the matter was brought before the court. Section 1(3) sets out a non-exhaustive welfare checklist of factors to consider when the court, in any disputed proceedings, is considering whether to make, vary, or discharge an order under section 8 of the

---

41 *Re A* [2001] Fam 147, 179. For ease of expression the term parents will be used to refer to the holders of parental responsibility even though not all parents have parental responsibility and some non-parents will have it with respect to a child in their care.
42 Reflected in professional guidance. GMC notes that the right to consent to medical treatment is an aspect of parental responsibility, GMC Guidance, *0-18 years: guidance for all doctors*, 2018, Appendix 2, https://www.gmc-uk.org/ethical-guidance/ethical-guidance-for-doctors/0-18-years accessed 16 April 2020. The BMA, *Children and Young People Toolkit*, 2010, last updated 2018, states that consent is provided by the holder of parental responsibility where this is in the best interests of the child, https://www.bma.org.uk/advice/employment/ethics/children-and-young-people/children-and-young-peoples-ethics-tool-kit/introduction accessed 16 April 2020.
43 *Re C* [2016] EWCA Civ 374, [43] (King LJ), quoting Sharpe J in the Family Court.
44 Law Commission (n 5) para 1.5.

Children Act or whether to make, vary, or discharge a public law order with respect to a child.[45] These factors are -

'(a) the ascertainable wishes and feelings of the child concerned (considered in the light of his age and understanding);
(b) his physical, emotional and educational needs;
(b) the likely effect on him of any change in his circumstances;
(c) his age, sex, background, and any characteristics of his which the court considers relevant;
(d) any harm which he has suffered or is at risk of suffering;
(e) how capable each of his parents, and any other person in relation to whom the court considers the question to be relevant, is of meeting his needs;
(f) the range of powers available to the court under this Act in the proceedings in question.'

The paramountcy of the child's welfare is thus applicable to any judicial determination of an issue concerning the upbringing of the child, whereas the welfare checklist is applicable in more limited circumstances including when a local authority or Trust have applied for a Specific Issue Order (SIO) which is opposed by the child's parents. The court is required to adopt the principles of the least intervention necessary, including the possibility of concluding that it should not intervene, applying the principle of no unnecessary order.[46] There must be a tangible benefit from making the order so that if there is no benefit from the order, an order should not be made. The welfare of children as determined in the case law concerning children's medical treatment is considered in detail in chapter three.

Responsibility to Support Parents to Fulfil Their Responsibilities

All children require universal services such as education and primary health care. Section 17 of the Children Act imposes a duty upon local authorities to provide services to safeguard and promote the welfare of children in need and support parents to care for their children. A child is 'in need' if

(a) '(a) he is unlikely to achieve or maintain, or to have the opportunity of achieving or maintaining, a reasonable standard of health or development without the provision for him of services by a local authority under this Part;

---

45 CA 1989 s 1(4).
46 CA 1989 s 1(5). Andrew Bainham has described this as a provision of common sense; there is no point in the court making an order unless to do so would enhance the welfare of the child, 'Changing Families and Changing Concepts: reforming the language of family law' (1998) 10 *Child and Family Law Quarterly* 1. However, it also reflects the principle that court orders are not necessarily the best way of securing the welfare of the child and that the court does not necessarily know better than the child's parents so should only intervene when it is satisfied that it is necessary to do so.

(b) his health or development is likely to be significantly impaired, or further impaired, without the provision for him of such services; or
(c) he is disabled,
and "family", in relation to such a child, includes any person who has parental responsibility for the child and any other person with whom he has been living.'

The duties imposed upon local authorities include taking reasonable steps, through the provision of services, to prevent children within their area suffering ill-treatment or neglect,[47] to provide services for disabled children,[48] and to reduce the need to bring proceedings including those for care orders or under the inherent jurisdiction of the High Court with respect to children.[49] As Judith Masson has explained, this creates a power which does not found a claim for a specific service or impose a duty to provide a specific service for a specific child.[50] Section 27 of the Children Act 1989 provides for co-operation between local authorities and other authorities including the NHS Trusts.[51] This permits the local authority to ask for help in the exercise of its functions under Part III of the Act, that is, their support of children and their families. Brenda Hale has explained that 'the concept of partnership', although not specifically articulated in the Children Act, is an 'underlying principle' of 'working together in the interests of the child'.[52] The principle of partnership thus applies to inter-agency co-operation to support authorities working with parents caring for children in need and more generally to work together with parents to prevent the need for compulsory action or court orders.

Wardship, New Orders and Inherent Jurisdiction

Prior to the Children Act, the courts had encouraged local authorities to use wardship[53] to fill the gaps in child protection legislation.[54] As Martin Parry has explained,

> For some local authorities, the wardship jurisdiction served as a supplement to the statutory care jurisdiction, whereas for others it served as a substitute for the inadequacies, perceived and real, of the legislation, which had for them become otiose.[55]

---

47 CA 1989 Sch 2 para 4(1).
48 CA 1989 Sch 2 para 6.
49 CA 1989 Sch 2 para 7.
50 Judith Masson, 'The Climbié Inquiry – Context and Critique' (2006) 33 *Journal of Law and Society* 221, 236.
51 CA 1989 s 27.
52 Brenda Hale, 'In Defence of the Children Act' (2000) 83 *Archives of Disease in Childhood* 463.
53 *Re D* [1977] Fam 158, 164.
54 *A v Liverpool City Council* [1982] AC 363, 373.
55 Martin Parry, 'The Children Act 1989: Local authorities, wardship and the revival of the inherent jurisdiction' (1992) 14 *Journal of Social Welfare and Family Law* 212, 212.

The Report of the Inquiry into Child Abuse in Cleveland had been critical of the ability of local authorities to use wardship which was denied to parents who wished to challenge local authority decisions with regard to the upbringing of the child in care.[56] The Law Commission in their working paper on *Wards of Court* considered that the use of wardship by local authorities to 'bypass the statutory child care system' was a 'major cause for concern'.[57] Pending reform of the law on wardship, the Law Commission proposed to 'incorporate the most valuable features' of wardship into the legislation whilst reducing the need to use wardship except in the most 'unusual and complex' cases.[58] The objective was to limit the use of wardship to those situations in which 'continuing parental responsibility of the court' was required[59] so that the use of wardship would not circumvent the statutory scheme established by the Children Act.

Section 8 of the Children Act introduced new orders, the Specific Issue Order (SIO) and the Prohibited Steps Order (PSO), both of which were 'modelled on the wardship jurisdiction'.[60] The Law Commission explained that, as with wardship, the objective of the orders was to enable anyone with a 'genuine interest' in the welfare of a child to apply for an order on an issue relating to his or her welfare.[61] At the time the Children Bill was before Parliament Lord Mackay explained that, in addition to applications to court to settle matters upon which those with responsibility for the care of a child are unable to agree, SIOs allow the court's agreement to be sought on serious issues affecting the upbringing of the child, giving as examples abortion and sterilisation.[62] Whilst the child's parents retain responsibility for the child's upbringing, an application for a SIO asks the court to determine a specific question in connection with parental responsibility, whilst an application for a PSO asks the court to prohibit the taking of a step that could be taken by a parent in meeting his parental responsibility for a child without the consent of the court.[63] The court can make a section 8 order in any family proceedings in which a question arises concerning the welfare of the child,

---

56 Butler-Sloss LJ, *Report of the Inquiry into Child Abuse in Cleveland* (Cm 412, 1988); Dawn Oliver 'Challenging Local Authority Decisions in Relation to Children in Care - Part 1' (1988) 1 *Journal of Child Law* 26.
57 John Eekelaar and Robert Dingwall, 'The role of the courts under the Children Bill' (1989) 139 *New Law Journal* 217 referencing Law Commission, *Review of Child Law: Wards of Court* (Law Com No 101, 1987).
58 Law Commission (n 5) para 1.4. Responses to the Law Commission Working Paper on *Wards of Court* (n 57) had supported reform but only after reform of the private and public law provisions, para 1.4.
59 Law Commission (n 5) para 4.40.
60 Law Commission (n 5) para 4.41.
61 Law Commission (n 5) para 4.41.
62 Lord Mackay (n 23).
63 CA 1989 s 8(1), consequently, along with the Child Arrangements Order, referred to as s 8 orders.

36 The Children Act 1989

upon application,[64] on the court's own volition,[65] under the inherent jurisdiction of the court,[66] in a freestanding application by an entitled applicant, or with leave.[67] SIOs and PSOs are private law orders, most usually used when those with parental responsibility for a child are unable to agree on a specific issue such as the child's schooling, religious upbringing, or immunisation. Whilst there are no limits upon applications by holders of parental responsibility, leave of the court is required before an application can be brought by a local authority[68] or anyone with a 'genuine interest' in the issue.[69] Leave is required for non-entitled applicants, both the local authority and NHS Trusts, to apply for a SIO,[70] for which s.10(9) requires the court to have regard to

(a) the nature of the proposed application for the section 8 order;
(b) the applicant's connection with the child;
(c) any risk there might be of that proposed application disrupting the child's life to such an extent that he would be harmed by it.[71]

The Law Commission stated that the requirement for leave was designed to be a 'filter' to prevent 'unwarranted interference' in a child's upbringing whilst ensuring that the welfare of the child can be effectively protected.[72] In the context of a child's medical treatment, the 'genuine interest' originates not from the Trust's status as a public body or doctors' status as employees of a public body but from the legal and professional duties of doctors to children in their care which may require state intervention in their family life.[73]

The expected reform of wardship was not forthcoming, and so it remains the case that, apart from the exceptions imposed upon local authorities, anyone with a legitimate interest in the child can institute wardship proceedings merely by issuing a summons without restrictions.[74] The Children Act, however, imposed restrictions upon the use of wardship by local authorities rather than removing those on parents. These were enacted 'in terms of the inherent jurisdiction, and in so doing the Act revives that wider jurisdiction whilst simultaneously severely limiting its application'.[75] Section 100(1) repealed the Family Law Reform Act

---

64 CA 1989 s 10(1)(a)
65 CA 1989 s 10(1)(b).
66 CA 1989 s 8(3).
67 CA 1989 s 10(2).
68 Although CA 1989 s 9(1) prohibits the court from making a s 8 order in respect of a child in care.
69 Law Commission (n 5) para 4.41.
70 CA 1989 s 10(2)(b). The persons who are entitled to apply for a specific issue order or prohibited steps order are specified in CA 1989 s 10(4).
71 CA 1989 s 10(9).
72 Law Commission (n 5) para 4.41.
73 The legal and professional duties of doctors are detailed in chapter four.
74 Senior Courts Act 1981 s 41.
75 Parry (n 55) 213.

1969, s.7, which had given the court the power to place a ward of court in the care, or under the supervision, of a local authority. The rest of the section prevents the court, in the exercise of its inherent jurisdiction, from placing a child in the accommodation of the local authority, in their care or under their supervision, from making a child who is the subject of a care order a ward of court or conferring on the local authority power to determine any question in connection with any aspect of parental responsibility for a child.[76] Together it was anticipated that the reforms would reduce the need for applications for the court to exercise its inherent jurisdiction.[77] Reflecting the aim that the exercise of the court's inherent jurisdiction is limited to the most serious of cases and because, in such cases, the local authority is seeking to intervene in fundamental decisions about a child's future without taking responsibility for the care of the child or acquiring parental responsibility for the child, the local authority must apply for leave for the court to exercise its inherent jurisdiction with respect to children.[78] This imposes a threshold requirement. For the local authority to be given leave to ask the court to exercise its inherent jurisdiction, the court must be satisfied that there is 'reasonable cause to believe that if the court's inherent jurisdiction is not exercised with respect to the child he is likely to suffer significant harm'[79] and the authority cannot achieve the result they wish to achieve by any other order the local authority is entitled to apply for.[80] Therefore, section 100 creates a statutory 'exception to the general position of unrestricted access to the inherent jurisdiction'.[81] Thus, the Children Act placed limits upon the access of the local authority to the courts' inherent jurisdiction and sought to limit the circumstances in which it would be necessary to invoke wardship. Investing local authorities with specific responsibilities in relation to child protection and welfare, Parliament specified the circumstances in which the local authority could use its compulsory powers to intervene in family life, one which depended upon an application brought to the court by the local authority.

Beyond the requirement to work in partnership with local authorities in the provision of support services and to help local authorities with their enquiries (considered below), the Children Act makes no specific mention of NHS Trusts. Trusts are able to apply on behalf of the treating doctors for the leave of the court to apply for a SIO. The limits imposed upon the local authority, with respect to applications for wardship or for the court to exercise its inherent jurisdiction, do not apply to NHS Trusts. As Lady Hale stated when giving the reasons for refusing permission to appeal to the Supreme Court in *Gard*, 'although a child can only be removed from home if it has been established that the child is likely to

---

76 CA 1989 s 100(2).
77 HL Deb, 6 December 1988, vol 502, col 493.
78 CA 1989 s 100(3).
79 CA 1989 s 100(4)(b).
80 CA 1989 ss 100(4)(a) and 100(5)(b).
81 *In the Matter of Charles Gard* [2017] EWCA Civ 410 [108].

suffer significant harm, the significant harm requirement does not apply to hospitals asking for guidance as to what treatment is and is not in the best interests of their patients'.[82] Trusts are entitled to ask a judge to decide about a child's future medical treatment which places the judge under a duty to do so. We return to the use of these orders in relation to children's medical treatment below. However, it is first necessary to consider the public law provisions under the Children Act.

The Public Law Provisions of the Children Act

Part IV of the Children Act sets out the public law powers for intervention by local authorities and courts in family life, providing for a range of orders for the compulsory intervention of the state, through the local authority, to safeguard and protect the welfare of children. When a local authority has 'reasonable cause to suspect that a child who lives, or is found, in their area is suffering, or is likely to suffer, significant harm', section 47 provides that the authority shall make enquiries to enable them to decide whether they should take any action to safeguard or promote the child's welfare.[83] When a local authority is conducting an enquiry, it is the duty of those listed in s.11, including NHS Trusts, to assist with those enquiries, in particular by providing relevant information and advice if asked to do so.[84] Enquiries should be directed at establishing whether the authority should apply to a court or exercise any of their other powers under the Act.[85] Thus, the principle of Working Together requires Trusts to support the local authority in determining whether to exercise its duties to protect children from harm.

The Children Act gives local authorities powers to intervene in family life, in the interests of the child's welfare, whilst placing limits upon the circumstances in which it can do so.[86] The process must be instigated by the local authority but requires the decision of a court. Care proceedings can only commence upon an application by the local authority or authorised person to court.[87] The first stage is a court hearing for a finding of fact to determine whether the threshold has been met before the court can consider whether it is in the welfare of the child to make an order. The threshold to be satisfied before the local authority, following

---

82 *In the matter of Charlie Gard (Permission to Appeal Hearing)*, 8 June 2017, https://www.supremecourt.uk/news/permission-to-appeal-hearing-in-the-matter-of-charlie-gard.html accessed 29 February 2020.
83 CA 1989 s 47(1) also when a child in their area is subject to an emergency protection order or is in police protection.
84 The persons listed in CA 1989 s 47(11) are any local authority; any local housing authority; the National Health Service Commissioning Board; any clinical commissioning group; Local Health Board; Special Health Authority; National Health Service trust or NHS foundation trust; and. any person authorised by the Secretary of State for the purposes of this section.
85 CA 1989 s 47(3) (i) & (ii).
86 Law Commission (n 5) para 1.5.
87 CA 1989 s 31(1).

investigations, can consider making a Care Order, Supervision Order, or Interim Order is set out in s.31(2) which provides,[88]

A court may only make a care order or supervision order if it is satisfied –
(a) that the child concerned is suffering, or is likely to suffer, significant harm; and
(b) that the harm, or likelihood of harm, is attributable to –
   (i) the care given to the child, or likely to be given to him if the order were not made, not being what it would be reasonable to expect a parent to give to him; or
   (ii) the child's being beyond parental control.[89]

Significant harm includes impairment of physical or mental health[90] compared with that which could reasonably be expected of a similar child,[91] for example, given the child's disabilities or medical condition. Failure to seek medical treatment may, as Judith Masson has suggested, meet this threshold.[92] As one of the requirements for the threshold for compulsory intervention relates to the standard of parental care, parental decisions and actions concerning their child's medical treatment may raise concerns and may require social service enquiry or intervention. In other cases, it may be that the parents lack the capacity to meet their child's needs or make decisions about their child's medical treatment.[93] However, the courts have made it clear that care proceedings are not the appropriate mechanism by which the local authority can secure medical treatment that it views as in the best interests of the child, unless there are care proceedings with a care plan which includes issues of medical treatment.[94] Neither are care proceedings the mechanism through which to secure the medical treatment proposed by professionals to which parents have disagreed.[95] As the court recognised in *Re C*,[96] the threat of care proceedings may undermine the trust and the 'co-operative relationship' between the health professionals and parents working together to care for the child.[97] If the court determines that the threshold has been met, the court must consider the welfare principle, welfare checklist, and no unnecessary

---

88 The threshold for an Emergency Protection Order is set out in CA 1989 s 44(1).
89 Case law considered by C Cobley and NV Lowe, 'The statutory "threshold" under section 31 of the Children Act 1989 – time to take stock' (2011) 127 *Law Quarterly Review* 396.
90 CA 1989 s 31(9).
91 CA 1989 s 31(10).
92 CA 1989 s 31(2)(b)(i).
93 Considered in chapter five.
94 *LA v SB & AB & MB* [2010] EWHC 1744, [15], considered in chapter three.
95 *Re O* [1993] 2 FLR 149, considered in chapter three.
96 [1997] 2 FLR 180.
97 As the parents of Ashya King explained, they feared that if they questioned the treatment plan that an Emergency Protection Order would be sought to take Ashya into care, Jo Bridgeman, 'Misunderstanding, threats, and fear, of the law in conflicts over children's healthcare: In the Matter of Ashya King [2014] EWHC 2964' (2015) 23 *Medical Law Review* 477.

order principle. As the purpose of this book is to explore parental, professional, and public responsibilities with respect to children's health and medical treatment, understanding this background is important to contextualise the cases, given that many of the cases which were formative of the approach of the courts in children's medical treatment cases were brought to court by local authorities with respect to children already in their care.[98]

The Children Act abolished the procedures by which local authorities had assumed parental rights over children in care of administrative action, of passing a resolution (at a council committee or sub-committee), or by virtue of the fact that the child had been in local authority care for three years.[99] When a Care Order is in place with respect to a child, the local authority gains parental responsibility, which is shared with the child's parents.[100] The local authority has a duty, as far as is reasonably practicable, to consult and consider the wishes and feelings of the child in care, the child's parents, and any other person who has parental responsibility or whose wishes and feelings may be relevant before making a decision with respect to the child.[101] The local authority further has the power to determine the extent to which parents may meet their parental responsibility for the child where that is necessary to safeguard or promote the child's welfare.[102]

The principle is that once a child is in local authority care, decisions about the child's upbringing should be made by those with parental responsibility rather than the court, so the Children Act places limits upon applications to court by the local authority with respect to children in care. A child in care may not be made a ward of court;[103] conversely, a care order will terminate wardship.[104] The court cannot, in the exercise of its inherent jurisdiction with respect to children, place a child in local authority care or make a child who is subject to a care order a ward of court.[105] If the child is in care, the local authority cannot apply for a SIO.[106]

Section 11 of the Children Act 2004 places a duty on public services including NHS Trusts and Foundation Trusts and their employees to ensure their functions are discharged having regard to the need to safeguard and promote the welfare

---

[98] Demonstrated in chapters three and five.
[99] Repealing by sch 11 of the CA 1989 Child Care Act 1980 s 3; Stephen Cretney, 'The Children Act 1948 - Lessons for Today' (1997) 9 *Child and Family Law Quarterly* 359.
[100] CA 1989 s 33(3). An Emergency Protection Order also confers parental responsibility upon the local authority, CA 1989 s 44(4)(c) and is permitted to take such action in meeting parental responsibility for the child as is reasonably required to safeguard or promote the welfare of the child, CA 1989 s 44(5)(b).
[101] CA 1989 ss 22(4) & (5).
[102] CA 1989 s 33(4). How this is applied with respect to decisions concerning a child's medical treatment is considered in chapter five.
[103] CA 1989 s 100(2)c.
[104] CA 1989 s 91(4).
[105] CA 1989 s 100(2).
[106] CA 1989 s 9(1).

of children,[107] although this does not create an enforceable duty.[108] The duty is to safeguard children, that is, both to protect them from maltreatment and impairment of health and development, and to promote their welfare, ensure that children have safe and effective care, and are enabled to have the best outcomes.[109] In the context of disagreements between parents and doctors about the provision of medical treatment to a child, MacDonald J said in the recent case of Tafida Raqeeb that this places the Trust under a duty to consider whether it is necessary to apply to court:

> To do otherwise in such circumstances is to leave a void in relation to consent. This cannot be consistent with the duty on the NHS Trust to ensure that its functions (in this case, the medical treatment of a child) are discharged having regard to the need to safeguard and promote the welfare of children, nor with the best interests of the individual child concerned. It would also have the effect, if no such application were made, of conferring on the parents an unimpeachable authority to make welfare decisions in respect of their children notwithstanding countervailing medical advice, which is not the position in law.[110]

Consideration is now given to the application of the private and public law provisions of the Children Act in the context of medical treatment.

The Children Act 1989 and Children's Medical Treatment

Parents have primary responsibility for making decisions about their child's healthcare and medical treatment. However, as explained in chapter one, the responsibility for making decisions about the medical treatment of a seriously ill child or child with a complex condition, together with the doctors upon whose expertise parent and child rely, is unique in parenting. Both the child and his or her parents depend upon the care of specialists with knowledge and expertise not possessed by parents. Health professionals also have specific legal and professional obligations to the child. They have legal and professional duties to have regard to the need to safeguard and promote the welfare of children. Consequently, they have public duties to children in their care, which require them, when they have

---

107 HM Government, *Working Together to Safeguard Children: A guide to inter-agency working to safeguard and promote the welfare of children* (2018) https://assets.publishing.service.gov.uk/government/uploads/system/uploads/attachment_data/file/779401/Working_Together_to_Safeguard-Children.pdf accessed 29 February 2020.
108 Judith Masson, 'The Climbié Inquiry – Context and Critique' (2006) 33 *Journal of Law and Society* 221, 241.
109 HM Government (n 107) 6.
110 *Tafida Raqeeb (by her Litigation Friend) v Barts NHS Foundation Trust* [2019] EWHC 2531 (Admin) & *Barts NHS Foundation Trust v Shalina Begum and Muhhamed Raqeeb & Tafida Raqeeb (by her Children's Guardian)* [2019] EWHC 2530 (Fam) [109].

42 *The Children Act 1989*

concerns that the child is at risk of significant harm, to inform the local authority, and they have professional duties, when they have concerns about a child's welfare arising from parental decisions about the child's medical treatment, to refer these to court for determination. The Children Act concern with both the welfare of the child and the protection of the child from harm is mirrored in the context of the provision of medical treatment to a seriously ill child, when issues of the child's welfare are removed from the privacy of the home to the public place of the NHS hospital, and where decisions of both parents and doctors about a child's medical treatment are exposed to scrutiny to ensure compliance with norms of child welfare.

It was envisaged by the Law Commission that questions about a child's medical treatment may be referred to court under the Children Act. As explained in chapter three, at the time of the review of child care law and the Children Act, with the exception of *Re E*, those cases concerning a child's medical treatment or health that had been referred to court had arrived there as a result of an application by the local authority for the court to exercise its wardship jurisdiction. However, these were not the cause for concern about local authority use of wardship noted above. The examples, given by Lord Mackay above, of the use of SIOs to determine questions of sterilisation and abortion reflected the facts of cases which had, at that time, been referred to court. *Re D*[111] and *Re B (1988)*[112] both concerned the sterilisation of a teenage girl with learning difficulties, whilst *Re G-U*[113] and *Re P*[114] both concerned the legality of the termination of the pregnancy of a teenager. Sterilisation and abortion are both major and irreversible procedures but do not necessarily indicate the need for the ongoing involvement of the court. Lord Mackay further noted that the inherent jurisdiction of the High Court would, subject to leave, still be available for a 'particularly difficult issue, such as an irreversible medical procedure'.[115]

Thus, 'major and irreversible treatment issues' can be brought before the court in an application for a SIO or, subject to the limitations imposed upon local authorities, in an application for the court to exercise its inherent jurisdiction or in wardship. Writing at the time, Michael Freeman suggested that the changes introduced by the Children Act could prevent the use of wardship in cases concerned with children's medical treatment.[116] In contrast, Jonathan Montgomery observed,

---

111 1976] Fam 185.
112 [1988] AC 199, these cases are considered further in chapter five.
113 [1984] FLR 811.
114 [1986] 1 FLR 272, decided 26 October 1981. These cases are considered further in chapter five.
115 Lord Mackay (n 23).
116 Michael Freeman, 'Care After 1991' in David Freestone (ed), *Children and the Law: essays in honour of HK Professor Bevan* (Hull University Press 1990) 130-171, 168-170.

health authorities are not within the definition of local authorities and the problems could be overcome by a change in practice, whereby health authorities make applications for wardship rather than referring the matter to the social services department of the local authority. Alternatively, the inherent jurisdiction of the court can be used to deal with specific matters. Unlike wardship, this will not involve continuing court supervision and because of this, it may be that the inherent jurisdiction will be increasingly used in preference to wardship.[117]

As the case law analysed in chapter three demonstrates, this is exactly what happened. Thus, the division of responsibilities was established between the public authorities, in which Trusts apply to the court in the interests of child welfare, referring the issue to and involving the local authority when parental behaviour presents concern of risking harm to the child. The role of doctors is to advocate for the welfare of the child, in most cases accommodating parental views, leaving any child protection issues to the local authority in the exercise of their statutory powers. Applications by local authorities in the exercise of their child protection duties in response to child neglect or abuse are clearly distinguishable from the protection of the interests of the child in relation to the provision of medical treatment. Questions about the medical treatment of a seriously ill child or a child with complex conditions or the termination of a child's pregnancy raise issues of both welfare and harm, of professional duties as well as parental responsibilities, and of public concern for the wellbeing of children.

Decisions about the best treatment that can be provided to a seriously ill child are intensely private and personal, entrusted to those most directly concerned for the welfare of the child. However, some decisions about a child's medical treatment need to be made in a public forum where the decision-maker can be held to account. These include serious and irreversible medical treatment decisions concerning children in care and also instances when those who are most directly concerned for the child's welfare, the child's parents and the doctors responsible for the care of the child, cannot agree. The Children Act provides the framework within which parents and professionals fulfil their duties to the child, a framework which recognises that the state, whether through the exercise of its powers by the local authority or by the court, has a responsibility and an interest in the welfare of children.

Conclusions

Nigel Parton, writing in 1991, said that the Children Act was concerned with 'constructing a new consensus' or a 'new set of balances' concerning the roles

---

[117] Jonathan Montgomery, 'Consent to Health Care for Children' (1993) 5 *Tolley's Journal of Child Law* 117, 121.

and responsibilities of parents and of the state in relation to the upbringing of children.[118] Noting that others had referred to the provisions of the Children Act as the privatisation of child law, Gillian Douglas considered it, consistent with the then Conservative Government's approach to public regulation, to represent the de-regulation of child law.[119] She explained,

> it is the interaction of the exercise of parental responsibility with the activities of others, and the balance to be struck between the two, which has provided this imagery. For the Act appears to cut back the powers of the state to interfere in parental upbringing of children; to strengthen the parental position against that of the state.[120]

In a similar vein, Stephen Cretney, writing at the time, observed that the Children Act, 'significantly redefine[d] the role both of the state and of the courts in relation to intervention in family life'. He considered that the role of the law and of the courts had been restricted, such that the law was 'in retreat from the private realm of family life'.[121] The threshold requirements to be surpassed before the local authority can ask the court to exercise its inherent jurisdiction or before the local authority can intervene in families in public law proceedings reflected the principle that it is 'important for the law in a free society expressly to protect the integrity and independence of families save where there is at least likelihood of significant harm to the child from within the family'.[122] Except for the public law powers conferred by the Children Act upon local authorities, intervention by the state, in the form of an application by a public institution to court for a judge to make a decision about the best interests of their child, is otherwise unparalleled in family life. The Trust is asking a judge to make a fundamental decision about a child's future, without acquiring parental responsibility for the child and without taking over responsibility for the care of the child. It is seeking to interfere with a decision of parents that is of fundamental significance to their child's life, indeed, may precipitate the end of their child's life. As noted in the quote above from MacDonald J in the case of Tafida Raqeeb, the professional duties of doctors encompass a public duty to ensure that children's welfare is promoted, and they are protected from harm. Furthermore, as the cases considered throughout this book demonstrate, many of the cases which influenced the approach and principles of the law governing the provision of medical treatment to children have been concerned with a child who is in the care of the state. These vulnerable children need to have independent decisions made about their welfare,

---

118 Parton (n 18) 148.
119 Douglas (n 13) 418.
120 Douglas (n 13) 419.
121 Stephen M Cretney, 'Defining the Limits of State Intervention: The Child and the Courts' in Freestone (n 116) 58.
122 HL Deb, 6 December 1988, vol 502, col 493.

which are determined in a public forum where the decision-maker can be held to account, ensuring that decisions about their future comply with socially acceptable standards for the care of children. The law, as it developed from the first reported case of *Re D* in 1976, is critically examined in the next chapter within its social and political context.

3 The Development of the Legal Framework for Children's Medical Treatment Cases

The Law Concerning Children's Medical Treatment

This chapter examines the development of the legal framework concerning the medical treatment of children establishing the balance of responsibilities between parents, professionals, public authorities, and the courts. It argues that, to understand the current principles and approach of the courts, it is necessary to understand the social, legal, and political context in which the law developed and the changing context within which it is currently applied. This chapter shows that the very first cases, decided when the law as it applied to medical practice was uncertain, amounted to a challenge to prevailing ideas about medical paternalism and parental authority. *Gillick* emphasised that parents have protective duties for the welfare of their child, not parental authority over them. In the cases that followed, the courts were asked to give guidance to those with responsibility for a child's medical treatment, and the approach of the court to the exercise of its inherent jurisdiction to protect the vulnerable is explained. This chapter then considers cases in which the courts rejected the argument that decisions about a child's medical treatment are matters for clinical judgement; questions about serious medical issues concerning a child in care or when those with primary responsibility disagree must be brought before the court to determine the welfare of the child in the exercise of the judicial duty to protect the vulnerable. This chapter concludes with a consideration of the judicial review cases which reflect the changing issues before the courts as the law has developed from challenges to underfunding of the NHS, to parental attempts to secure treatment in another health authority, and most recently cases in which parents have sought to take their child abroad for treatment.

Parental Authority and Potential Criminal Liability

When the court was asked in *Re B (1981)*[1] to make decisions about the medical treatment of a child, it was in order to clarify the legal obligations of doctors,

---

1 [1981] 1 WLR 1421.

parents, and social services to the child. Questions about the relationship between criminal liability and medical practice were prevalent, following the contemporaneous prosecution of paediatrician Dr Arthur, who had prescribed nursing care and the administration of a sedative to John Pearson, a baby with Down's Syndrome, following his parents' rejection of him.[2] The charge of murder in that case was amended to attempted murder, as the post-mortem raised questions about the cause of death, a charge of which Dr Arthur was acquitted. Farquharson J opened his direction to the jury by saying that the case was of 'enormous importance' because it raised 'serious questions affecting the practice of the medical profession, as well as matters that gravely affect the interests of the public at large', concerning the duties of a doctor to a child with disabilities whose parents do not want that child to survive.[3] The judge reminded the jury of the case for the defence that following the birth of a child with Down's Syndrome, the doctor would seek to determine what was in the best interests of the child who, if his or her parents did not want to care for him, had a very remote chance of being fostered or adopted into another family and thus in all likelihood would be 'placed in some form of institution'.[4] Dr Arthur maintained that his professional conscience was clear as he had acted as a responsible paediatrician respecting the authority of the parents.[5]

In the context of the debate prompted by *R v Arthur*, when the parents of Baby Alexandra, who also had Down's Syndrome, refused their consent to surgery to remove an intestinal blockage, the hospital informed the local authority, which then applied for her to be made a ward of court. Her parents were of the view that the best course of action for her was to be allowed to die, sedated to ensure she did not suffer any pain.[6] The judge authorised the operation. When Alexandra was transferred for the court-authorised procedure, the surgeon at that hospital declined to operate out of respect for the wishes of her parents. The surgeon explained that he considered that the 'great majority of surgeons faced with a similar situation' would have reached the same decision.[7] Whilst a surgeon at the hospital where she had been born and another at a different local hospital were prepared to operate, there is evidence to support the view of the surgeon who declined to operate. Michael Freeman has written that the British Paediatric Association's response to the case was that parents should decide whether a

---

2 *Re B* (n 1) followed the charge but preceded the trial of Dr Arthur, *R v Arthur* (1981) 12 BMLR 1.
3 *R v Arthur* (n 2) 1.
4 *R v Arthur* (n 2) 5.
5 Arthur Osman, 'Conscience is clear, murder case doctor says' *The Times* (3 April 1981). A British Medical Journal editorial of the time emphasised the need for socially acceptable standards to guide doctors, arguing that there was no reason to consider that judges were better placed than parents to reach a humane decision, Editorial Comment, 'The Right to Live or the Right to Die' (1981) 283 *British Medical Journal* 569.
6 *Re B* (n 1). The context in which decisions were made about Alexandra's quality of life is considered in chapter six.
7 *Re B* (n 1) 1423.

severely impaired baby should be treated.[8] The British Medical Association's ethical guidance, then stated in the *Handbook of Medical Ethics,* was that the decision must ultimately be for parents, although the doctor's primary concern was the needs and rights of the child.[9] This advice, by virtue of its lack of clarity, could be criticised for leaving the decision to the individual doctor according to their personal values.

The medical evidence was unanimous that the procedure was clinically indicated. The different view within the medical evidence was not whether it was in Baby Alexandra's best interests to have life-saving surgery given her potential future quality of life with Down's Syndrome but whether to respect parental authority. The matter was brought back before the judge, who then decided that the parental wishes should be respected, indicating that the judicial, as well as professional, duty was to respect parental authority. Determining the appeal brought by the local authority, Templeman and Dunn LJJ held that the judge had erred, as it was his duty to reach an independent assessment of the best interests of the child and not to accede to professional respect for parental authority. The court authorised the procedure, protecting the right to life and the future of a vulnerable child unable to articulate her own interests, paving the way for the protective approach of courts to the interests of the individual child in medical treatment cases. Following the procedure, Alexandra was temporarily taken into care in the exercise of the public authority's protective duties to the child, although a few months later she was returned to the care of her parents.[10]

Janet Read and Luke Clements have noted that the cases of *R v Arthur* and *Re B* resulted in unprecedented 'public interrogation' of medical practice, brought the law into cases of ethical controversy which had previously been dealt with privately between parents and doctors, and raised questions about the duties and responsibilities of local authorities.[11] Writing soon after, Michael Freeman observed that an organisation was formed to promote the rights of parents to decide and quoted an article from *The Times* which described the Court of Appeal's decision as a 'cruel folly' for failure to appreciate the 'moral capacities of ordinary people'.[12] Ian Kennedy placed the decisions of the parents within the context of the then-prevailing attitudes to, lack of support for the care of, and prospect of living in an institution for, children with disabilities:

---

8 Michael Freeman, 'Freedom and the Welfare State: Child-rearing, parental autonomy and state intervention' (1983) 5 *Journal of Social Welfare and Family Law* 70, 88, referencing *The Times* (19 August 1981).
9 Freeman (n 8) 88, referencing the 1981 edition, paras 5.11, 5.12.
10 Freeman (n 8) 88 referencing *The Observer* (5 December 1982).
11 Janet Read and Luke Clements, 'Demonstrably Awful: The Right to Life and the Selective Non-Treatment of Disabled Babies and Young Children' (2004) 31 *Journal of Law and Society* 482, 501.
12 Michael Freeman, *The Rights and Wrongs of Children* (Frances Pinter, 1983) 261 referencing *The Times* (14 September 1981) and Claire Tomalin, 'Alexandra: The Cruel Folly' *The Times* (1 September 1981).

As a society we offer parents little or no support, whether in the form of practical help or professional advice, which may persuade them to keep the baby at home despite any initial decision not to do so. And the fate which awaits the baby, if it is not kept at home, is for the most part one which many parents and others would think was not far removed from a living death, lost in the back wards of some soulless institution.[13]

It was with respect to these cases[14] that Ian Kennedy and Michael Freeman, both writing in the 1980s, presented the arguments that doctors needed a socially, ethically, and legally acceptable framework within which to work, reflecting good practice and protecting the interests of their patients and society more generally. However, these cases also led them to observe that the development of this framework for practice was not best achieved through decisions of the court in individual cases. The Court of Appeal in *Re B* may have eventually reached the right conclusion for Alexandra focused upon her best interests, although that only occurred because of the proactive intervention by the local authority in the exercise of its protective responsibilities to the child. The Court of Appeal judgment in *Re B* set the law in the direction of development through individual cases, drawing upon and developing existing legal principles and processes, reflecting the ordinary standards of the day. The changing standards by which decisions are reached was commented upon by Wall LJ in his observations on *Re B* in a Court of Appeal judgment in 2005,

> Was it in her interests to have the operation, and live the life of a Down's Syndrome child, or not to have the operation, and die literally within a week? Put in those stark terms, the answer in 2005 may seem much clearer than it was in 1981, given in particular our increased knowledge of the educational and social goals which many Down's Syndrome children are capable of achieving. The answer was, however, perfectly clear to this court, and the local authority's appeal was allowed.[15]

That judges must reflect the standards of the day was emphasised by their Lordships in *Gillick*,[16] a case which raised very different issues from *R v Arthur* and *Re B* but was equally determinative of the approach to be taken in cases concerned with children's medical treatment.

---

13 Ian Kennedy, *The Unmasking of Medicine* (Granada, 1981 revised 1983) 94.
14 And *Re D* [1976] Fam 185, considered below.
15 *Re Wyatt* [2005] EWCA Civ 1181 [67].
16 *Gillick v West Norfolk and Wisbech Area Health Authority and another* [1986] AC 112.

The Impact of *Gillick*[17]

As is well known, the question for the courts in *Gillick*, was whether a doctor can lawfully prescribe contraception for a girl under 16 years of age, without the knowledge or consent of her parents.[18] The DHSS Guidance which was the subject of challenge by Victoria Gillick stated that, although it would be an exceptional case in which a doctor would provide contraception to a girl under the age of 16 without parental consent, 'in the last resort'[19] the decision whether or not to prescribe contraception was a matter of clinical judgment. Whether a girl under the age of 16 should be provided with contraception was, Victoria Gillick argued, a social not a clinical judgement which parents rather than doctors should make with respect to their children.[20] Lord Fraser placed the issues in *Gillick* within the context of the changed nature of the parent/child relationship from the absolute power of the authoritarian Victorian father to the responsible parent who nurtured their child's independence. Notions of parental authority had become outmoded. Lord Scarman set the issues in the case against the background of the development of the contraceptive pill making contraception a medical matter, the growing independence of young people, and the changed status, by which he meant liberation, of women.[21] It was important, his Lordship stressed, that the common law adapted to societal change so that the law met the needs of society. The emphasis by the majority upon parental rights existing in order to enable them to fulfil their duties to their children,[22] and which must be exercised for the welfare of the child,[23] placed limits upon the parental authority which Victoria Gillick was asserting and which had prevailed prior to the Court of Appeal determination in *Re B*. At the same time, the decision of the majority that the guidance was lawful, and that a doctor unable to persuade a child to inform her parents could lawfully provide contraceptive advice and treatment without her parents' knowledge or consent, could be interpreted as an example of the law leaving questions of social, rather than clinical, judgement to doctors.

Some obiter comments from the majority support this view.[24] The majority, Lords Fraser, Scarman, and Bridge, formulated the decision about the provision

---

17 *Gillick* (n 16).
18 *Gillick* (n 16) (Lord Fraser) 162.
19 Circular HSC (IS) 32, 1980 revising section G of DHSS Memorandum of Guidance on family planning services (HN (80) 46), May 1974; *Gillick* (n 16) 164.
20 Jane Lewis and Fenella Cannell, 'The Politics of Motherhood in the 1980s: Warnock, Gillick and Feminists' (1986) 13 *Journal of Law and Society* 321, 326.
21 *Gillick* (n 16) (Lord Fraser) 172; (Lord Scarman) 182.
22 *Gillick* (n 16) (Lord Fraser), 170.
23 *Gillick* (n 16) (Lord Scarman) 184. Subsequently put on a statutory footing by the Children Act 1989.
24 In the minority, Lord Brandon focused upon questions of criminal liability whilst Lord Templeman considered that parents were better placed than doctors to try to prevent girls from engaging in sexual intercourse, although contraception could lawfully be provided if, by

of contraception as a matter of clinical judgement.[25] Lord Fraser observed that the medical profession had been entrusted with discretionary powers going beyond clinical judgement, and they could be entrusted with this responsibility.[26] Lord Scarman observed that by upholding the guidance as lawful, their Lordships were leaving 'the law in the hands of the doctors', but that was the price of keeping the law in line with social experience.[27] The exercise of professional judgement in accordance with good medical practice was sufficient to protect the interests of girls. The medical profession was 'a learned and highly trained profession regulated by statute and governed by a strict ethical code which is vigorously enforced'; failure to meet these ethical standards would amount to professional misconduct.[28] As Ian Kennedy has explained, it is not clear from the judgments of the majority whether the intention was to replace the authority of the parent with the authority of the doctor, giving the responsibility to the doctor to determine the best interests of the child, or whether the role of the doctor was to determine best clinical interests, leaving the competent girl to determine where her best interests lie.[29] Stephen Gilmore has argued that it was the former that *Gillick* was concerned with competing claims of adults to know a child's best interests. He argued that their Lordships were concerned with the protection of child welfare and determined that the boundary of parenting lies at the point at which the parental protective role is no longer required.[30] This, he argued, was the way the issue was presented by both the supporters and opponents of Victoria Gillick.[31] One interpretation of the case, therefore, is that *Gillick* supports professional power or control over parental authority rather than supporting the autonomy or rights of the competent child. Whilst their Lordships' speeches could have been clearer as to whether the judgment protected professional authority or the autonomy of the competent child, strictly speaking it was not necessary to decide in order to answer the question before the court. What was clear was the balance of responsibilities between parents and doctors on this issue. The parental role should be understood as one of protection, not authority.

---

their combined efforts, they could not do so, such that contraception was the only way of protecting against pregnancy.
25 Without, as S.P. De Cruz identified, amounting to a 'doctor's charter to prescribe contraceptive advice and treatment without regard to parental wishes', 'Parents, Doctors and Children: The Gillick Case and Beyond' (1987) *Journal of Social Welfare and Family Law* 93, 107.
26 *Gillick* (n 16) 174.
27 *Gillick* (n 16) 191.
28 *Gillick* (n 16) 191.
29 Ian Kennedy, 'The Doctor, the Pill, the 15-year-old Girl' in Ian Kennedy, *Treat Me Right: Essays in Medical Law and Ethics* (OUP, 1988, reprinted 2001) 52-118, 94-5.
30 Stephen Gilmore, 'The Limits of Parental Responsibility' in Rebecca Probert, Stephen Gilmore and Jonathan Herring (eds), *Responsible Parents and Parental Responsibility* (Hart 2009) 63, 64.
31 Gilmore (n 30) 71.

Lack of Guidance

Gillick was concerned with the respective duties of parents and professionals in relation to the developing capacities of older children. Soon after *Gillick*, there followed two reported cases, *Re C* and *Re J (1991)*, concerned with the life-sustaining treatment of children in which the court noted the lack of guidance for those required to make such decisions. In both cases, the child had been made a ward of court, whilst the local authority retained 'care and control' over the child. Neither child had left the hospital since birth. Court involvement was inevitable; as a ward, all major decisions about the child's upbringing had to be made by the court. Sixteen-week-old C, who was considered to be terminally ill, had been made a ward of court at birth, at a point when her medical condition was not anticipated, as social services had formed the view that her parents would have 'great difficulty' caring for her.[32] Questions arose about her future medical treatment, specifically what treatment should be administered if she suffered an infection or illness. The local authority social worker thought that C should be treated as any other child, whilst the local authority legal department thought that C should 'receive such treatment as is appropriate to her condition'. Lord Donaldson MR agreed with the view of the legal department and held that C should be treated in accordance with the report of the paediatrician instructed by the Official Solicitor. Balcombe LJ highlighted the lack of guidance from the legislature for courts or others – parents, professionals, local authorities – in such cases.[33] In his Lordship's opinion, the judge had adopted the correct approach in undertaking a best interest analysis. The purpose of the judgment of the court was to explain clearly the reasons for the decision of the court and the course of treatment to be administered to a baby in the care of the state, ensuring that the decision could be subject to scrutiny and was socially acceptable.

In the second reported case, the following year, five-month-old J, who had severe brain damage due to a shortage of oxygen arising from breathing difficulties following his premature birth, had been made a ward of court for 'extraneous reasons' not detailed in the judgment.[34] Balcombe LJ explained that 'J's mother has many problems and cannot cope on her own', whilst J's father had a 'better comprehension of what is here at stake'.[35] His parents had in the past been prepared to accept the recommendations of his doctors, at other times supporting the position of the Official Solicitor who appealed against the order permitting the withholding of artificial ventilation from J. Lord Donaldson noted that the Official Solicitor had asked for guidance on 'the generality of the problem', noted as lacking in C. With consideration of the relationship between doctors, parents, and the court with respect to such decisions, the presumption in favour of a course of action which will prolong life and consideration of the quality of life

---

32 [1990] Fam 26, 31.
33 *Re C* (n 32) 38.
34 *Re J* [1991] Fam 33, 40.
35 *Re J* (n 34) 50.

from the assumed point of view of the child, Lord Donaldson MR sought to assist those who have to make such decisions by offering some clarification.[36] The court rejected the submission of Mr Munby QC, Counsel for the Official Solicitor, that the absolutist approach based upon the principle of the sanctity of life meant that a court is 'never justified in withholding consent to treatment which could enable a child to survive a life-threatening condition', whatever pain or side-effects and whatever the expected quality of the life of the child.[37] The alternative submission, that the court could sanction the withholding of life-saving treatment only when the child's quality of life would demonstrably be intolerable, was likewise rejected.[38] Their Lordships emphasised that the approach to be taken, in wardship cases, was to give paramount importance to the best interests of the child. In the determination of best interests there should be a 'very strong presumption in favour of a course of action which will prolong life'. The judge should also take into account the pain and suffering caused by the treatment and the quality of life which the child will experience if life is prolonged, from the assumed point of view of the child.[39] But that 'intolerability' was not, as had been submitted to the court, a 'quasi-statutory yardstick.'[40]

Further, Lord Donaldson MR observed that in the ideal situation, the provision of medical treatment to a child occurs through a partnership between doctors and parents. In doing so, he distinguished the duties of parents, doctors, and court. Whilst parents and the court, which 'takes over the rights and duties of the parents', must give consent to a child's medical treatment according to their judgement of best interests, the legal duty of the doctor is to care for the child according to 'good medical practice recognised as appropriate by a competent body of professional opinion'.[41] Doctors, parents, and the court each have distinct duties to the child and, in the ideal circumstances, work together in partnership to secure the course of action that is in the best interests of the child. Whilst parents and the court must determine the child's best interests, neither parents nor the court can require doctors to administer a treatment that is 'medically contra-indicated' or which they could not 'conscientiously administer'. *Re J (1991)*, together with the second *Re J (1993)*, Fam 15, considered in chapters four and six over which Lord Donaldson presided and affirmed those principles,[42] was to have a profound and enduring effect upon the principles and approach of the courts in children's decision-making cases. Determined in wardship proceedings with the consequence that the responsibility of the judge was to undertake the best interest analysis, decisions about the future medical treatment of both children were brought before the courts by local authorities who had legal

---

36 *Re J* (n 34) 47.
37 *Re J* (n 34) 42.
38 *Re J* (n 34) 44, with reference to the Court of Appeal in *Re B* (n 1).
39 *Re J* (n 34) 46.
40 *Re J* (n 34) 46.
41 *Re J* (n 34) 41 quoting, of course, *Bolam v Friern Hospital Management Committee* [1957] 1 WLR 582, considered in chapters four and seven.
42 *Re J* (n 34) considered in chapters four and six.

responsibilities to them. Both were babies with disabilities about whom, in the context of prevailing attitudes to disability, the professionals caring for them had concluded they would not have a quality of life and whose parents were unable to make decisions about their future treatment. Viewed thirty years later, the decisions that it was lawful and in the best interests of the babies to withhold artificial ventilation as long as those clinically responsible for them, in the exercise of their professional judgement, considered that was in their best interests, may not appear to be an effective exercise of the courts protective jurisdiction. As explained in chapter six, the conclusion of each child's best interests followed from an uncritical acceptance of the medical view of disability formed within prevailing attitudes that children with disabilities did not have lives that were worth living. Attitudes have changed, but what has endured is the understanding that it is the role of the court to exercise its protective jurisdiction and the approach and principles applied in fulfilling this responsibility.

Aside from *Gillick*,[43] by the time the Children Act 1989 came into force in October 1991, there had been ten reported cases concerning the provision of medical treatment to a child. As just explained, *Re C*[44] and *Re J (1991)*[45] both concerned the withholding of life-sustaining treatment from a baby, both wards of court. Baby Alexandra had been made a ward of court upon application by the local authority when it was consulted about her care.[46] There had been two cases concerning proposed sterilisations of a child with learning difficulties. *Re D* had been referred to court by an educational psychologist employed by the local authority; *Re B (1988)* was in local authority care.[47] Both were made a ward of court so that the court could make the decision. *Re P* and *Re B (1991)* were made wards so that the court could determine the application concerning the termination of pregnancy,[48] whilst the court in *Re G-U* stressed that local authorities needed to understand that when a child is a ward of court, no major decision can be made affecting that child without the involvement of the court.[49] Two cases concerned refusals of consent to treatment by older children; *Re R*, who was in local authority care was made a ward of court for decisions to be made about the administration to her of anti-psychotic medication.[50] The application

---

43 *Gillick* (n 16). In the 1980s there were also two unsuccessful applications for leave to apply for judicial review. Brought within a few months of each other, both concerned delays to heart surgery for a child due to a lack of intensive care nurses to staff beds in a paediatric intensive care ward at a Birmingham hospital, *R v Central Birmingham Health Authority, ex parte Walker; R v Secretary of State for Social Services and another, ex parte Walker* 3 BMLR 32; *R v Central Birmingham Health Authority ex parte Collier*, 6 January 1988 unreported, official transcript on Westlaw, see further below.
44 *Re C* (n 32).
45 *Re J* (n 34).
46 *Re B* (n 1).
47 [1988] AC 199.
48 *Re P* [1986] 1 FLR 272; *Re B* [1991] 2 FLR 426 (decided May 1991).
49 [1984] FLR 811.
50 [1992] 1 FLR 190 (decided July 1991).

for authority to administer blood to A in the treatment of leukaemia despite his refusal was made by the health authority;[51] all of the other applications had been made by the local authority. In that case the local authority had sought, but Ward J declined to make, an order for care and control, considering it inappropriate to 'introduce motions of that sort'.[52] The specific issue of the administration of blood in the treatment of leukaemia could be addressed in wardship proceedings without affecting his parents' responsibility for the care of their son.

All decisions were made by the court in the exercise of its wardship jurisdiction, establishing the protective role of the court to the interests and welfare of children. As Hedley J later observed in *Wyatt*, the responsibility had not been placed with the judiciary by an Act of Parliament; rather the court has a 'historic duty of overseeing the best interests of those who, for whatever reason, cannot make decisions for themselves'.[53] More recently, reviewing the 'evolution' of the inherent jurisdiction and wardship, Hayden J acknowledged that

> though it is difficult to be definitive as to the nature of the inherent jurisdiction or to prescribe its parameters, it can perhaps most conveniently be defined as the route by which the Court may make orders in relation to specific individuals and their affairs that are not governed by individual statute.[54]

The protection of the interests of children when issues arise as to their medical treatment, either because the child is in the care of the state or when there is disagreement about the treatment that is in the best interests of the child by those primarily responsible, given effect through the involvement of public authorities and then the courts, was thus established.

In the cases which followed the implementation of the Children Act 1989 the question was addressed of the procedure by which children's medical treatment cases should be considered. In *Re O*,[55] Johnson J considered the exercise of the court's inherent jurisdiction following an application under s.100 of the Children Act to be the most appropriate procedure, whereas Booth J in *Re R*,[56] agreed with Counsel for the local authority that an application for a SIO was the most appropriate procedure for such cases. Procedural issues were revisited, more recently, by Mostyn J in *Re JM*;[57] reported judgments in the intervening years suggesting that applications for a SIO are rare.[58] Mosytn J observed that the

---

51 [1993] 1 FLR 386 (decided September 1990).
52 *Re E* (n 51) 395.
53 *Portsmouth NHS Trust v Wyatt & Wyatt, Southampton NHS Trust Intervening* [2004] EWHC 2247 [33].
54 *Gloucestershire County Council v Re K* [2017] EWHC 1083 [16].
55 [1993] 2 FLR 149.
56 [1993] 2 FLR 757.
57 [2015] EWHC 2832.
58 Exceptions being *Re C* [2000] 2 WLR 270; *Re K, W and H* [1993] 1 FLR 854; *Re MM* [2000] 1 FLR 224. In a 2004 review, Stephen Gilmore observed that the case law revealed

court's inherent jurisdiction may not be used to 'bypass' legislation but may be used to 'fill gaps in, or to supplement, a statutory scheme'.[59] On the other hand, he recognised that whilst it might seem that cases concerning the medical treatment of a child 'fall squarely' within the scope of s.8 as the determination of a specific question that has arisen concerning an aspect of parental responsibility, the legislature when passing the Children Act might not have had in mind the situation in which an NHS Trust seeks permission to carry out serious medical treatment upon a child contrary to the wishes of the child's parents, in this case removal of an aggressive cancerous tumour from J's jaw and reconstruction using bone from his leg. That is indeed possible given that, as explained in chapter two, at the time the legislation was being developed there had been no comparable cases. Mostyn J concluded that if the Trust is seeking final binding declarations, it should apply for leave for an application for a SIO and combine that with an application for declaratory relief in the exercise of the court's inherent jurisdiction.[60] It should be noted that this conclusion was reached in the context of cuts to civil legal aid, which meant that legal aid was not available in applications for s.8 orders but may be available, subject to means testing, in cases concerning the exercise of the court's inherent jurisdiction. The views expressed by Mostyn J may be the reason why GOSH applied for declarations under the inherent jurisdiction of the court and for a SIO in the case of Charlie Gard. Notably, however, there was no mention of the SIO in the judgment of Francis J at first instance. That the Trust had applied for a s.8 order was revealed in questioning before the Supreme Court.[61] When there is an issue to be determined concerning the medical treatment of a child, the application most often appears to take the form of an application, in the case of the local authority with leave, for the court to exercise its inherent jurisdiction rather than an application for the court to make the child a ward of court or seeking leave to apply for a SIO under s.8 of the Children Act. Although the revelation in *Gard* may suggest that judgments cannot be considered a reliable guide.[62]

'some uncertainty concerning the nature and scope of the order', Stephen Gilmore, 'The nature, scope and use of the specific issue order' (2004) 16 *Child and Family Law Quarterly* 367.
59 *Re JM* (n 57) [22], [23].
60 *Re JM* (n 57) [24]-[27]. The exercise by the court of its inherent jurisdiction is subject to *Practice Direction 12D – Inherent Jurisdiction (including Wardship) Proceedings*, https ://www.justice.gov.uk/courts/procedure-rules/family/practice_directions/pd_part_12d accessed 28 March 2020.
61 The hearing in the application for permission to appeal can be watched via the video on the Supreme Court website, https://www.supremecourt.uk/watch/charlie-gard/080617-p m.html accessed 29 February 2020.
62 Rob George has argued that the remedies within the Children Act mean that it is inappropriate for the court to continue to rely upon its inherent jurisdiction, 'The Legal Basis of the Court's Jurisdiction to Authorise Medical Treatment of Children' in Imogen Goold, Jonathan Herring and Cressida Auckland (eds), *Parental Rights, Best Interests and Significant Harms: Medical Decision-Making on Behalf of Children Post-Great Ormond Street Hospital*

A declaration made by the court in the exercise of its inherent jurisdiction is permissive, giving the doctor the protection of the court if they treat the child in accordance with the declaration when the parent has not consented. In contrast, when making a Specific Issue Order, the court determines the matter, the specific question on the aspect of parental responsibility that has arisen and may make directions giving guidance as to how it is to be carried out. The next question determined was the approach to be adopted by the courts in resolving these cases.

Decision-Making by the Court

The involvement of the court in cases concerned with the medical treatment of a child has to be understood alongside, but in comparison with, cases concerned with adults who lack capacity. The *Bolam* test equally applies to the standard of professional competence in the diagnosis and treatment of children, and *Sidaway*, understood in subsequent cases broadly to apply *Bolam* to the provision of information about treatment, was, until *Montgomery*, equally applicable to the provision of information to parents about their child's treatment.[63] The application of the *Bolam* test to the legality of the withdrawal of artificial nutrition and hydration from patients in a persistent vegetative state in *Bland* in 1989,[64] and to the determination of whether sterilisation was in the best interests of an adult who lacked capacity in *Re F* in 1990,[65] limited the review of such decisions by the court. Encouraged as good practice, the review of such decisions by the courts was as a consequence limited to the question whether the conclusion that the procedure was in the best interests of the patient was in accordance with a competent body of professional opinion. In contrast, the provision of treatment to children who lack the capacity to make decisions about their own medical treatment, which must be treatment in accordance with a reasonable body of professional opinion, is dependent upon the determination of parents or the court of the treatment option that is in the best interests of the child. The provision of medical treatment to a child therefore involves clinical judgement, professional judgement, and parental or judicial judgement. Parents have a particular interest, and expertise, in the wellbeing of their child, giving them a claim to know what is best given the particular needs of their child and their values and beliefs. When a child

---

v Gard (Hart, 2019) 67-83. The potential of the Children Act in relation to decisions concerning the medical treatment of children is explored in Jo Bridgeman, 'The Provision of Healthcare to Young and Dependent Children: The Principles, Concepts, and Utility of the Children Act 1989' (2017) 25 *Medical Law Review* 363.

63 *Bolam v Friern Hospital Management Committee* (n 41); *Sidaway v Board of Governors of the Bethlem Royal Hospital* [1985] 2 WLR 480; *Montgomery v Lanarkshire Health Board* [2015] UKSC 11, on the duties of doctors see further chapter four.

64 *Airedale NHS Trust v Bland* [1993] 2 WLR 316, (Lord Keith) 363, (Lord Goff) 376, (Lord Lowry) 378, (Lord Browne-Wilkinson) 387.

65 *Re F* [1990] 2 AC 1, (Lord Brandon) good practice, 56–7 (Lord Bridge) although not necessary in practice should be invoked, 51.

is in care, or those with primary responsibility for the child's wellbeing cannot agree on the course of treatment, the role of the court is not to review parental decisions or professional judgement but to reach an independent determination of the best interests of the child to fulfil the duty of the state for the protection and wellbeing of children. As with the decisions of parents and professionals, what is considered to be best in any individual case will be a judgement reached within the particular legal, political, social, and historical context of the time.

The first reported case in which the decision of the child's parent and doctor was referred to court, *Re D* in 1976, concerned non-therapeutic sterilisation rather than the medical treatment of a child.[66] The decision of D's mother and paediatrician to subject D to a sterilisation operation was challenged in legal proceedings initiated by an educational psychologist from the local education authority. Heilbron J observed that

> [t]his is an application to invoke the wardship jurisdiction of this court in entirely novel circumstances. The case is primarily of great importance to the child concerned… [but] … it also raises a matter of principle of considerable public importance.[67]

As a novel application, the first question was whether this was an appropriate case for wardship, the ancient jurisdiction originating in the obligation of the sovereign to protect persons and property and in particular those unable to look after themselves, which passed to the Family Division of the High Court in 1970.[68] The judge concluded that wardship was appropriate, as the proposed operation, if performed for non-therapeutic reasons and without D's consent, would be a violation of 'a basic human right, namely, the right of a woman to reproduce'.[69] The judge could not 'conceive of a more important step' than the proposed non-consensual non-therapeutic sterilisation of the child.[70]

Arguments that the view of either the child's parents or clinicians should prevail in disputed cases were rejected early in the case law. In *Re E*, in September 1990, 15-year-old A had been made a ward of court so that a court could resolve issues about his medical treatment, specifically the administration of blood in the treatment of leukaemia to which A was refusing to consent.[71] Ward J rejected the submission made on behalf of A's parents that proceedings were an abuse of process, expressing the view that the case was a proper exercise of the court's inherent jurisdiction.[72] The court, the judge said, was exercising the prerogative of the Crown delegated to judges to protect the welfare of the ward by making

---

66 *Re D* (n 14), considered in detail in chapter five.
67 *Re D* (n 14) 187.
68 *Re D* (n 14) 192-3.
69 *Re D* (n 14) 193.
70 *Re D* (n 14) 196.
71 *Re E* (n 51), previous applications had all been made by local authorities.
72 *Re E* (n 51) 391.

an objective decision placing the welfare of the child as the first and paramount consideration.[73] The alternative argument, that decisions about a child's medical treatment were matters of clinical judgement into which the court should not get involved, was made in *Royal Wolverhampton Hospital NHS Trust v B*.[74] The Trust had made an urgent, out of hours, application for orders authorising them to withhold ventilation from five-month-old E despite the refusal of the consent of her parents. In his submissions, Peter Jackson QC for the Official Solicitor argued that it was an 'exceptional case', which if reported might have the unintended consequence of establishing the 'route that NHS Trusts took whenever there was a difficulty between themselves, parents, and children in this situation'. He argued that it was not necessary for the court to make the declaration sought and that it was a matter of clinical judgement. In other words, the submission was that doctors could act in accordance with their professional judgement and that it was not necessary for a difference of opinion between doctors and parents on the issue of withholding life-sustaining treatment from a child to be referred to court. Bodey J concluded,

> In circumstances of parental/expert disagreement, and the sad absence of trust, it does seem to me that the best interests of E do indicate, on balance, that the Court should respond positively to the Health Authority's application, rather than say, in effect, that it is a matter for the clinicians' clinical judgment and not a matter in which the Court proposes to take any part.[75]

The case of *Re T* and the European Court of Human Rights (ECtHR) decision in relation to David Glass were central to establishing that decisions about a child's medical treatment are not purely matters of clinical judgement. The Court of Appeal judgment in *Re T* has been much criticised by academics for the application of best interests to the facts,[76] but the case clearly established that decisions about medical treatment are wider than clinical considerations. The ECtHR, in the case of David Glass, established that doctors cannot treat the child in the best interests of that child as they consider it to be without authority from either the child's parents or the courts.

---

73 *Re E* (n 51) 391-2.
74 [2000] 1 FLR 953.
75 *Royal Wolverhampton Hospitals NHS Trust* (n 74) 956.
76 Michael Davies, 'Selective Non-Treatment of the Newborn: In Whose Best Interests - In Whose Judgement' (1998) 49 *Northern Ireland Legal Quarterly* 82; Sabine Michalowki, 'Is it in the best interests of a child to have a life-saving liver transplantation?' (1997) 9 *Child and Family Law Quarterly* 179; Michael Freeman, 'Can we leave the best interests of very sick children to their parents?' in Michael Freeman (ed), *Law and Medicine, Current Legal Issues 2000* (OUP 2000) 257-268; Jonathan Herring, 'The Human Rights Act and the welfare principle in family law – conflicting or complementary?' (1999) 11 *Child and Family Law Quarterly* 223; Marie Fox and Jean McHale, 'In Whose Best Interests?' (1997) 60 *Modern Law Review* 700.

T had been born with a life-threatening liver condition, biliary atresia, for which he had surgery when he was three months old. This surgery was not successful, but his parents decided, in light of the pain and distress it had caused him, that they would not agree to a liver transplant. Concerned about the parents' decision, his consultant paediatrician sought legal advice and the matter was referred to the local authority child protection team. The local authority applied for leave for the court to exercise its inherent jurisdiction. The Court of Appeal allowed the appeal against the decision of Connell J, who had decided that the decision of the mother to refuse her consent against the unanimous medical advice was not reasonable. Butler-Sloss LP explained that the authorities clearly established that when decisions about a child's medical treatment were before the court in the exercise of the court's inherent jurisdiction, the court was to reach an independent determination as to the welfare of the child. The judge had taken the wrong approach in assessing the mother's decision against clinical opinion, concluding that he should consent to the operation on the basis of the 'clinical assessment of the likely success of the proposed treatment' and without consideration of the factors relevant to the decision of reasonable parents.[77]

The decision of the ECtHR in 2004,[78] with respect to the treatment of David Glass, was concerned with the balance of responsibilities for making decisions about the medical treatment of dependent children. David Glass was aged 12 years at the time of the treatment in question and 18 years old when the European Court ruled on his case. David had been born with severe physical and mental disabilities including cerebral palsy, hydrocephalus, epilepsy, curvature of the spine, a dislocated hip, visual impairment, and limited cognitive function. He was cared for at home by his mother with the help of family members and community health services. The issue arose from disagreements about his treatment when David developed septicaemia and recurrent respiratory tract infections following a tonsillectomy. After a number of admissions to hospital during which his condition failed to improve, the doctors treating him at St Mary's Hospital in Portsmouth formed the view that he was dying, that it was not appropriate to provide intensive care, and that morphine should be administered to alleviate pain and suffering. His mother, Carol Glass, disagreed with the assessment that he was dying, and her solicitor wrote a letter on her behalf to the hospital expressing her refusal to consent to the administration of morphine. Upon his next re-admission, diamorphine was administered despite his mother's refusal and a Do Not Resuscitate Order (DNR) put on his notes without her knowledge. A meeting to discuss his care was attended by the police, and a fight broke out on the wards between family members and his doctors as his family tried to resuscitate him. After his discharge, the Director of the Trust wrote to Carol Glass, informing her that the hospital would only be able to provide palliative care for David

---

[77] Re T [1997] 1 WLR 242, 250.
[78] Glass v United Kingdom [2004] 1 FLR 1019, concerned with events in the summer of 1998, considered in judicial review proceedings in the domestic courts in July 1999, see below p 69–70.

Development of Legal Framework 61

in the future so that if she wished for more active care, David should be taken to a hospital elsewhere.

Her complaint not having been addressed in domestic proceedings for judicial review, Carol Glass complained to the European Court of Human Rights.[79] The ECtHR held that administration of diamorphine to David against the continued opposition of his mother was an interference with his right to respect for private life, specifically his right to physical integrity. Doing so without seeking consent from the court was not necessary in a democratic society and amounted to a breach of David's Article 8 right. In terms of the balance of responsibilities in respect of the current legal framework for children's medical treatment decision-making,[80] this is a significant decision.[81]

The breach of David's human rights was by doctors who genuinely believed that they were acting in the best interests of a seriously ill child and, following advice from the Official Solicitor, believed that they were entitled to do so. The ECtHR judgment detailed extracts from David's medical notes, which testified to the confidence of his doctors, on the basis of this advice, in their ability to treat according to their assessment of his best interests. In his medical notes, Dr Walker recorded,

> I have told [Carol Glass] that we can give morphine to alleviate distress even vs. their wishes (and we can – I am assured by the Official Solicitor that no judge has ever overturned a doctors' decision to withdraw treatment/alleviate symptoms) but we wouldn't without telling them.[82]

Dr Hallett wrote: 'In the event of total disagreement we should be obliged to go to the Courts *to provide support for decision* [to use morphine]'.[83] In other words, that if they wished to administer morphine or to withdraw treatment against his

---

79 The complaint that the actions of the doctors had amounted to a breach of Articles 2 (right to life), 6 (right of access to court), 13 (right to effective remedy), and 14 (not to be discriminated against in the enjoyment of Convention rights) were held to be manifestly unfounded. The ECtHR focused upon the complaints of the child, whereas in the later case concerned with the future medical treatment of Charlie Gard, the ECtHR considered only the complaints by the parents. The question whether the parents had standing to make a complaint on their child's behalf arose because Charlie's parents challenged decisions of the court made according to his best interests which were agreed by the Guardian who had been appointed to represent his interests in the domestic courts. David Glass had not been individually represented in the domestic proceedings which took the form of judicial review.
80 The limitations of the decision of the ECtHR are considered in Jo Bridgeman, 'Caring for Children with Severe Disabilities: Boundaried and Relational Rights' (2005) 13 *The International Journal of Children's Rights* 99.
81 The discussion of the decision by A C Elias-Jones and J Samanta showed that the significance of the judgment was in the clarification brought to the respective responsibilities and the role of parents, doctors, and the court, 'The implications of the David Glass case for future clinical practice in the UK' (2005) 90 *Archives of Disease in Childhood* 822.
82 *Glass* (n 78) [14].
83 *Glass* (n 78) [16].

mother's wishes, the matter should be brought before the court but that a court would support the view of the doctors. The doctors treated David according to their judgement of his best interests on the understanding that clinical judgement prevailed.

The ECtHR decision confirmed that the framework of English law, established in the cases considered in this chapter, complied with the Convention but that domestic law had not been followed. That legal framework is that responsibility for deciding which of the appropriate treatment options is in the best interests of the child rests with parents, not doctors, and, in the event of a disagreement, with the court. The ECtHR explained that the framework within English Law for decision-making about the medical treatment of a child was that of parental 'authority to act on his behalf and to defend his interests', including his right to physical integrity under Article 8, through consent to medical treatment.[84] Except in an emergency, doctors cannot treat contrary to parental objection but are required to refer the matter to court.[85] Clinical judgement, medical authority, does not prevail. The doctors had failed to comply with the law when they treated David according to their judgement of his best interests, failing to respect the decision of his mother or seek the view of the court. The duty of doctors is to identify the appropriate treatment options and which of the options is, in their professional judgement, best, providing information and working in partnership with parents to enable them to decide which of the treatment options are in the best interests of the child in light of the values, beliefs, knowledge, and experience of the decision-maker. When the doctors cannot accept the parental decision, it is the duty of the Trust to refer the matter to court, at which time the judge takes over the responsibility for determining the best interests of the child, ensuring that decisions about a child's medical treatment are made according to the ordinary standards of the day.

In *An NHS Trust v AB*, Counsel submitted that the principle that neither parents nor the court can require a doctor to treat contrary to their professional judgement meant that applications such as that before the court, that it was lawful to move to palliative care, served no purpose and should only be made when there was a difference of medical opinion.[86] King LJ responded:

> The courts have long recognised that in a dispute in relation to serious medical treatment the matter should be placed before the court. Principle and common humanity demand that parents who find themselves in such desperate circumstances should have an opportunity to have their views considered by the courts and that the medical team should not be able to have the 'final say' and to make life and death decisions with which they disagree'.[87]

---

84 *Glass* (n 78) [70].
85 *Glass* (n 78) [75].
86 [2016] EWCA Civ 899 [30].
87 *An NHS Trust v AB* (n 86) [32].

It is notable that the 'permissive order' which Bodey J made in *B* above was to enable the child's doctors to treat her according to their determination of her best interests. Such orders, combined with the principle noted above from *Re J* that neither parents nor the court can require doctors to treat contrary to their clinical judgement, might give the impression that the approach taken in cases concerning children differs little from that which then applied with respect to adult patients who lacked capacity when treatment was lawful as long as the decision that the treatment was in the patient's best interests was in accordance with a competent body of professional opinion. As Barbara Hewson, who was Counsel before the ECtHR in *Glass,* observed of the judgment, the law as summarised by the ECtHR in *Glass* could be viewed as amounting to no more than that the issue must be referred to court before 'maternal opinion' can be overridden.[88] However, as King LJ stated in *AB,* consideration of a child's medical treatment by the court ensures that there is an independent review of all of the evidence, the professional judgement of the treating doctors, the parental view of their child's best interests, second opinions, independent experts, and that there is compliance with professional guidance. It also provides the opportunity for the court to reach a decision, focused upon determination of the best interests of the child, following consideration of the submissions from both parties and of the Guardian as an independent representative of the child. The role of the court in such cases is to protect the vulnerable and reach an independent judgement of the best interests of the child and not just to ensure that the decision as to best interests accords with a competent body of professional opinion. It is also to ensure that decisions about a child's medical treatment and his or her best interests accord with socially acceptable standards for the treatment of children. Furthermore, requiring cases to be referred to court ensures that decisions, both in cases of disagreements and those involving a vulnerable child in the care of the state, are given reasoned justification in published judgments enabling public scrutiny and debate upon the issues raised.

Judicial Determination of Best Interests

Once the jurisdiction of the court has been invoked, the responsibility for the decision about the child's medical treatment is removed from his or her parents, and the duty rests with the court to reach an independent decision. As Lord Donaldson MR stated in *Re R,* the court does not 'step into the shoes of the parent'. The jurisdiction of the court is not derived from parental rights and responsibilities, rather it 'derives from, or is, the delegated performance of the duties of the Crown to protect its subjects and particularly children who are the generations of the future'.[89] As long ago as *Re D* in 1976, Heilbron J stated that

---

88 Barbara Hewson, 'When maternal instinct outweighs medical opinion' (2004) 154 *New Law Journal* 522.
89 *Re R* (n 50) 200.

it was 'beyond dispute' that in wardship proceedings the welfare of the child was the paramount consideration.[90] Shortly afterwards, Lord Hailsham in the House of Lords in Re B (1988)[91] stated that whether the term wellbeing, welfare, or interests was used, and each could be considered synonymous, that was the paramount consideration in wardship proceedings.[92]

Balcombe LJ observed in Re W that, when the issue concerned the upbringing of the child, s.1(1) of the Children Act gave statutory effect to the paramountcy of the welfare of the child.[93] The local authority wanted to know whether it would be lawful to move W, who was receiving treatment for anorexia, to a named treatment unit contrary to her wishes.[94] The Court of Appeal in Re W was concerned, amongst other things, with the powers of the court in a case concerning the medical treatment of a child where it had been asked to make decisions with respect to a child by the holder of parental responsibility, following the Children Act, in light of Gillick and the interpretation there given to s.8 of the Family Law Reform Act 1969.[95] Nolan LJ emphasised that, whereas Gillick had been concerned with the extent of parental rights over the welfare of the child, Re W concerned the exercise of the court's jurisdiction,[96] in which the court had powers that were 'theoretically limitless'.[97] As Nolan LJ explained, the court has the power and responsibility, when it considers it to be necessary for the best interests of the child, to override the views of both the child and the parent.[98] Furthermore, their Lordships emphasised, the powers of the court exceed those of natural parents, in that the court can override consent to medical treatment provided by a child aged 16 or older or Gillick competent, whereas those with parental responsibility cannot.[99]

In determining applications concerning the medical treatment of a child, the judiciary focus upon their duty to protect through an independent analysis of the best interests of the child.[100] The standard, derived from the speech of Lord Upjohn in J v C, is that of the 'judicial reasonable parent', 'reflecting and adopting the changing views as the years go by of reasonable men and women, the parents of children, on the proper treatment and methods of bringing up children'.[101] The Court must decide 'exercising the authority of the Crown as national', rather

---

90 Re D (n 14) 194.
91 Re B (n 47).
92 Re B (n 47) 202.
93 Re W [1993] Fam 64, 85.
94 Re W (n 93) 73.
95 Lord Donaldson MR was also responding to criticism of his earlier judgment in Re R (n 50).
96 Re W (n 93) 93.
97 Re W (n 93) 81.
98 Re W (n 93) 93.
99 A refusal of medical treatment by a child can be overridden by those with parental responsibility as well as the court, Re W (n 93) 83-4.
100 Re E (n 51) 391.
101 Re D (n 14) 194, Heilbron J quoting Lord Upjohn in J v C [1970] AC 668, 722-723.

than natural, parent.[102] The standard is that of the 'wise parent',[103] taking a broad view of the evidence of the welfare of the child.[104]

Recently, the High Court has accepted the application of the propositions developed by the courts to guide their decision-making in cases of withdrawing or withholding treatment to the determination of the provision of treatment to children. Originating in the judgments of the Court of Appeal in the cases of *Re J (1991)*[105] and *Re J (1993)*,[106] the legal principles were set out as 'intellectual milestones' by the Court of Appeal in *Wyatt*[107] and as ten propositions by Holman J in *Re MB*,[108] recently affirmed as the correct legal framework by the Court of Appeal, Supreme Court, and ECtHR in the Charlie Gard case.[109] When the matter is brought before the court, the court must decide it, and the duty of the judge is to exercise an 'independent and objective judgment' to determine the course of action that is in the best interests of the child. Best interests must be assessed from the assumed point of view of the child and in the widest sense and include every kind of consideration capable of affecting the decision. Non-exhaustively these include medical, emotional, sensory (pleasure, pain and suffering), and instinctive (the human instinct to survive) considerations'[110] arrived at through a balance sheet of benefits and burdens. With reference to Lord Donaldson in *Re J (1991)*,[111] the judge is directed, beyond best interests, to consider the child's quality of life from the perspective of the child and to recognise the strong, but not irrebuttable, presumption in favour of the prolongation of life. Judgments are informed by the medical opinion of the child's treating team, and it is common practice for the medical evidence to include second

---

102   *Re R* (n 50) 202.
103   *Re D* (n 14) 194.
104   *Re T* (n 77) 254.
105   *Re J* (n 34).
106   *Re J* [1993] Fam 15.
107   *Wyatt & Another v Portsmouth Hospital NHS & Another* [2005] EWCA Civ 1181, [87] approving Hedley J in the court below *Portsmouth NHS Trust v Wyatt* [2004] EWHC 2247.
108   [2006] EWHC 507, [16].
109   *In the Matter of Charles Gard* [2017] EWCA Civ 410; *In the matter of Charlie Gard (Permission to Appeal Hearing)*, 8 June 2017, https://www.supremecourt.uk/news/permission-to-appeal-hearing-in-the-matter-of-charlie-gard.html: *Charles Gard and Others v United Kingdom*. Application no. 39793/17, 28 June 2017, http://hudoc.echr.coe.int/eng#{"documentcollectionid2": ["DECGRANDCHAMBER","ADMISSIBILITY","ADMISSIBILITYCOM"],"itemid": ["001-175359"]}.
110   *An NHS Trust v A* [2007] EWHC 1696, [40]. Examples of which are *Donald Simms and Jonathan Simms v An NHS Trust and Secretary of State for Health*; *PA and JA v An NHS Trust and Secretary of State for Health* [2002] EWHC 2734, the application of which is considered in chapter seven and *Tafida Raqeeb (by her Litigation Friend) v Barts NHS Foundation Trust* [2019] EWHC 2531 (Admin) & *Barts NHS Foundation Trust v Shalina Begum and Muhhamed Raqeeb & Tafida Raqeeb (by her Children's Guardian)* [2019] EWHC 2530, considered in chapter six.
111   *Re J* (n 34) 46.

opinions and evidence from independent experts. Consideration is also given to parental views and opinions, depending upon the court's assessment of those views.[112] More recently, it has become common for judgments to cite from the speech of Lady Hale in the Supreme Court in *Aintree University Hospital NHS Foundation Trust v James* that the question to be asked is 'whether it is lawful to give the treatment, not whether it is lawful to withhold it'. If the treatment is not in the best interests of the child, the court is not able to give consent and it is lawful to withdraw or withhold it. Furthermore, it will not be lawful to give the treatment.[113] In *An NHS Trust v A*,[114] Holman J explained that he considered the propositions to be a fair and accurate summary of the law and equally applicable as a guide for deciding cases whether it was the doctors or the parents who wished for treatment to be administered, withheld, or withdrawn. More recently, Mostyn J in *Re JM* explained that he viewed these propositions as a 'fuller explication' of the principle of the paramountcy of the welfare of the child guiding the court in the exercise of its powers equally applicable to judicial decisions on the provision of treatment as to decisions concerning the withholding or withdrawal of treatment.[115] With reference to the judgment of Thorpe LJ in *Re A*,[116] Holman J in *Re MB*[117] suggested that in the preparation of their case the parties should draw up a balance sheet. Thorpe LJ had suggested that a balance sheet should set out actual benefits against actual dis-benefits and possible benefits and disadvantages with an estimate of their probability to arrive at a sum of certain and possible benefits against certain and possible disadvantages.[118] Balance sheets are included in some judgments but not uniformly.[119] Once referred to the court, in contrast with other issues of a child's upbringing which may be brought to court for resolution upon which there is little expert evidence, determination of the child's best interests is inevitably focused upon the medical evidence – evidence which clinicians are better placed than the child's parents to secure and to understand. It is argued in the chapters which follow that the issue in each the case and the approach adopted to the evidence has to be understood within the prevailing social, political, and cultural context which informs judgements about the appropriate treatment and care of children. However, there are cases in which the judge has uncritically accepted the medical evidence and thereby has not ensured the interests of the child have been protected. Furthermore, it is argued that the

---

112 *Re T* (n 77) 250.
113 [2013] UKSC 67, particularly paras [19], [21], [22], [39].
114 [2007] EWHC 1696, [40].
115 *Re JM* (n 57) [14].
116 [2000] 1 FLR 549.
117 *Re MB* (n 108) [58]-[60].
118 *Re A* (n 116).
119 Holman J included the balance sheet draw up by the Guardian in *Re MB* (n 108), stating that he had found the balance sheets drawn up enormously useful when considering the evidence, reaching his decision, and preparing his judgment, and suggested that the preparation of such should become part of the preparation of the case, [58].

focus upon best interests has resulted in a failure to evaluate the duties of doctors to children in their care and the consequent balance of responsibilities between parents, doctors, public authorities, and the courts.

Judicial Review

One of the key arguments of this book is that it is necessary to understand that cases concerning the future medical treatment of children are of different types, they are not all disputes between doctors and parents about the child's best interests. Further, it is necessary to understand the legal, political, social, and historical context for the cases which established the framework of the law through which such cases are decided as well as the effect of changes to the context in which the law has been applied in subsequent cases. That context includes the NHS as a public institution, public responsibilities of local authorities and the courts for the protection of children, and the public interest in ensuring that children are cared for according to the reasonable standards of the day. For these reasons it is also necessary to consider the role of the courts in the judicial review of the decisions of Trusts as public bodies. These cases also reflect the changing nature of the issues which require authoritative resolution. The first set of cases involves unsuccessful attempts to challenge the allocation of resources which had delayed the provision of medical treatment to children. This is followed by cases in which the process for determining disputes between parents and children was settled. And thirdly, of recent incarnation, actions by parents seeking to remove their child overseas for treatment or care are covered.

In *R v Central Birmingham Health Authority, ex parte Walker* (1987),[120] and *R v Central Birmingham Health Authority, ex parte Collier* (1988),[121] the parents of a two-month-old baby and a four-and-a-half-year-old child, respectively, applied for judicial review of the decision of the same health authority to delay the children's heart surgery. The delay was a result of decisions about the allocation of available funds which meant that although there were surgeons available, the children could not be safely cared for due to lack of intensive care beds and nurses. The proceedings amounted, therefore, to a challenge to the consequences of an underfunded health service by the parents of seriously ill children to whom surgery offered the prospect of recovery.[122] In the High Court in *Walker*, Macpherson J observed that the decision to delay heart surgery was 'unfortunate, disturbing, and in human terms, distressing' but not justiciable as it was not illegal, procedurally deficient, nor unreasonable. Leave to apply for judicial review was refused and upheld on appeal. In the application the following year, following three delays to heart surgery desperately required by Matthew Collier at the same hospital

---

120 3 BMLR 32.
121 [1988] 1 WLUK 690.
122 David died after undergoing the surgery which had been delayed five times, 'Heart baby challenge', *The Guardian* (7 December 1987).

and similar reasons, the court viewed the situation as no different in any relevant respect. Counsel had explained that it was general knowledge that the health authority had insufficient resources, and the purpose of the proceedings was to secure more resources to enable the procedure to go ahead. Ralph Gibson LJ said that he could not express a view on the national allocation of resources nor upon the decisions of those responsible for distributing the resources made available to the health authority. Against the background that the children's heart unit in Birmingham had become a 'symbol of National Health Service malaise' in which the sickest children were in competition for beds due to chronic underfunding,[123] and encouraging the health authority to provide an explanation, whilst being unable to require it to do so, Ralph Gibson LJ observed,

> If I were the father of this child, I think that I would want to be given answers about the supply to, and use of, funds by this health authority. No doubt the health authority would welcome the opportunity to deal with such matters so that they could explain what they are doing and what their problems are. But this court and the High Court have no role of general investigator of social policy and of allocation of resources. The court's jurisdiction, as is very well known, is limited to dealing with breach of duties under law, including decisions made by public authorities which are shown to be unreasonable.[124]

The approach adopted was followed by the Court of Appeal in the next case, although leave was given for judicial review of the decision of the health authority not to fund further cancer treatment for ten-year-old Jaymee Bowen.[125] A few years earlier, Jaymee had been treated for non-Hodgkin's lymphoma with common acute lymphoblastic leukaemia but had subsequently developed acute myeloid leukaemia which had been treated with chemotherapy, complete body irradiation, and a bone marrow transplant. Nine months later she relapsed, and her treating doctors considered that further active treatment was not in her clinical best interests and that she should be given palliative care. Her father sought an extra-contractual referral for experimental treatment. Like *Walker* and *Collier*, this was a legal challenge to a funding decision and hence, the prioritisation of scarce resources. However, while the doctors in *Walker* and *Collier* considered surgery to be in the best interests of the children, Jaymee's treating doctors did not consider the experimental treatment to be in her best interests. In the Queen's Bench Division, Laws J had allowed the application for certiorari,

---

123 Deirdre Fernand, 'A baby waiting for his turn to live – Which sick child will be given a vital heart operation?' *Sunday Times* (31 January 1988).
124 Stephen Brown LJ observed that the application was misconceived in light of *Walker* but observed that the hope was that the proceedings would put pressure on the hospital to perform the operation. Matthew Collier underwent heart surgery but died from complications, Paul Hoyland and Patrick Wintour, 'Hole-in-heart child loses fight for life', *The Guardian* (21 February 1988).
125 *R v Cambridge District Health Authority, ex parte B* [1995] 1 FLR 1055.

quashing the health authority's decision on the grounds that the health authority had given insufficient consideration to the views of her father.[126] Furthermore, the judge held that the decision interfered with Jaymee's right to life, an interference which required substantial justification by the health authority in the form of an adequate explanation for their decision to decline to fund the treatment.[127] The Court of Appeal allowed the appeal considering that the health authority was very aware of the views of the father and that it was 'totally unrealistic' to expect the health authority to provide the court with a detailed account of its resource allocation decisions.[128]

It was never judicially determined whether the experimental treatment, formulated as a judicial review of the allocation of resources, was supported by a competent body of professional opinion, nor whether it was in Jaymee's best interests to be administered with the experimental treatment. Had the court concluded that it was not in her best interest to receive the treatment, it would not have been lawful to provide it. The question whether it was in her best interests would have required careful examination of the different medical opinions of the doctors who had been caring for her, of the doctor who was prepared to treat her, and whether the administration of the experimental treatment was supported by a competent body of professional opinion.[129] Whether it was in Jaymee's best interests to receive the treatment may appear to have been moot in the context of the absence of funds to pay for the treatment although the decision of the health authority not to fund the treatment followed from the decision of her doctors that it was not in her best interests to receive the experimental treatment, a decision which should have been subject to judicial scrutiny. It may have revealed that this was not an appropriate treatment option. Following the publicity given to her case, Jaymee's treatment was funded by an anonymous benefactor, and she lived for a further year before dying from the side-effects of the treatment. The Panorama documentary in which both Jaymee and the health authority chief executive were interviewed was seen as encouraging public debate of the rationing, which had always happened in the NHS.[130]

That the best interests of a child should be determined in family proceedings was confirmed by the courts when Carol Glass, in judicial review proceedings, challenged the decision of Portsmouth Hospitals NHS Trust that they would only be able to offer her son, David Glass, palliative care in the future. Scott Baker J held that the decision was not susceptible to review. It related to past events which would not arise again; it would be difficult to frame a declaration which did not limit doctors in providing appropriate treatment for any future situation,

---

126 *Ex parte B* (n 125) 1063.
127 *Ex parte B* (n 125) 1065.
128 *Ex parte B* (n 125) 1073.
129 This aspect of the case is addressed in chapter seven.
130 Panorama, *The Story of Child B*, 26 October 1995 reviewed in 'Rational Rationing', *The Times* (27 October 1995).

and if there was a disagreement between doctors and his mother in the future it would be determined according to the best interests of the child. The Court of Appeal in *Glass* stressed that such cases were to be brought before the court by an application to the Family Division for a SIO, declaration under the court's inherent jurisdiction, or in wardship, and that judicial review was not the appropriate procedure by which to make decisions about a child's medical treatment.[131]

As demonstrated above, the best interests of the child as determined by the court in the exercise of its inherent jurisdiction has been the focus of cases concerned with the medical treatment of children, consistent with the view that it is best interests and not the allocation of resources which determines treatment decisions concerning children both on the wards and in the courtroom. However, research by Simon Mellor and Sarah Barclay identified that concerns about allocation decisions affecting the quality of care were a common source of developing conflicts surrounding the care of children.[132] Central to recent cases such as those about the future medical treatment of Ashya King and Charlie Gard were parental concerns that their child was not being offered the best treatment available. Simon Mellor and Sarah Barclay also identified discussions about withholding or withdrawal of treatment as particularly difficult, and parents have expressed concerns that these discussions have been driven by allocation decisions. For example, the father of OT expressed the view that the Trust's position that ventilation should be withdrawn was driven by resources, and the Trust viewed OT as a 'bed-blocker'.[133]

However, following from the unsuccessful challenge to the best interest principle in *Gard* and *Evans,* the parents of Tafida Raqeeb challenged, in judicial review proceedings, the decision of Barts that it was not in her best interests to be transferred to Italy for continued ventilation.[134] MacDonald J concluded that the decision of the Trust to prevent the transfer to another hospital pending a determination of the court of Tafida's best interests was amenable to judicial review, relating as it did to a decision of her treating doctors acting as employees of the Trust, a public body with statutory functions under the National Health Service Act 2006.[135] He accepted the argument made on behalf of her parents that the Trust had acted unlawfully in failing to consider Tafida's directly enforceable rights according to Article 56 of the Treaty for the Functioning of the European Union relating to the provision and receipt of services in another Member State or whether there were public policy justifications for that interference.[136]

---

131 *R v Portsmouth Hospitals NHS Trust, ex parte Glass* [1999] 2 FLR 905, 909.
132 Simon Meller and Sarah Barclay, 'Mediation: an Approach to Intractable Disputes Between Parents and Paediatricians' (2011) 96 *Archives of Disease in Childhood* 619, 619.
133 *Re OT* [2009] EWHC 633 [12].
134 *Tafida Raqeeb* (n 110), in proceedings that were heard together the Trust applied for a SIO and declarations under the court's inherent jurisdiction that continued ventilation was not in Tafida's best interests, considered in chapter six.
135 *Tafida Raqeeb* (n 110) [141].
136 *Tafida Raqeeb* (n 110) [144].

However, the judge concluded that had the Trust done so, they would have reached the same decision to comply with the national requirement to refer the question of Tafida's best interests to the court. This was because the Trust would have considered that the derogation of her right was justified by preventing her transfer, pending the decision of the court on the best interests application. As a consequence no remedy was granted as, had the Trust acted lawfully, Tafida would still have been in the same position.[137] MacDonald J was able to limit the reach of his conclusion given that, as Barend Van Leuwen has argued, free movement arguments are no longer likely to be available given that free movement of services is not in the negotiations with the EU following the decision to leave the European Union.[138] However, the submissions which MacDonald J dismissed, based on discrimination under the Equality Act 2010 and contravention of the NHS Constitution, remain for development, along with new arguments, in future cases. Given the unassailable position of the best interests principle, there will inevitability be further cases in which parents have secured second opinions, and the child has been accepted for treatment abroad under different regulatory regimes, funding models, and value systems, and consequently, further arguments in judicial review of the decision of the Trust as a public body.

Conclusion

The best interests analysis, applied in cases from *Re D* in 1976 to the recent high profile cases over 40 years later of *Charlie Gard, Isaiah Haastrup, Alfie Evans* and *Tafida Raqeeb*, across cases concerned with the provision, withholding, and withdrawal, of medical treatment, is firmly established as the 'lodestar'[139] or 'gold standard'[140] for judicial determination. The approach that the courts take to a determination of best interests is rooted in the early case law in which local authorities, fulfilling their public duties, referred cases to court for the exercise of the judicial protective duties to the child in wardship. Whilst cases are now referred to court by the Trust which has an interest in the case by virtue of the legal duties of doctors to children in their care, or the local authority when it shares parental responsibility with the child's parents, the approach of the courts has continued to be that of protecting the interests of the vulnerable. Through this case law, the responsibilities of parents, professionals, public authorities, and the courts for children's medical treatment have been established; the balance of

---

137 *Tafida Raqeeb* (n 110) [141]. *Tafida Raqeeb* (n 110) [155], [157].
138 Barend Van Leuwen, 'Free movement of life? The interaction between the best interests test and the right to freely receive services in Tafida Raqeeb' [2020] Public Law 398.
139 *NHS Trust v Baby X and others* [2012] EWHC 2188, [6]; *Alder Hey Children's NHS Foundation Trust v Evans* [2018] EWHC 308, [47].
140 *In the Matter of Alfie Evans*, 20 March 2018, https://www.supremecourt.uk/news/permission-to-appeal-determination-in-the-matter-of-alfie-evans.html accessed 3 March 2020.

responsibilities between whom have to be understood as changing in response to the social, legal, and political context in which they are exercised.

To understand these cases as a professional challenge to parental decisions about the best interests of their child, with responsibility handed to the judge, who decides following a presentation of each side's account of the child's best interests, fails to recognise the responsibilities of all involved in the provision of medical treatment to a child to protect their interests and wellbeing according to the ordinary standards of society. Consideration of the best interests of the child has to be placed within the context not only of parental responsibilities but also of the legal duties of professionals and public responsibilities for the welfare and protection of children. The legal and professional duties of doctors to children in their care are the subject of the next chapter.

4 The Legal Duties of Doctors to Children in Their Care

The Legal Duties of Doctors to Children in Their Care

As examined in chapter three, the law concerning the provision, withdrawal, and withholding of medical treatment from children appears to be clear and straightforward, framed early in the jurisprudence and developed in subsequent cases. The duty of all, parents, health professionals,[1] and judges, as stated in case law and professional guidance, is to act according to the best interests of the child. But, as parents and carers have other duties to their child,[2] such as to seek medical advice in the first place, so too do doctors, similarly framed at the boundaries by the ordinary principles of criminal and civil law but also supplemented by standards of professional conduct.[3] The purpose of this chapter is to situate the duty to act in the best interests of the child within the context of the wider legal and professional duties owed by doctors to children in their care. It must be emphasised that this is not to argue for a shift in focus from the child (best interests) to doctors (professional duties). Nor is it an argument for greater deference by judges to the medical profession or that judges should 'blindly accept assertions of good medical practice' without evaluating the evidence[4] – to the contrary. It is to argue that the legal framework which has developed through the case law, focused upon the best interests of the child and academic critique of legal and ethical best interests, needs to be set within the context of professional as well as parental duties to the child and that cases should examine the fulfilment of professional duties to the child separately from, and in addition to, the child's best interests.

---

1 The care of children with serious illnesses and complex conditions will be provided by a multi-disciplinary team, all members of which have legal and professional duties to the child, however, the focus of this chapter is upon the duties of doctors.
2 The term parent will be used in this chapter to refer to those with decision-making responsibility in relation to a child's medical treatment arising from parental responsibility, although this can also be held by a non-parent and also by the local authority as explained in chapter two.
3 *Re W* [1993] Fam 64, 76, 78.
4 Margaret Brazier and José Miola, 'Bye Bye Bolam: A Medical-Litigation Revolution?' (2000) 8 *Medical Law Review* 85-114, 86.

74 *Legal Duties of Doctors to Children*

In his October 2005 judgment concerning the medical treatment of Charlotte Wyatt, Hedley J considered an application by her parents, given evidence of improvement in her condition, for a discharge of the declaration which authorised withholding of ventilation, and an application by the Trust for a declaration that in the event of an irreconcilable difference her doctors should decide about her treatment. Discharging the declaration, Hedley J was concerned to explain the nature and limits of the duties of doctors. The judge emphasised that the doctor's duty is to his or her patient. Doctors have a 'professional duty' to act in the best interests of the child[5] and advise parents accordingly about the medical facts and the decision to be made.[6] Further, Hedley J stressed, it is the responsibility of doctors to work in partnership with the child's parents,[7] through a process of discussion and negotiation, to agree a treatment plan reflecting their parental and professional judgment of the best interests of the child, accommodating parental wishes as far as 'professional judgment and conscience' allows.[8] Robin Downie and Jane Macnaughton have explained that a judgement is a claim made in a situation of uncertainty but on the basis of some evidence.[9] A professional judgement, they continued, is one made in a professional context in which 'the uncertainty derives from the professional context and the evidence or relevant considerations are acquired by means of professional knowledge and skills'.[10] The professional judgement of doctors is informed by clinical knowledge and professional experience. Doctors will also exercise professional judgement in accordance with the values of the profession as detailed in *Good Medical Practice*.[11] Diagnosis, identification of treatment options, assessment of which of the available options is clinically best, and treatment that is in the overall best interests of the child are thus professional judgements, informed by medical knowledge, experience, and critical reflection in the context of uncertainty about the efficacy of treatment, side effects, and pain and suffering.

This chapter situates the best interest analysis within the legal and professional duties of doctors to children. This chapter considers the duty of care owed by doctors to patients, the duty to act in the best interests of the child, including the good practice, but not a legal duty, to work in partnership with parents and to facilitate the participation of older children, the duty to consider the transfer of the patient when there is another doctor willing to treat, the duty to refer questions about a child's medical treatment to court, and the limits imposed by acting

---

5 *Re Wyatt* [2005] EWHC 2293, [29].
6 *Re W* (n 3) 78.
7 *Re Wyatt* (n 5) [29].
8 *Re Wyatt* (n 5) [41].
9 Robin Downie and Jane Macnaughton, 'In Defence of Professional Judgement' (2013) 15 *Advances in Psychiatric Treatment* 322, 322.
10 Downie and Macnaughton (n 9) 322.
11 GMC, *Good Medical Practice,* last updated April 2019 https://www.gmc-uk.org/ethical-guidance/ethical-guidance-for-doctors/good-medical-practice accessed 16 April 2020.

in accordance with professional judgement or conscience. It also considers good practice guidance to doctors.

Duty of Care to Child

Doctors owe their patients a legal duty to take reasonable care not to cause them harm. Failure to fulfil the standard of care may result in civil liability for professional negligence. The duty of doctors to take reasonable care not to cause harm to their patients is a long-established recognisable duty situation.[12] Consequently, the primary question is whether the doctor has fulfilled the standard of care owed. The standard of reasonable care imposed by the law, established by *Bolam*, is to act in 'accordance with good medical practice recognised as appropriate by a competent body of professional opinion'[13] using medical knowledge and clinical judgement. This standard applies not only to the provision of treatment but also in making a diagnosis, identifying viable treatment options and forming an opinion as to which of the viable options is clinically best for the patient. In their diagnosis, identification of treatment options and provision of treatment, doctors must act 'in accordance with a practice accepted as proper by a responsible body of medical men skilled in that particular art',[14] which must be 'responsible, reasonable, and respectable' and, in the assessment of the risks and benefits, 'capable of withstanding logical analysis'.[15]

Diagnosis, identification of treatment options, and provision of treatment involve professional judgement drawing upon medical knowledge and expertise but also the assessment of the risks and benefits; consequently, they are judgements upon which there is scope for differences of medical opinion. The standard of care recognises that these are medical decisions within the specific competence of doctors, requiring expertise which others, including the child's parents, do not possess. When questions about the standard of care are before the court, the responsibility of the judge is to evaluate the evidence that the practice adopted was in accordance with a competent body of medical opinion.[16] In *Bolitho*, Lord Browne-Wilkinson noted that in *Bolam*, the judge had referred to the accepted practice being proper practice according to a '*responsible* body' or '*reasonable* body of opinion', whereas in *Maynard*,[17] the House of Lords had referred to a 'respectable' body of professional opinion. Whatever their differences, the terminology of proper, appropriate, and accepted treatment and responsible, reasonable, and respectable body of professional opinion are all aimed at capturing the same essence, that the risks and benefits have been weighed and a defensible

---

12 *Darnley v Croydon Health Services NHS Trust* [2018] UKSC 50, [16].
13 *Re J* [1991] Fam 33, 40.
14 *Bolam v Friern Hospital Management Committee* [1957] 1 WLR 582, 587.
15 *Bolitho v City & Hackney HA* [1998] AC 232, 243.
16 Brazier & Miola (n 4) 86. This is considered in the context of innovative treatment in chapter seven.
17 *Maynard v. West Midlands Regional Health Authority* [1984] 1 WLR 634.

conclusion has been reached which is supported by other experts in the field.[18] The terms 'appropriate treatment' and 'reasonable body of opinion' are used in this book to refer to a professional judgement which accords with the standard of care imposed by the law.

The cases which are the subject matter of this book are not concerned with whether the doctor providing the treatment had met the legal standard of care, although concerns about the treatment the child had previously been provided with may form part of the background to the case,[19] or parental concern about the quality of care their child was receiving may have fuelled the dispute about the treatment to be provided.[20] The link between the legal duty of care and treatment decisions is that decisions are made as to which treatment option is in the best interests of the child from those treatment options identified as appropriate according to a reasonable body of opinion. As Jonathan Montgomery suggested in his commentary on the Charlie Gard case, the question remained whether the treatment plan of the US doctor would have fulfilled the standard of care so to have avoided liability in negligence, had administration of it caused Charlie harm.[21] In the terminology used before the Court of Appeal in that case, the question was whether it was a 'viable' therapeutic option.[22] A further example is *Re AA*,[23] in which Bodey J made the declaration sought by the Trust that it was lawful to insert an Implantable Cardioverter Defibrillator (ICD) into seven-year-old AA, which was 'standard management' to monitor and normalise the rhythm of the heart. All the medical evidence before the court, including the expert for the Guardian, supported this management of AA's condition. The evidence of Dr K, the consultant paediatric cardiologist treating AA, and his colleagues that this was appropriate treatment was supported by the peer-reviewed literature. Dr K considered that it would be 'medically negligent' to discharge AA without implanting an ICD.[24] In contrast, there was no doctor before the court willing to prescribe or fit the wearable device the parents wanted for their daughter. Dr K had not, nor would he, prescribe the device for a child with AA's condition, as it was a temporary measure for patients waiting for other treatment.[25] It could

---

18 *Bolitho* (n 15).
19 *King's College NHS Trust v Thomas & Haastrup* [2018] EWHC 127.
20 *Re OT* [2009] EWHC 633; *Bolton NHS Foundation Trust v C and LB and PT* [2015] EWHC 2920; *County Durham and Darlington NHS Foundation Trust v SS, FS and MS* [2016] EWHC 535.
21 Jonathan Montgomery, 'The 'tragedy' of Charlie Gard: a case study for regulation of innovation?' (2019) *Law, Innovation and Technology* 155, 170.
22 The term used before the Court of Appeal in *In the Matter of Charles Gard* [2017] EWCA Civ 410.
23 *Re AA* [2015] EWHC 1178.
24 *Re AA* (n 23) [10], [11].
25 *Re AA* (n 23) [26]. The court will not sanction parental rejection of mainstream medical approaches for the treatment of their child in the absence of medical evidence that their alternative is an appropriate treatment option, *Re C* [1999] 2 FLR 1004; [2000] 2 WLR 270; *In the Matter of JA* [2014] EWHC 1135, *An NHS Trust v SR* [2012] EWHC 3842.

not be in AA's best interests to follow the course her parents sought, given the absence of evidence that it was an appropriate treatment for her condition and supported by a reasonable body of opinion.

Duty to Act in the Best Interests of the Child

As Lord Donaldson MR stated in *Re J (1991)*[26] and repeated as part of his ratio in *Re J (1993)*,[27] 'the fundamental duty' owed by a doctor to patient is, subject to obtaining the necessary consent, to 'treat the patient in accordance with his own best clinical judgment'.[28] In *Wyatt*, referring to an earlier part of Lord Donaldson MR's judgment, Hedley J stated that the duty of doctors is to act 'in what he sees as the best interests of the child: no more and no less'.[29] As Lord Donaldson MR also identified in *Re J (1991)*, in practice, the treatment of a child requires doctors to work in partnership with the child's parents, given their respective expertise and responsibilities.

Working in partnership with parents requires doctors to share their expertise about the appropriate treatment options and which of the options is, in their professional judgement, in the child's best interests. The current law requires doctors to provide information about the 'material risks' of the treatment they consider to be clinically best for the child. It further requires doctors to provide information about reasonable alternatives or variants of significance to the reasonable parent in the position of the parent or of which the doctor is, or should reasonably be, aware that the particular parent is likely to attach significance.[30]

In strict legal terms, the decision as to which of the appropriate treatment options is in the best interests of a young child is for parents to make in the exercise of parental responsibility. This reflects the reality that parents know their child and best know his or her personality, character, experiences, and needs. Furthermore, it recognises that decisions about medical treatment are personal decisions, made taking into account individual values, beliefs, and preferences identified on behalf of young children by their parents. In practice, however, decisions about a young child's medical treatment are usually reached together by parents and doctors, each bringing different knowledge, expertise, and skills with respect to the specific needs of the particular child arising from their respective roles, responsibilities, and relationships with the child. In the majority of cases, doctors are able to work together with parents, together agreeing upon the treatment, from the appropriate treatment options, that they consider to be in the best interests of the child, altering the treatment plan in response to the specific needs of the individual child.

---

26 *Re J* (n 13).
27 [1993] Fam 15.
28 *Re J* (n 27) 27. And again in *Re R* [1991] 1 FLR 190.
29 *Re Wyatt* (n 5 [40].
30 *Montgomery v Lanarkshire Health Board* [2015] UKSC 11 [87].

Recognising that decisions about medical treatment are personal decisions reached according to individual values and beliefs means that, in practice, doctors do provide a treatment which, in their professional judgement, is not clinically best for the child in order to accommodate parental beliefs and values. The cases concerned with the administration of blood to a child whose parents are Jehovah's Witnesses are examples of doctors modifying the treatment plan in order to accommodate parental wishes.

In the first reported case, *Re S* in 1992,[31] the medical evidence before the court was provided by the consultant paediatrician and the senior lecturer in paediatric oncology who shared responsibility for S's care. The consultant 'emphasised that he had gone a long way to vary what would have been the conventional treatment to reflect the convictions of the parents'.[32] Following consultation with colleagues at a specialist centre, the consultant had tried non-conventional treatment for which no scientific evidence existed and had let S's haemoglobin level fall below the level at which a blood transfusion would be usually be administered. However, leave of the court was sought, for the administration of blood in an emergency, when the consultant considered that S's condition had deteriorated to such an extent that palliative care was the only other option. He explained that whilst he respected the parental convictions, his first duty was to his patient and that duty required that S be provided with intensive treatment, although in the future and out of respect for the parental beliefs, he would continue to avoid administering blood if it were possible to do so.[33]

Ten-month-old R was receiving treatment for B-cell lymphoblastic leukaemia. Her parents, who were Jehovah's Witnesses, were unable to consent to the administration of blood, which had been given upon admission in order to save her life. The medical evidence was that blood products could be necessary at any point over the two-year course of treatment; without blood the treatment would be unsuccessful. Her parents did not want her doctors to have blanket authority to administer blood, believing that advances in medical science may identify alternatives. Booth J made a SIO permitting the administration of blood without the consent of R's parents when, in the professional opinion of those medically responsible for her care, her condition was life-threatening. In other circumstances, to respect her parents' beliefs, her doctors should discuss with the parents all alternative forms of management, administering blood only if there was no reasonable alternative.[34]

---

31 [1993] 1 FLR 376. *Re O* [1993] 2 FLR 349 was decided the following year.
32 *Re S* (n 31) 378.
33 *Re S* (n 31) 378.
34 Orders are now commonly made in such terms when parents cannot consent to the administration of blood due to their religious beliefs ensuring that the parents are consulted if the situation is not immediately life-threatening and blood or blood products used only if there is no clinically appropriate alternative, *Birmingham Children's NHS Trust v B & C* [2014] EWHC 531; *An NHS Foundation Trust v Mrs T & Mr T* [2016] EWHC 2980.

In the most recent case, at the time of writing, *Cardiff and Vale University Health Board v T and H*,[35] MacDonald J granted the application permitting the administration of blood to three-and-a-half-week old, T, who was ventilator dependent with cardiac failure and reduced lung function due to a congenital disorder. His mother had been told earlier that week that T would need a blood transfusion in the near future and was told the day before the application that the administration of blood should not be delayed. An iron preparation had not improved his condition. That morning, T had suffered a cardiac arrest, and the multi-disciplinary team caring for him considered that administration of blood was urgently required to prevent further cardiac arrest and address the potentially fatal complications of anaemia and low blood pressure. The evidence before the court from his consultant neonatologist was that they were minimising the administration of blood and had let his haemoglobin levels fall lower than usual, but that modifying the treatment provided to accommodate parental beliefs had led to T becoming acutely unwell, and his treating team was of the view that without a transfusion, T's life was at a very significant risk.[36]

The children in these cases had not been provided with the treatment that their treating doctors considered to be clinically optimal, as the treatment had been modified to accommodate the parental view of the child's best interests given their religious beliefs. However, when in their professional judgement to continue to respect parental wishes would be to put the child at risk of significant harm, the application has been made to the court. The declarations enabled the doctors to treat and avoid the risk of the child suffering significant harm but not to provide clinically optimal treatment, given that the administration of blood would continue to be avoided when possible to accede to the parental view, given their beliefs, of the child's best interests.[37]

The analysis of the case law in this book demonstrates that the early cases were concerned with questions whether the proposed course of treatment was best for the child as with the proposed sterilisation of *Re D*, or with quality of life as in *Re B (1981)* and the treatment to be administered to children with life-limiting conditions, *Re C*, *Re J (1991)*, and *Re J (1993)*. However, medical practice has developed as seen in the more recent cases before the courts, and issues about a child's medical treatment are now more usually brought before the courts when the treating doctors can no longer accede to parental wishes or when a decision about the treatment for a serious medical condition or life-changing intervention has to be made with respect to a child in care. The understanding that these cases are solely about the best interests of the child is a consequence of the courts' application of the best interests test to determine the issue, to which the evidence

---

35 [2019] EWHC 1671.
36 *Cardiff and Vale University Health Board* (n 35) [11].
37 Caroline Bridge has argued that the compromise endorsed by the court causes the child suffering, 'Religion, Culture and Conviction – The Medical Treatment of Young Children' (1999) 11 *Child and Family Law Quarterly* 1.

and argument are directed. To give separate consideration to professional duties to the child in their care and then best interests would serve to clarify the professional judgements about appropriate treatment options from which the choice is made according to best interests.

Information, Participation, and Decision-Making

A very young child depends upon their parents to advocate for them and to articulate their individual needs. For this reason it is important that cases involving serious medical treatment or life-changing interventions of children in the care of the state are brought before the courts, to ensure that their interests are protected and so that decisions made about them can be subjected to public scrutiny and decision-makers can be held to account. As *Gillick* recognised, as a child develops the capacity to understand their condition and its treatment, good parenting and good medical practice requires that their ability to participate in decisions about their medical treatment is fostered, even if they do not have the legal capacity to take responsibility. Parents and health professionals need to be attentive to the individual child in order to consider the extent to which a child is able, and wishes, to participate in decisions about their medical treatment. Furthermore, as *Gillick* and section 8 of the Family Law Reform Act 1969 recognise, the older child will have the capacity to make decisions about their medical treatment;[38] here the partnership shifts with consideration needing to be given to the extent to which the child wishes their parents to participate in decisions about their medical treatment.

It is notable that there is a limited body of case law concerned with the treatment decisions of older children. There are seven cases listed in the appendix concerning the refusal of medical treatment by a teenager who may have been *Gillick* competent in the last twenty years[39] in comparison with the flurry that followed *Re R* and *Re W*[40] in the 1990s and which established the law relating to the powers of holders of parental responsibility and the court when an older child has refused their consent to medical treatment for a serious medical condition.[41] The explanation may be that these early cases gave parents the power to override

---

38 And will also be owed a duty of confidentiality, *R. (on the application of Axon) v. Secretary of State for Health & Another* [2006] EWHC 37. For a discussion of the potential application of *Montgomery* to children given the abilities of others to give consent to treatment in their best interests see Emma Cave and Craig Purshouse, 'Think of the Children: Liability for Non-Disclosure of Information Post-Montgomery' (2020) 28 *Medical Law Review* 270.
39 *Re P* [2003] EWHC 2327; *An NHS Foundation Trust v A and Others* [2014] EWHC 920; *In the Matter of JA* [2014] EWHC 1135; *An NHS Foundation Hospital v P* [2014] EWHC 1650; *Plymouth Hospitals NHS Trust v YZ and ZZ* [2017] EWHC 2211; *University Hospitals Plymouth NHS Trust v B* [2019] EWHC 1670; *An NHS Trust v CX* [2019] EWHC 3033.
40 *Re R* [1992] 1 FLR 190; *Re W* [1993] Fam 64; or *Re E* [1993] 1 FLR 386 which preceded them.
41 *Re K, W and H* [1993] 1 FLR 854; *Re S* [1994] 2 FLR 1065; *Re L* [1998] 2 FLR 810; *Re M* [1999] 2 FLR 1097.

the refusal of a child whether *Gillick* competent or not to give consent, although not the provision of consent, so that it is not necessary to go to court to obtain consent to recommended medical treatment. It may be that greater recognition of the rights of the child means that their decisions about their medical treatment are respected. Alternatively, it may be that through good medical practice, including the provision of information and discussions with different members of the treatment team, a treatment plan can be agreed that is acceptable to all. Authorising the administration of an antidote to 14-year-old YZ who had taken an overdose,[42] MacDonald J noted that the application to court had been made as the optimum time for its administration had expired. The reason for this was that the staff had used the time to engage in lengthy discussions with YZ using a variety of strategies in an attempt to get her to agree to tests and, if necessary, treatment. Her mother agreed that she should be tested and treated. The judge expressed the view that although it was best practice to try to secure the agreement of a young person to their medical treatment, it was 'unfortunate' that the matter was not brought before the court until the window for optimum treatment was almost closed.[43] A further example is *An NHS Foundation Trust v A and Others*,[44] in which Hayden J observed that without the treatment at issue, the fitting of a feeding tube, A's body had begun to shut down and it was believed when the application had been filed a month before that she would only live for two to three months without it. The judge noted that her consultant had spent some time trying to persuade A and her mother to accept his advice. The judge observed that whilst it was good practice to spend time trying to find an agreed way forward, crucial time had been lost trying to get agreement when this was unlikely to ever occur.[45] We would not therefore now expect the judge to note without comment, as in *Re L*, that one of the reasons L lacked the understanding necessary to make a decision about her treatment was that she had not been told the manner of her death should she not have the surgery to which she had refused consent.[46] Neither would we now expect a judge to accept that one reason S lacked understanding that without further blood transfusions in the management of beta thalassemia she would die was because she had not been informed.[47]

Transfer to a Doctor Prepared to Take Over Care of the Child

A child who is seriously ill or has a complex medical condition will be cared for by a multi-disciplinary team. Discussions about treatment options within the

---

42 *Plymouth Hospitals NHS Trust v YZ and ZZ* [2017] EWHC 2211.
43 *Plymouth Hospitals NHS Trust* (n 42) [18].
44 [2014] EWHC 920.
45 *An NHS Foundation Trust* (n 44) [18].
46 *Re L* (n 41) 812.
47 *Re S* (n 41).

multi-disciplinary team will reassure doctors that their professional judgement about appropriate treatment options accords with a reasonable body of opinion in the face of medical uncertainty. Whilst not a legal obligation, when parents seek for their child to receive treatment which the responsible doctors consider is not appropriate but about which there is scope for uncertainty, second opinions will often, as a matter of good practice, be sought from experts in other specialities and in other hospitals.[48] Second opinions may reassure the parents that the course of treatment proposed by the treating doctors is best for their child. Second opinions may confirm the professional judgement of the treatment team, may present an alternative way forward that they feel able to try or lead the treatment team to re-assess their original view. It may be that the treatment team maintain their judgement but that the process of securing second opinions led to the identification of a doctor elsewhere prepared to treat in the way that the parents wish. In *Re J (1993)*, Lord Donaldson suggested that if that were the case, the Trust would have to consider its current responsibilities to the child and to other children who may need its facilities, whilst the parents would have to consider the advice from the Trust and any risks involved in a transfer.[49]

Transfer of the child to another doctor prepared to take over the care of the child has been at issue in some of the recent cases. As noted above, the central issue in the case concerning the future medical treatment of Charlie Gard was whether the nucleoside bypass therapy offered by the US doctor was a viable therapeutic option.[50] In the cases concerning Alfie Evans and Isaiah Haastrup, the offer to care for them followed not from medical or scientific expertise in the treatment of the child's condition but a different moral or ethical approach in the jurisdiction in which they practised.[51] As MacDonald J stated in his judgment, dismissal of the application by the Trust in relation to the future care of Tafida Raqeeb had the effect that life-sustaining treatment had to be continued either within the NHS Trust or by the hospital in Italy which had agreed to accept her.[52] Had different positions held by the medical experts on Tafida's care been purely a question of different moral or ethical values, MacDonald J would no doubt have reached the same conclusion he did in relation to the care of Alfie Evans. However, there was sufficient evidence before the court that there were children with similar conditions to Tafida receiving long-term ventilation at home in this jurisdiction to lead to the conclusion that the withdrawal of ventilation was not, at that point in time, in her best interests.

---

48 GOSH's position statement of the 13 July 2017, [15], https://www.serjeantsinn.com/news/charlie-gard-position-statements/ accessed 29 February 2020.
49 *Re J* (n 27) 28.
50 *In the Matter of Charles Gard* (n 22).
51 *Haastrup* (n 19) [83]-[84].
52 *Tafida Raqeeb v Barts NHS Foundation Trust* [2019] EWHC 2531 (Admin); *Barts NHS Foundation Trust v Shalina Begum and Muhhamed Raqeeb & Tafida Raqeeb* [2019] EWHC 2530 (Fam), [188].

As had occurred in all these cases, when there are disagreements about the medical treatment that should be provided to the child, such that the partnership between parents and professionals is no longer effective or when there is a serious treatment decision with respect to a child in care, there is a responsibility on the part of the Trust to refer the matter to court.[53] Court orders are permissive. They do not affect the doctors' duty to act in accordance with their professional judgement.[54]

Professional Judgement and Conscience

The balance of responsibilities between parents, courts, and doctors, and recognition of the specific expertise brought by doctors to the medical encounter is emphasised in the principle that whilst parents and the court can give or withhold consent to the treatment proposed by the doctors, neither can require doctors to treat contrary to their clinical or professional judgement. This principle originated in the judgment of Lord Donaldson MR in *Re J (1991)*,[55] repeated as part of his ratio in *Re J (1993)*, in which the issue was whether, in the exercise of its inherent jurisdiction, a judge could require a doctor to provide treatment which in their clinical judgement is not in the best interests of the patient.[56] In his Lordship's opinion it would be an

> abuse of power as directly or indirectly requiring the practitioner to act contrary to the fundamental duty which he owes to his patient. This, subject to obtaining any necessary consent, is to treat the patient in accordance with his own best clinical judgment, notwithstanding that other practitioners who are not called upon to treat the patient may have formed a quite different judgment, or that the court, acting on expert evidence, may disagree with him.[57]

Lord Donaldson continued to say that parents cannot insist on treatment, and doctors can refuse to administer treatment which they consider to be 'medically contra-indicated' or which they could not '*conscientiously* administer'.[58] In *Wyatt*, Hedley J adopted the latter phraseology, that a doctor cannot be required to act contrary to his or her professional conscience.[59] This formulation has not been generally adopted, and judges more usually have stated that the court cannot

---

53 As considered in chapter three.
54 *Portsmouth NHS Trust v Wyatt* [2004] EWHC 2247.
55 *Re J* (n 13).
56 *Re J* (n 27) 26-7.
57 *Re J* (n 27), 27.
58 *Re J* (n 13) (Lord Donaldson MR), emphasis added, 41; repeated as part of his ratio in *Re J* (n 27), 27.
59 *Re Wyatt* (n 5) [32].

require doctors to treat contrary to their professional[60] or clinical[61] judgement. However, professional conscience captures the nature of the professional judgement which is protected, noting that there are numerous exercises of professional judgement in the provision of medical treatment. Hedley J explained that the exercise of professional conscience is an 'intellectual' process in which the doctor must take account of all the circumstances, professional guidance, and second opinions, to arrive at a conclusion as to the patient's best interests and consider whether there is a 'reasonable basis' for the provision of the treatment even if he is inclined against it.[62] The judge explained that professional conscience is more of an intuitive than rational confirmation of the intellectual conclusion and 'honed by experience of patients, exposure to the practice of colleagues, and the ethos of his work'.[63]

In his fourth published judgment on the issue of the medical treatment of Charlotte Wyatt should she suffer a respiratory crisis, Hedley J repeated the fourfold categorisation of the circumstances in which parents and professionals may be disagreed over the medical treatment of a child, originally stated in his first judgment upon Charlotte's treatment a year earlier.[64] These were (i) where the parents refuse consent to recommended treatment, failure to administer which would be an affront to that doctor's conscience; (ii) where the doctor disagrees with the parental decision to refuse consent to recommended treatment; (iii) where parents request treatment which is not recommended by the doctor but to administer it would not be an affront to conscience; and (iv) where to provide the treatment the parents' request would be an affront to conscience.[65]

Hedley J thought that most disagreements would fall within categories (ii) or (iii) and, consistent with what is argued above, the doctors giving evidence in the case agreed that they would, 'in the last resort', accommodate the parental request.[66] Disagreements which fall into categories (ii) and (iii) are examples when the doctor, respecting the contribution of parents to decision-making, the uncertainties in clinical judgement, and that their judgement may be informed by values which differ from those of the parents, accedes to the parental view. Hedley J tentatively concluded that a case fell within the fourth category when the doctor considered the treatment requested by the parent is '*inimical* to the best interests

---

60 *Re R* (n 28) 201; *King's College Hospital NHS Foundation Trust v MH* [2015] EWHC 1920 [34], quoted in *GOSH v NO & KK & MK* [2017] EWHC 241 [23] and *A Local Authority and An NHS Trust v MC & FC & C* [2017] EWHC 370 [42]; *An NHS Trust v BK, LK & SK* [2016] EWHC 2860 [1]; *Haastrup* (n 19) [1]; *An NHS Trust v A & B & C* [2018] EWHC 2750 [30].
61 *A National Health Service Trust v D* [2000] 2 FLR 677, 686; *R v Portsmouth Hospitals NHS Trust, ex parte Glass* [1999] 2 FLR 905, 908; *Re L (Medical Treatment: Benefit)* [2004] EWHC 2713 [30].
62 *Re Wyatt* (n 5) [34].
63 *Re Wyatt* (n 5) [35].
64 *Portsmouth NHS Trust* (n 54) [18].
65 *Re Wyatt* (n 5) [30].
66 *Re Wyatt* (n 5) [31].

of the patient, and that his professional conscience, intuition, or hunch, confirms that view'.[67] It is in those circumstances, Hedley J explained, that the doctor cannot be compelled to provide the requested treatment, although another doctor should not be prevented from providing the treatment. In practice, this view will be confirmed or otherwise by consulting experts from other disciplines and other hospitals. If, having done so, the doctor remains of their original opinion, but there is a doctor who is prepared to treat, they come under a duty to consider a transfer.[68]

The explanation Hedley J gave of professional conscience in medical decisions made it clear that he was referring to the discharge of professional duties rather than a process of examining individual or personal conscience.[69] As Hedley J used the term, professional conscience is different from generalised claims based upon the *personal* values of professionals as, for example, in the conscience clauses in the Abortion Act 1967 or the Human Fertilisation and Embryology Act 1990.[70] The judge may have been invoking what Jonathan Montgomery has referred to as 'conscientious professional discretion'.[71] It involves a professional judgement as to the limits of what is professionally acceptable given the diagnosis and prognosis. Moral values are an inevitable aspect of judgements of professional conscience, but this is a professional, and not a personal, conclusion. In identifying four circumstances in which disagreement may arise between parents and doctors, Hedley J used the term 'professional conscience' to distinguish those situations in which, in the exercise of their professional judgement, the doctor can accede to the parental wishes, from those in which, in their professional judgement, they cannot do as the parents request.

Stephen Smith has considered the nature of individual claims of conscience, principally with reference to *Aintree v James*.[72] He argued that individualised claims of conscience arise when the doctor does not object to a particular

---

67 *Re Wyatt* (n 5) [36].
68 *Ms B v An NHS Hospital Trust* [2002] EWHC 429 [100 (viii)], although a case concerned with the decisions of a competent adult, this must equally be so in the treatment of children who should not be denied treatment merely because they lack the capacity to decide for themselves.
69 There are different views on the meaning and scope of the concept of professional conscience which is as yet under-theorised in the academic literature, see Sara Fovargue, Sheelagh McGuinness, Alexandra Mullock, Stephen Smith (eds), 'Conscience and Proper Medical Treatment Special Issue (2015) *Medical Law Review*.
70 As explored by Sara Fovargue and Mary Neal, '"In Good Conscience": Conscience-based Exemptions and Proper Medical Treatment' (2015) 23 *Medical Law Review* 221; Mary Neal and Sara Fovargue, 'Conscience and Agent-Integrity: A Defence of Conscience-Based Exemptions in the Health Care Context' (2016) 24 *Medical Law Review* 544.
71 Jonathan Montgomery, 'Conscientious Objection: Personal and Professional Ethics in the Public Square' (2015) 23 *Medical Law Review* 200, 201.
72 *Aintree University Hospitals NHS Foundation Trust v James* [2013] UKSC 67, which concerned the lawfulness of withholding treatment in the event of a deterioration in the condition of an adult patient in a minimally conscious state; Stephen Smith, 'A Bridge too Far: Individualised Claims of Conscience' (2015) 23 *Medical Law Review* 283; Stephen Smith,

treatment in all instances but in the particular circumstances of the particular patient so that the treatment previously provided has now become 'objectionable'; it has become 'a 'bridge too far'.[73] This may be because the child's condition has deteriorated so that treatment once in the child's best interests or within the range of appropriate treatment options can no longer be provided with a good conscience. This may be, for example, because it is sustaining the life of a child for whom there are no appropriate treatment options, who has no conscious interaction, no ability to breathe independently, and no prospect of recovery.[74] In such cases, doctors do not object to the provision of life-sustaining intervention in general, indeed, often they will have been providing it to the patient. But, due to a change in circumstances, the point has been reached at which it is contrary to their professional judgement, to their professional conscience, to provide it in the particular circumstances that now prevail. A line has been crossed so that continued treatment is, in the judgement of the responsible doctors, no longer 'within the bounds of what is proper in a clinical sense'.[75]

The decision that to provide or continue treatment is contrary to their professional conscience has to be understood within the social and political context, of approaches to parenthood, and the nature of the doctor/patient relationship within which the judgement is reached. The principle that parents or the court cannot require a doctor to treat contrary to their professional judgement suggests that the doctor is the dominant partner, that medical opinion prevails. Yet, once it is recognised that doctors will provide treatment they consider is not clinically best for the child, respecting parental judgements of their child's best interests, the balance looks more equal. To recognise that the principle is that doctors cannot be required to treat a child contrary to their professional conscience or in a way they consider to be *contrary* or *inimical* to the child's best interests suggests a more balanced partnership than the legal principle as it is usually expressed. Similarly as Stephen Smith has argued, to approach the issue as solely that of best interests means that the question that is not addressed is the extent to which the doctors have been required to provide treatment they object to, in his terms, that is contrary to their individual conscience. As has been argued, in the current time, the evidence before the courts suggests that the practice is to refer the question to court when doctors have reached the view that what the parents want is contrary to or inimical to the best interests of the child, which is far from saying that there is a disagreement over what is best. But, inevitably, when this point has been reached it is also the case that the provision of treatment or continued treatment is not in the child's best interests.

'Individualised Claims of Conscience, Clinical Judgement and Best Interests' (2018) 26 *Health Care Analysis* 81.
73 Smith, 'A Bridge too Far' (n 72) 284.
74 *Re A* [2016] EWCA Civ 759, considered further in chapter six.
75 Smith, 'A Bridge too Far' (n 72) 285.

Good Medical Practice Guidance

As well as complying with the minimum standards established by the law and in order to fulfil their professional duties, doctors are required to comply with guidance issued by the General Medical Council (GMC). By virtue of s.35 of the Medical Act 1983, the GMC has the 'power' to provide advice on 'standards of 'professional conduct, performance, and medical ethics' and medical professionals risk their registration if they seriously or persistently fail to follow *Good Medical Practice*.[76] *Good Medical Practice* sets out the professional values and behaviours expected from doctors who must use their professional judgement to apply the principles to their practice. As Charles Foster and José Miola have observed, that it is possible for a doctor to be acting unethically, risking professional sanction for failure to comply with standards of professional ethics, despite acting lawfully, is 'structurally sound'; the standard set by professional ethics should be higher than the minimum established by the law.[77]

Elaborating the principles of *Good Medical Practice,* the GMC has specific guidance on safeguarding and protecting the health and wellbeing of children and young people, *0 – 18 years: guidance for all doctors*.[78] It applies to all doctors not just those whose work routinely involves children. All doctors need to be aware of the needs of children when they see patients who are parents or carers, who are cared for by children or young people, or who may represent a danger to children or young people. With reference to relevant legislation and a handful of cases, *0-18 years* is focused upon guidance based upon ethical principles of good practice such as respect and honesty. These include treating children as individuals with rights to whom doctors should listen, taking account of what the child patient has to say about the things that affect him or her, and guiding doctors to effective and honest communication that respects the views of children and responds to their concerns.[79] The case law referenced is primarily the early cases concerning the legal framework for the treatment of 16- and 17-year-olds.[80] The guidance advises doctors that they may have to seek legal advice if the parents of a child who lacks capacity cannot agree with each other or both refuse their consent, and in England and Wales, if a competent young person refuses treatment the doctor considers to be in their best interests.[81] However, when considering doing so, the doctor is advised first to seek the advice of the multi-disciplinary

---

[76] GMC, *Good Medical Practice*, https://www.gmc-uk.org/ethical-guidance/ethical-guidance-for-doctors/good-medical-practice accessed 16 April 2020.
[77] Charles Foster and José Miola, 'Who's in Charge? The Relationship Between Medical Law, Medical Ethics and Medical Morality' (2015) 23 *Medical Law Review* 505, 514.
[78] GMC Guidance, *0-18 years: guidance for all doctors,* 2018, https://www.gmc-uk.org/ethical-guidance/ethical-guidance-for-doctors/0-18-years accessed 16 April 2020, the guidance came into effect on 15 October 2007 and was updated in May 2018.
[79] GMC, *0-18 years* (n 78) paras 3, 7, 14.
[80] GMC, *0-18 years* (n 78) para 28.
[81] GMC, *0-18 years* (n 78) paras 27, 31, 33.

team, experienced colleagues, an independent advocate, named or designated doctors for child protection, or professional or regulatory bodies.[82]

Doctors may also consult guidance provided by other professional bodies such as the British Medical Association's (BMA) *Children and Young People Ethics Toolkit*[83] and on topics specific to children such as the non-therapeutic circumcision of children.[84] There are a number of guidance documents on caring for children at the end of life, from the GMC, National Institute for Health and Care Excellence (NICE),[85] and the Royal College of Paediatrics and Child Health (RCPCH).[86] The GMC Guidance, *Treatment and care towards the end of life: good practice in decision-making*,[87] which offers guidance in relation to all patients, states that it is based on long-established ethical principles and takes account of, and is consistent with, current law but is not a statement of the legal principles or a substitute for legal advice. It emphasises the professional obligation to take account of 'up-to-date, authoritative' clinical guidance, and when there are uncertainties about the range of treatment options, to seek advice or second opinions from colleagues with relevant expertise, who may be from another discipline.[88] Paragraphs 90-108 address decisions concerning neonates, children, and young people focused upon capacity, parental responsibility, and best interests, and referring users back to *0-18 years*.

The Royal College of Paediatrics and Child Health (RCPCH) first issued its guidance on *Withholding or Withdrawing Life Saving Treatment in Children: A Framework for Practice* in 1997, following soon after the early case law which had concerned such cases. The current guidance, *Making Decisions to Limit Treatment in Life-Limiting and Life-Threatening Conditions in Children: A Framework for Practice*, seeks to provide an ethical and legal framework for good

---

82 GMC, *0-18 years* (n 78) para 32.
83 BMA, *Children and Young People Ethics Toolkit*, last updated March 2019, https://www.bma.org.uk/advice/employment/ethics/children-and-young-people/children-and-young-peoples-ethics-tool-kit, accessed 16 April 2020. The purpose of which is to identify the key factors for doctors to take into account when making decisions, and direct to other sources of advice, frequently the GMC guidance.
84 BMA, *Children and Young People Ethics Toolkit* (n 83).
85 NICE, *End of life care for infants, children and young people with life-limiting conditions: planning and management*, 2016, https://www.nice.org.uk/guidance/ng61 accessed 16 April 2020. Evidence based guidelines which make recommendations that practitioners should take into account in exercising their judgement.
86 RCPCH, *Making Decisions to Limit Treatment in Life-Limiting and Life-Threatening Conditions in Children: A Framework for Practice*, 2015, https://adc.bmj.com/content/100/Suppl_2/s1.full.pdf+html accessed 16 April 2020.
87 https://www.gmc-uk.org/ethical-guidance/ethical-guidance-for-doctors/treatment-and-care-towards-the-end-of-life accessed 16 April 2020. Came into effect in July 2010, replacing *Withholding and Withdrawing Life-Prolonging Treatments* (2002), notably there is very little law referenced in these sections.
88 GMC (n 87), para 94.

practice.[89] The stated purpose of the guidance is to provide a framework for the making of decisions that are in the best interests of the child and in accordance with good clinical practice.[90]

With the exception of the RCPCH guidance on withholding or withdrawing life-sustaining treatment, professional guidance is rarely referred to in the judgments concerning children's medical treatment.[91] This is presumably because the guidance, although underpinned by the law, is good practice guidance rather than legal obligations. In that respect, to demonstrate their good practice, the GMC Guidance *0-18 years* was referred to in the GOSH position statement in the Charlie Gard case. GOSH referred to the requirement to act in the child's best interests and put the child first whilst considering the parents and others close to the child to support their claim that their approach had been focused throughout upon the interests of Charlie.[92] Given the dominance within the law of the best interests principle, consideration is now given to what the guidance has to say about best interests.

Professional Guidance on Best Interests

The GMC Guidance *0-18 years* states that the 'guiding principle' in all decisions affecting children and young people is their best interests.[93] It advises that parents are usually best placed to determine the best interests of their child and should make decisions on their child's behalf until the child is able to make their own decisions.[94] It continues to explain that in assessing best interests, beyond what is clinically indicated, consideration should be given to

a. the views of the child or young person, so far as they can express them, including any previously expressed preferences
b. the views of parents
c. the views of others close to the child or young person
d. the cultural, religious, or other beliefs and values of the child or parents
e. the views of other healthcare professionals involved in providing care to the child or young person, and of any other professionals who have an interest in their welfare

---

89 RCPCH, *Making Decisions to Limit Treatment in Life-Limiting and Life-Threatening Conditions in Children: A Framework for Practice*, 2015, https://adc.bmj.com/content/10 0/Suppl_2/s1.full.pdf+html accessed 16 April 2020. The second edition was published in 2004.
90 RCPCH (n 89) 6.
91 The ECtHR referred to guidance from the GMC, BMA and RCPCH in setting out the domestic framework in *Glass v United Kingdom* [2004] 39 EHRR 15.
92 GOSH position statement of the 13th July, [11] https://www.serjeantsinn.com/news/c harlie-gard-position-statements/ accessed 29 February 2020.
93 GMC, *0-18 years* (n 78) para 8.
94 GMC, *0-18 years* (n 78) para 21.

90 *Legal Duties of Doctors to Children*

    f. which choice, if there is more than one, will least restrict the child or young person's future options.[95]

Other relevant information may also be considered. To the extent that consideration should be given to the ascertainable views of the child or young person, this reflects s.1(3)(a) of the Children Act 1989, although the guidance goes further by directing doctors to consider previously expressed preferences. The current law considers the views of parents as to the best interests of their child but not the views of those close to them. Section 1(3)(d) of the Children Act directs welfare assessment to the 'background and characteristics' of the child, which should include consideration of the 'cultural, religious, or other beliefs and values of the child' although not those of his or her parents. Determination of the best interests of the child takes into account the views of other healthcare professionals involved in providing care to the child, although the focus in the cases is upon the clinical assessment of doctors rather than other health professionals who have an interest in the welfare of the child. The guidance also goes beyond the law by specifically advising doctors to select the option which will least restrict the child's future options. Recognition that the views of parents and others involved in the care of the child or with interest in his or her welfare are intrinsic to the assessment of the child's best interests is akin to the assessment of the best interests of an adult who lacks capacity under the terms of the Mental Capacity Act 2005. Practitioners will have a view as to what is clinically best for the child and, drawing upon their experience and values, what they consider to be in the best interests of the child given the potential benefits and burdens, the possible outcomes, and the expected effect upon quality and quantity of life. But the guidance directs doctors beyond those factors to incorporate the views of child, parents, and carers, which should result in a more relational than individualistic assessment.

    The BMA Toolkit[96] also directs doctors to factors within the Children Act welfare checklist, specifically, the child's own wishes, feelings and values (where these can be ascertained), physical and emotional needs, and religious or cultural background. Like the GMC guidance, doctors are encouraged to select a treatment that is least restrictive of the patient's future choices; to consider the views of parents and others who are close to the patient about what is likely to benefit the patient; the views of other health care professionals involved in providing care to the child and of any other professionals who have an interest in the welfare of the child. However, the BMA Toolkit also brings into the assessment of best interests clinical judgementof the effectiveness of the proposed treatment compared to other treatment options and the likelihood and likely extent of any degree of improvement in the patient's condition if treatment is provided, both factors which are relevant to identifying the treatment options from which to determine which is in the best interests of the child. Doctors are directed to consider the

---

95 GMC, *0-18 years* (n 78) para 12.
96 BMA, *Children and Young People Ethics Toolkit* (n 83).

patient's ability to understand what is proposed and weigh up the alternatives which are relevant to capacity, not best interests. Encouraging doctors to provide additional support or explanations to enhance the child's potential to participate in the decision is consistent with the child's UNCRC right to participate, but is a matter of effective communication, not best interests. In sum, the BMA guidance confuses issues of clinical judgement, capacity, participation, and communication with best interests.

The Royal College of Paediatrics and Child Health framework for good practice on limiting life-sustaining treatment explains that the legal principles originate from both case law and statute and that both the legal and the ethical principle governing decisions is the best interests of the child, giving recognition to the rights of the child and their family.[97] Ethical obligations, the guidance states, are based on the duty of care which parents and professionals owe to the child, the child's rights, and the law, all of which are centred upon the best interests of the child.[98] The guidance recognises the 'unique role' of parents in determining their child's best interests, although also that in most cases parents and professionals work in 'partnership' to secure the best interests of the child.[99]

The guidance makes repeated reference to the duty to act in accordance with the best interests of the child. In the introductory paragraphs, it states that this applies to all members of the treating team.[100] Further, that best interest of the child is the 'ethical and legal rationale for all treatments'.[101] In the section on fundamental considerations of the ethical framework, it provides that the best interests of the child must be the 'paramount concern' of health professionals.[102]

The guidance explains that,

> Throughout this document the term 'best interests' has been used in the sense used in law (the five-point welfare check list of the Children Act 1989; the nine-point check list of the Mental Capacity Act 2005 as applied to over 16-year olds) and in published professional guidance (GMC *End of life Care* 2010; GMC *0–18 years: guidance for all doctors* 2007). No single formula applies, but determination of clinical best interests involves balancing benefits and burdens (of whatever type) of treatments and outcomes, whilst considering the ascertainable wishes, beliefs and values and preferences of the child and their family, the cultural and religious views of the latter, the views of those providing care for the child and what choice is least restrictive of future options.'[103]

---

97 RCPCH (n 89) 4.
98 RCPCH (n 89) para 2.4.1.
99 RCPCH (n 89) para 2.4.1.
100 RCPCH (n 89) 4.
101 RCPCH (n 89) 6.
102 RCPCH (n 89) para 2.4.1.
103 RCPCH (n 89) 6.

The reference to the absence of any single formula may amount to a recognition of the differences between the Children Act, Mental Capacity Act 2005, and GMC guidance. The welfare checklist in s.1(3) of the Children Act provides a non-exhaustive seven-point checklist, and the differences between that provision and the GMC guidance are noted above. The Mental Capacity Act 2005, which applies to children aged 16 and 17 and adults, is based much more than the Children Act in consideration of the past as well as present wishes of the patient, beliefs and values of the patient that would have influenced their decision, and other factors that the patient would be likely to consider had they been able to, factors recognised in the GMC guidance.

The RCPCH guidance recognises the value judgements involved in the determination of best interests,

> All decisions about best interests of a child involve value judgements about what is of value in life, how best to promote the child's interests, and how different or competing interests should be weighed against each other. [104]

The guidance alerts doctors to consider whether different conclusions about a child's best interests have been reached because they are informed by different values as much as by different understandings of the relevant facts. It is notable that in comparison with the wide range of factors to which doctors are directed by the good medical practice guidelines, the evidence from medical practitioners before the court as to the child's best interests is narrowly focused upon the child's medical condition, prognosis, pain and suffering, and in more recent cases, upon the capacity for the child to benefit from human interaction.

Professional Duties to Children in their Care

The partnership between parents and professionals in the provision of care is framed by both parental responsibility and the legal and professional duties of doctors to the child in their care, by the Children Act 1989, common law and professional ethics. The focus in judgments, professional guidance, and academic analysis, upon the child's best interests, has resulted in neglect to consider the legal and professional duties of doctors to children in their care. It is the unique relationship of care in which doctors have legal and professional duties to children which justifies the intervention of the State into family life, in the form of the decision of the court upon application by the Trust, when doctors cannot agree to the treatment preferences of parents, and requires a judgment of the court when an issue arises concerning the serious medical treatment or intervention with respect to a child in care. Public responsibilities to protect the welfare of the child are the focus of the next chapter.

---

104 RCPCH (n 89) para 2.4.2.

5 Protecting the Interests and Welfare of Vulnerable Children

Public Responsibilities for Children's Health

Accounts and analysis of children's medical treatment cases typify them as disputes between parents and doctors, that is, parental responsibility in conflict with the professional duty to act in accordance with the best interests of the child.[1] This characterisation fails to recognise the duties of doctors alongside the responsibilities of the local authorities and the courts to protect the wellbeing of children. Whilst the primary responsibility for children rests with their parents, parents depend upon others for help and support in raising their children. All parents will be able to access advice and support from Health Visitors and General Practitioners, most will use education services, and children's wellbeing will be enhanced by access to public parks and museums. The emphasis of the New Labour government between 1997 and 2010 that *Every Child Matters* was aspirational in its aim to support the families of all children to improve child outcomes, and the focus upon wellbeing has been narrowed in the era of austerity to child protection issues.[2] Whilst policy changes affect its implementation, the framework of the Children Act 1989, within which social services work, specifically tasks them with supporting children in need, supporting their care within the family, avoiding compulsory intervention where possible, and when it is necessary to adopt the least interventionist approach. However, the Children Act 1989 and 2004 place specific duties upon other public services to work together with local authorities to protect children and their welfare. This requires doctors, in fulfilment of their legal and professional duties to children, to make judgements about raising concerns with social services and, when the concern about child wellbeing is specifically in relation to medical treatment, to seek advice about a referral to

---

1 For Example, Margaret Brazier and Emma Cave, *Medicine, Patients and the Law* (Manchester University Press, 2016) ch14; Jo Bridgeman, *Parental Responsibility, Children and Healthcare Law* (Cambridge University Press, 2007).
2 Nigel Parton, ''The Changing Politics and Practice of Child Protection and Safeguarding in England' in Stephen Wagg and Jane Pilcher (eds), *Thatcher's Grandchildren? Politics and Childhood in the Twenty-First Century* (Palgrave Macmillan, 2014) 45–68, 62.

court. GMC, *Protecting Children and Young People: the responsibilities of all doctors*, provides:

> All children and young people are entitled to protection from abuse and neglect. *Good medical practice* places a duty on all doctors to protect and promote the health and well-being of children and young people. This means all doctors must act on any concerns they have about the safety or welfare of a child or young person.[3]

Case law reveals a much greater proportion of cases, than the conceptualisation of the law governing children's medical treatment would suggest, brought to court by the local authority in respect of children in care or in whose upbringing the local authority is involved due to concerns relating to the child's medical condition. It is argued that it is crucial to understand the responsibilities of the state towards children, that is, the public law dimensions of children's healthcare law and how these sit alongside and also frame the legal and professional duties of health professionals to children in their care. It is these public responsibilities, and the balance of responsibilities between parents, carers, local authorities, and the courts for the protection of the welfare of children, that justifies intervention by the state in family life. This chapter explores these cases, analysing children's healthcare law through consideration of the public, the social and political, rather than the more traditional ethical, role of the law.

First, the early cases that established the principles of children's healthcare law, as examined in chapter three, are revisited. The analysis here demonstrates that, because of the involvement of public authorities, these cases are examples of the state's role in protecting children rather than disputes between parents and professionals. The cases of *Re R* and *Re W* clarified the ability of the local authority, as a holder of parental responsibility, to consent to the medical treatment of a child. The court placed limits upon the authority of all holders of parental responsibility in the sterilisation cases, although the courts then provided ineffective protection of the interests of the young women through a failure to evaluate critically the evidence in the context of lack of support for the family and societal perceptions of the poor quality of life of people with disabilities. Cases of the withdrawal or withholding of life-sustaining treatment from children in care raise the question of the scope of s.33, which confers parental responsibility upon the local authority. It is argued that if the court is to be effective in its protection of vulnerable children in the care of the state and often their vulnerable parents, judges need to undertake a more critical examination of the evidence and ensure that the parental views are heard on the issue of withholding or withdrawing

---

3 GMC, *Protecting Children and Young People: the responsibilities of all doctors*, published July 2012, came into effect September 2012 and last updated May 2018, 6, https://www.gmc-uk.org/ethical-guidance/ethical-guidance-for-doctors/protecting-children-and-young-people accessed 29 February 2020 developing GMC *Good medical practice* (2013) para 27.

life-sustaining treatment. Finally, the professional duty identified by the GMC to consider informing social services is considered in cases where parental disengagement, pre-existing beliefs about the child's medical condition, and parental interference with medical treatment present cause for concern that parental care is presenting a significant risk of harm to the child.

Public Responsibilities in the Early Case Law

It is notable that the early cases, in which the legal framework and principles for judicial decision-making were developed, were brought to court by local authorities to enable the court to make decisions about the child's treatment. In some of these cases, the child was already in local authority care or a ward of court for reasons unrelated to the treatment at issue. In both *Re C* and *Re J (1991)*, the child had been made a ward of court, whilst the authority retained 'care and control' of the child. Neither child had left the hospital since birth. Sixteen-week-old C had been made a ward of court prior to birth at a point at which her medical condition was not anticipated, as social services had formed the view that her 'parents would have great difficulty in caring for her' for reasons unrelated to her medical condition.[4] Five-month-old J, who had severe brain damage due to a shortage of oxygen arising from breathing difficulties following his premature birth, had been made a ward of court for reasons unrelated to his medical condition.[5] Decisions about the withholding of life-sustaining treatment were thus made by the court upon application by the local authority in wardship proceedings.

Sixteen-year-old G-U was a ward of court and in local authority care when the termination of her pregnancy was arranged by the local authority,[6] and 15-year-old P was in local authority care following a conviction for theft and made a ward of court for the court to determine whether her pregnancy should be terminated.[7] D was cared for by her mother supported by a range of community professionals, although it was the insistence of D's local authority educational psychologist that the proposed sterilisation was not in her best interests that resulted in the matter being brought before the court.[8] In *Re B (1988)*, the council applied for an order to make B a ward of court and for leave for her to undergo the sterilisation operation.[9] B had been in local authority care, in a residential home for children and adults with learning difficulties, since the age of 4. It was envisaged that she would continue to live there for the foreseeable future as she was not expected to be able to live independently or with her family. Public authorities had not been involved in the care of *Re B (1981)*, which concerned baby Alexandra born with

---

4 *Re C* [1990] Fam 26, 31, considered in more detail in chapter six.
5 *Re J* [1991] Fam 33, considered in more detail in chapter six.
6 [1984] FLR 811.
7 [1986] 1 FLR 272.
8 [1976] Fam 185.
9 [1988] AC 199.

Down's Syndrome who required surgery to remove an intestinal blockage, until the local authority, informed of her parents' refusal of consent, applied for her to be made a ward of court so that the court could determine the issue.[10]

Baby Alexandra was taken into care following the court authorised surgery. The part of the order giving the authority leave to commence adoption proceedings was not put into effect as she was, a few months later, returned to her parents' care.[11] The application of the local authority for the transfer of care and control of D was dropped. Other than the specific issue of sterilisation there were no concerns about the mother's care of her daughter, which was supported by the 'various professions, persons, and agencies concerned with the welfare of children'.[12] Both cases prompted debate about whether decisions with life-changing effects upon children's lives should be left to doctors and parents. For example, it was suggested that the decision to sterilise a child required 'strict guidelines', 'stringent safeguards', and 'independent review'.[13] A discussion paper proposed the development of a Code of Practice to provide guidance but did not materialise.[14]

The process in these early cases was for the local authority to ask for the child to be made a ward of court, with the consequence that all major decisions about the child's upbringing had to be made by the court. In wardship, the court is under a duty to reach a decision as to the course of action, which is in the best interests of the child. Although there may have been differences of opinions amongst those caring for the child, these were not traditional 'dispute' cases. These cases can also, perhaps more accurately, be understood as cases in which the state, through the public authorities involved in the care of the child and then the court, was seeking to ensure that the interests of vulnerable children were protected. How effective the court was in doing so is addressed below.

Given the changes brought about by the Children Act, it was inevitable that the cases which followed immediately afterwards sought to clarify the responsibilities of the local authority, health authorities, parents, and the court. Questions about the orders to be sought in such cases, public law orders such as an Emergency Protection Order (EPO) or Interim Care Order (ICO), the private law Specific Issue Order (SIO), or declarations in the exercise of the inherent jurisdiction of

---

10 [1981] 1 WLR 1421.
11 Michael Freeman, 'Freedom and the Welfare State: Child-rearing, parental autonomy and state intervention' (1983) 5 *Journal of Social Welfare and Family law* 70, 88 referencing *The Observer* (5 December 1982).
12 *Re D* (n 8) 188.
13 Editorial, 'A wise and compassionate decision' *The Times* (18 September 1975); Martin Huckerby, 'High court forbids sterilization of handicapped girl aged 11' *The Times* (18 Sept 1975); Editorial, 'Sterilization – the need for safeguards' *The Times* (22 July 1975).
14 Michael Freeman referred to the Department for Health and Social Security Discussion Paper, *Sterilisation of Children Under 16 years of age* in Michael Freeman, 'Sterilising the Mentally Handicapped' in Michael Freeman (ed), *Medicine, Ethics and the Law* (Stevens & Sons, 1988) 55–84, 60.

the court were considered in two cases concerning the administration of blood soon after the Children Act was in force, *Re O*[15] and *Re R*.[16] In both, the hospital had sought the advice of the local authority when parental decisions about the child's medical treatment presented cause for concern that the child was being put at risk of permanent harm. Whilst, in both cases, it was the local authority which made the application to court, and the appropriate order was an issue before the court, in both cases the child's parents were 'caring, committed, and capable'. There were no general safeguarding concerns so that public law orders were not appropriate; the court could resolve the single issue for determination by the use of the private law orders or the exercise of its inherent jurisdiction to protect the vulnerable.

This chapter next considers specific issues in the body of case law in which the local authority initiated proceedings in order to ensure that the welfare of the child was determined by an independent judge in the public forum of the court, starting with treatment decisions concerning vulnerable teenagers.

Vulnerable Young Women in Local Authority Care

In a case decided just before the Children Act came into force, social services had been involved in the care of 15-year-old R for over 12 years. For a time, R, who had poor and sometimes violent parental relationships and difficulties establishing boundaries, had been on the 'at risk' register as a possible victim of emotional abuse.[17] In the four months prior to the application to court, R had been in voluntary care, in a children's home under a Place of Safety Order, cared for under an ICO, had been detained under s.2 of the Mental Health Act, and, at the time of the application, was in an adolescent psychiatric unit specialising in disturbance problems in young people. The consultant responsible for her care wanted permission from the local authority, which had legal responsibility for her under the ICO, to administer anti-psychotic medication. Permission was given. However, following a conversation with R, a duty social worker formed the view that she did not fulfil the requirements of ss.2 or 3 of the Mental Health Act 1983. Consequently, the social services department decided that the local authority could not give permission to administer drugs to R against her will. Her consultant was concerned that without medication R would lapse into a psychotic state, deteriorating to a condition where she may have to be sectioned and be at serious risk of suicide. He was of the view that they could only continue to care for her at the unit if they could administer medication with or without her consent. In wardship proceedings commenced by the local authority, Waite J held that R lacked capacity and consented to the administration of medication. The Official Solicitor appealed, asking for guidance as to whether R was *Gillick*

---

15 [1993] 2 FLR 149.
16 [1993] 2 FLR 757.
17 *Re R* [1992] 1 FLR 190, 192.

competent and upon the extent of the powers of the court in such cases. The Court of Appeal agreed that Waite J had been correct to conclude that R was not *Gillick* competent and that administration of the medication was in her best interests. Further, obiter, that the powers of the court to act in the best interests of the child included the power to override decisions of *Gillick*-competent children in wardship or applications made under s.8 of the Children Act.

Re R was followed soon after by *Re W*. At the time of the proceedings, W, her older sister, and younger brother had been in care for seven and a half years. W had had a particularly difficult time. Following the deaths of their mother and then their father, the children spent three months in temporary foster care before being placed with permanent foster parents. There W was bullied. W developed depression and a nervous tic for which she was referred to a family consultation clinic. The children were moved to new foster parents. A year later, her foster mother had surgery for breast cancer and, a few months later, W's grandfather, to whom she was very close, died. This was described by Lord Donaldson as the 'last straw' for W. Anorexia nervosa manifested itself a few months later for which W received first out-patient, then in-patient, treatment over some two years prior to the court proceedings. The Court of Appeal was concerned with W's appeal against the order of Thorpe J, made upon application by the local authority, authorising W's transfer from the specialist residential unit for children and adolescents to a unit specialising in the treatment of eating disorders.[18] Her testamentary guardian, her aunt, was, Lord Donaldson MR explained, 'faced with an appalling dilemma'. She wanted to respect W's wishes but was concerned that others in the unit were hindering W's recovery and she did not want W to die.[19]

When a child is in the care of the local authority, the local authority gains parental responsibility which it then shares with the child's parents.[20] Section 33(3)(b) and 33(4) give the local authority the power, where it is necessary to do so in order to safeguard or promote the child's welfare, to determine the extent to which the child's parent may meet their parental responsibility for the child.[21] The local authority's application for leave under s.100 for the court to exercise its inherent jurisdiction arose given the need to understand the balance of powers when parental responsibility, a concept introduced by the Children Act,[22]

---

18 *Re W* [1993] Fam 64, 74. Although, as W's health had deteriorated significantly since the ruling of Thorpe J the Court of Appeal had made an emergency order authorising her treatment at the specialist unit, 74.
19 *Re W* (n 18) 74.
20 CA 1989 s 33(3)(a).
21 Or guardian, special guardian or a person who has parental responsibility by virtue of CA 1989 s 4A.
22 The uncertainty of the law at the time led to the applications of the independent trust concerning three children aged 14 and 15 years in respect of whom the local authority had a Secure Accommodation Order and were housed in a specialist unit for 'unmanageable' adolescents. Thorpe J viewed the applications as 'misconceived and unnecessary' given the consent of the parents of the children to the administration of medication, in light of *Re R, Re K, W and H* [1993] 1 FLR 854, 855.

was shared by the local authority with the parent or guardian, in the context of a refusal of consent by a 16-year-old who was viewed, by the consultant psychiatrist who examined her on the instructions of the Official Solicitor and by Thorpe J, as competent to make a decision about her treatment.[23] The Court of Appeal confirmed that decisions about a child's medical treatment are made in the exercise of parental responsibility, although the court distinguished *Gillick* which would have suggested that once a child has sufficient intelligence and understanding to make a decision the parental right to decide gives way to the decision of the child. *Gillick* had been concerned with the balance of responsibilities between parents and doctors. This case was concerned with the powers of the court, but the judgment, obiter, extended to the powers of holders of parental responsibility. Most clearly stated in the judgment of Lord Donaldson, the Court of Appeal held that in the case of refusal of consent to medical treatment, not only the court, in the exercise of its inherent jurisdiction, but also those with parental responsibility including the local authority, can give consent enabling doctors to treat. Further, and again obiter, given that the powers of the court in the exercise of its inherent jurisdiction were unlimited, the court could also override a competent consent.[24]

Re R and *Re W* have been much criticised in the academic literature from a variety of perspectives, including their effect upon respect for the autonomous decision of the mature minor[25] and recognition of children's rights,[26] and in comparison of giving and refusing consent to recommended treatment.[27] However, commentators have not addressed the balance of responsibility between parents, the local authority, and the courts in relation to vulnerable children in care established in these cases. For different reasons and in different circumstances, neither R's parents nor W's guardian was able to care for them, with the consequence that both were in the care of the local authority who gained rights before, and responsibilities after, the Children Act. In both cases, the local authority brought the issues of the welfare and care of vulnerable children before the court. Not only did the court give guidance on the powers of those with parental responsibility and the courts, but those decisions were made publicly and subject to debate and, it should be acknowledged, much critical commentary. Whilst the Court of Appeal can be criticised for going further than was necessary to decide each case and for appearing to depart from *Gillick*, it should be acknowledged that the Court of Appeal was specifically asked for guidance in light of the Children Act and emphasised that *Gillick* had been concerned with the balance

---

23 *Re W* (n 18) 84.
24 Applied recently in *University Hospitals Plymouth NHS Trust v B* [2019] EWHC 1670; *An NHS Trust v CX* [2019] EWHC 3033.
25 For example, Margaret Brazier and Caroline Bridge, 'Coercion or caring: analysing adolescent autonomy' (1996) 16 *Legal Studies* 84.
26 For example, Gillian Douglas, 'The Retreat from *Gillick*' (1992) 55 *Modern Law Review* 569.
27 Explored in Stephen Gilmore and Jonathan Herring, '"No" is the hardest word: consent and children's autonomy' (2011) 23 *Child and Family Law Quarterly* 3.

of responsibilities between parents and doctors, whereas the issue in these cases was the powers of the court and how these fit with the responsibilities of holders of parental responsibility. As Margaret Brazier and Caroline Bridge observed, whilst it is possible to critique the reasoning in these two cases, it is much harder to disagree with the result, which they further suggest would be agreed by the majority of people, reflecting the ordinary standards of the day.[28] On the specific facts of these cases, the reasonable parent may understand the protective approach adopted by the judges in the attempt to save the lives of these young women in the care of the state who had had extremely difficult childhoods and were then in desperate circumstances.[29]

Sterilisation

There are five reported cases concerning proposals to sterilise a child with learning difficulties before her 18th birthday, the first in 1976 and the others between 1988 and 1993.[30] The limited number of reported cases does not mean that there have been few instances of sterilisation of children with learning difficulties. Writing at the time, Robert Lee and Derek Morgan cited figures of 36 sterilisations performed on young women under the age of 18 in 1973–4, and 90 of women under the age of 19 in the mid-1980s.[31] In their study, Stansfield et al. found a total of 73 referrals to the Official Solicitor between 1988 and 1999. In 50 of these cases there was an application to court, and 39 resulted in a court hearing of which the court ruled in 31 cases that sterilisation was in the best interests of the person with learning disabilities. These cases concerned people aged 12–41, with 27 cases involving children, in respect of whom the court approved sterilisation in nine cases with sterilisation considered to be therapeutic in relation to two further children.[32] Their review of the case files led them to conclude that a substantial proportion concerned people with significant learning difficulties who lacked the capacity to consent to sterilisation raising the question as to whether they had the capacity to consent to sexual intercourse. Furthermore, there was little evidence that the majority of those who were sterilised were involved in a sexual relationship or were likely to be in the future. The evidence in the files also suggested some cases of abuse.

---

28 Brazier and Bridge (n 25) 84.
29 The cases that followed in the 1990s and the emphasis in more recent cases upon the provision of information and discussion with young people are considered in chapter four.
30 *Re D* (n 8); *Re B* (n 9); *Re M* [1988] 2 FLR 497; *Re E* [1991] 2 FLR 585; *Re HG* [1993] 1 FLR 587.
31 Robert Lee and Derek Morgan, 'Sterilisation and Mental Handicap: Sapping the Strength of the State?' (1988) 15 *Journal of Law and Society* 229, 234 citing Clare Dyer, 'Sterilisation of Mentally Handicapped Women' (1987) 294 *British Medical Journal* 825.
32 AJ Stansfield, AJ Holland, ICH Clare, 'The sterilisation of people with intellectual disabilities in England and Wales during the period 1988 to 1999' (2007) 51 *Journal of Intellectual Disability Research* 569.

The context in which these applications were brought to court was a history of segregation of people with disabilities, negative views about disability amongst professionals, ignorance of disability amongst the public generally,[33] and limited services for disabled children and their families. In the 1980s, and therefore at the point that most of the cases were decided, government policy was to draw back the state including the closure of large institutions in which disabled children and adults had been living.[34] Children with learning difficulties were no longer to be admitted long term into a hospital. The move to local authority residences was insufficiently resourced, and the support provided to mothers caring for their disabled children at home was inadequately supported.[35] Janet Read and Luke Clements further observed that, whilst there was greater recognition in the 1980s of the expertise and knowledge of parents, '[u]nfortunately, a more appreciative approach to parents sometimes went hand-in-hand with a failure to recognize that theirs and their children's rights and wishes were not always coterminous'.[36] In all cases but the first, *Re D*,[37] applications were made to court just before the age of majority, and in all cases, except *Re D*, the proposed sterilisation was authorised as being in the best interests of the young woman. In *Re D*, Heilbron J fulfilled her responsibility, distinct from that of the local authority or parents, to protect the vulnerable through an independent and objective review of best interests. The other cases demonstrate a failure to examine critically the medical evidence and a concern for the burden upon those caring, reflective of then-prevailing attitudes of the personal tragedy of disability.

D's local education authority educational psychologist, the former and present headmaster of her school, and her social worker had a different view from her mother and consultant paediatrician of D's current and future abilities. Following a meeting at which they were unable to change her mother's mind, a request was made for an independent review of the decision, which was referred to the local authority's specialist in community medicine. Consistent with the respect given at that time to parental authority, this concluded that they could not interfere with the decision of D's mother made together with the paediatrician. Having sought legal advice, the educational psychologist applied to make D a ward of court so that the court could determine whether the proposed sterilisation was

---

33 Janet Read and Luke Clements, 'Demonstrably Awful: The Right to Life and the Selective Non-Treatment of Disabled Babies and Young Children' (2004) 31 *Journal of Law and Society* 482, 495.
34 Although concerned with the care of adults not children, for example through the development of the policy of community care effected by the National Health Service and Community Care Act 1990.
35 J Ryan and F Thomas, *The Politics of Mental Handicap* (Free Association Books, 1987) 118, 154; Jane Lewis, '"It All Really Starts in the Family...." Community Care in the 1980s' (1989) 16 *Journal of Law and Society* 83.
36 Read and Clements (n 33), 498. A point they make in relation to non-treatment but equally valid in this context.
37 *Re D* (n 8).

in her best interests. In her judgment, Heilbron J countered the argument of the consultant paediatrician that the decision was a matter for clinical judgement as long there was consent, with the observation that the reasons given for sterilising D were both clinical and social and thus the decision was not solely a matter of medical expertise. Heilbron J noted that D's 'caring and devoted', if 'overzealous', mother was genuinely seeking to do her best for her daughter,[38] and praised the exemplary care provided to D through the co-operation of a range of professionals and services. On the facts, the judge concluded that the sterilisation operation was not necessary, medically indicated, nor in D's best interests[39] and consequently declined to authorise the operation.[40] Although the reason the majority of applications were brought just before the child's 18th birthday was uncertainty at the time as to the powers of the court in relation to adults who lacked competence,[41] D's mother, not convinced by the decision of the court as to her daughter's best interests, expressed the intention to subject her daughter to the procedure upon the discharge of wardship when she reached majority.[42]

Lord Templeman was a lone voice amongst their Lordships considering an appeal against the authorisation of a sterilisation operation upon a ward, 17-year-old Jeanette, in *Re B*, when he expressed the opinion that, in all cases, the sterilisation of a child with learning difficulties should only be performed with the authorisation of a Family Division judge. It was, his Lordship said, a 'drastic step' for an individual, which raised issues of law, ethics, and medical practice such that the procedure should only be authorised by a judge following a full investigation in which[43]

> The girl will be represented by the Official Solicitor or some other appropriate guardian; the parents will be made parties if they wish to appear and where appropriate the local authority will also appear. Expert evidence will be adduced setting out the reasons for the application, the history, conditions, circumstances, and foreseeable future of the girl, the risks and consequences of pregnancy, the risks and consequences of sterilisation, the practicability of alternative precautions against pregnancy, and any other relevant information.[44]

---

38 *Re D* (n 8) 192.
39 *Re D* (n 8) 196.
40 *Re D* (n 8) 194.
41 This was clarified by the House of Lords in *Re F* [1990] 2 AC 1 which held that a doctor could lawfully administer treatment to an adult patient who lacked the capacity to make a decision as long as it was in the best interests of the patient according to a competent body of professional opinion. Since 2007, any proposals come within the Mental Capacity Act 2005.
42 M Huckerby, 'High Court forbids sterilization of handicapped girl aged 11' *The Times* (18 September 1975). Notably, by continuing wardship, D's interests could continue to be protected until she reached the age of majority.
43 *Re B* (n 9) 206.
44 *Re B* (n 9) 206.

Both the requirement for judicial authorisation and this account of the factors relevant to judicial determination suggest a process which protects the interests of the child, placing limits upon the powers of parents, professionals, and public authorities with respect to an invasive procedure undertaken to remove the ability to reproduce. The judgments, however, show that the courts were not effective in their protection of the interests of young women with learning difficulties.

The House of Lords in *Re B* dismissed the appeal of the Official Solicitor against leave given in wardship proceedings for the operation to be performed. Their Lordships emphasised that the wellbeing, welfare, or interests of the child were the paramount consideration.[45] There has been extensive academic criticism of the approach adopted by the House of Lords to B's best interests. Their Lordships emphasis upon her mental age failed to recognise her experience of life or behavioural skills.[46] In emphasising her lack of comprehension of the link between sex, pregnancy, and childbirth, their Lordships did not question whether she had received appropriate sex education.[47] They noted her sexual drive but did not consider whether she had the ability to give consent to sexual intercourse and consequently her vulnerability or the need to protect her from sexual assault. Dismissing the practical feasibility of contraception, sterilisation was perceived as the only viable option to avoid any reduction in her liberty which would have a detrimental effect upon her quality of life.[48] Their Lordships arrived easily at the conclusion that the 'last resort' of sterilisation was the 'least detrimental alternative'. Lord Oliver contrasted the use of the contraceptive pill as 'speculative, possibly damaging, and requiring discipline over a period of many years from one of the most limited intellectual capacity' with sterilisation as a 'safe, certain, but irreversible' response to the 'vulnerability of this young woman' and 'her need for protection' from the 'potentially frightening consequences of her becoming pregnant'.[49] Similarly, the speeches of their Lordships were dismissive of the basic human right of a woman to reproduce, which had been recognised by Heilbron J in *Re D*, considering this to be no relevance to a person they considered unable to make the choice to reproduce.

Writing at the time, Norma Martin noted that the Court of Appeal decision had prompted much debate and adverse comment from those representing people with learning disabilities. As a consequence, she considered that the House of Lords 'strove to distance themselves from the emotive rhetoric of the public debate' and quieten the controversy surrounding the case by stressing that the case was about an individual's welfare, not eugenics. Furthermore, she argued that their Lordships sought to present their decision as consistent with the policy

---

45 *Re B* (n 9) 202.
46 Kirsty Keywood, 'Sterilising the Woman with Learning Difficulties – In Her Best Interests?' in Jo Bridgeman and Susan Millns (eds), *Law and Body Politics: Regulating the Female Body*, (Dartmouth, 1995) 125-150, 130.
47 Keywood (n 46) 130.
48 *Re B* (n 9) 202–3.
49 *Re B* (n 9) 210.

of de-institutionalisation, increasing freedom and enhancing the quality of life.[50] It is difficult to argue with Ian Kennedy, who expressed the opinion that the application of best interests in *Re B* was a 'somewhat crude conclusion of social policy' which failed to hold to account those who proposed to sterilise her.[51] Kirsty Keywood argued that the House of Lords in *Re B* drew upon the medical model of learning disability, with disability understood as inherent in the individual rather than in social, economic, and political structures. Kirsty Keywood observed that B's life story was told as one of 'deficiency and abnormality', her needs presented in medical terms, and the applicability of rights claims was rejected.[52] She noted that only two years earlier, the House of Lords had decided *Gillick* in which they had curtailed parental authority, emphasised the autonomy of minors, and appeared to empower them to make decisions about their health in partnership with medical professionals. In contrast, Kirsty Keywood observed, 'young women like Jeanette seemed conspicuously absent from such analysis'.[53] There was no acknowledgement that, like non-disabled young women, Jeanette would too develop her capacities to make decisions and take care of herself and no consideration of the support that might enable her to do so. Whilst *Gillick* was concerned with the question whether doctors could be entrusted with the responsibility for the welfare of a child who had the capacity to make her own decisions such that she could do so without having to inform her parents, in *Re B*, the judgment of the court aligned with the conclusions of her carers and the medical view of disability steeped within the prevailing attitudes about the quality of lives of people with disabilities.

Despite the view of Lord Hailsham in *Re B* that the distinction between therapeutic and non- therapeutic was 'totally meaningless',[54] soon after, Sir Stephen Brown P in *Re E*,[55] made this distinction and limited the role of the court to cases of non-therapeutic sterilisation. Noting the exception as stated in *Re E* for therapeutic sterilisation, within the context of an application to court for a SIO rather than in wardship, Peter Singer QC said in *Re HG* that one of the responsibilities of holders of parental responsibility was to seek a decision of the court on the question of the non-therapeutic sterilisation of a child.[56] Formally the application was made by 17-year-old T with her father as her next friend.[57] The local authority which funded T's accommodation was joined as a party but indicated early in

---

50 Norma Martin, '*Re B (a child)*' [1987] 9 *Journal of Social Welfare Law* 369.
51 Ian Kennedy, 'Patients, Doctors and Human Rights' in Ian Kennedy, *Treat Me Right: Essays in Medical Law and Ethics* (Clarendon Press, 1988, reprinted 2001), 385–413, 395–6.
52 Kirsty Keywood, '*Re B (A Minor) (Wardship: Sterilisation)*]1988]: "People Like Us Don't Have Babies"' in Jonathan Herring and Jesse Wall (eds), *Landmark Cases in Medical Law* (Hart, 2015) 39–62, 45.
53 Keywood (n 52) 53.
54 *Re B* (n 9) 204.
55 [1991] 2 FLR 585.
56 [1993] 1 FLR 587, 595.
57 For the practical reason of eligibility for legal aid.

the proceedings that it did not want to participate, content to leave the decision to the court without making further submissions. In reaching the conclusion that sterilisation was in her best interests, the judge gave weight to the 'legitimate aspirations and anxieties of the parents' recognising the difficulties her family, who had initiated the application, had had over the years in getting appropriate medical attention for T and in 'seeking to cope with her within the family'. Supporting the view that the conclusion in these cases was led by concern for the convenience of those caring, if well intentioned, in the prevailing climate of lack of support for care, the judge also noted but gave less weight to the evidence that T was receiving the best possible care in a residential school, that the local authority were not persuaded, and dismissed as 'textbook points' the evidence of the doctor instructed by the Official Solicitor.[58] The judicial view was thus that sterilisation was too serious an invasion to allow parents to authorise, and unlike those involving adults, decisions about best interests were not left to be determined by a competent body of professional opinion according to the *Bolam* test.[59] However, like those concerning adults, these cases reveal a lack of critical appraisal of medical opinion[60] and demonstrate an understanding of sterilisation as protection in the effort to care, reflecting the then view of disability and the privatisation of responsibilities to care, protect, and nurture within the family. As Kirsty Keywood has argued, these cases demonstrate a 'reification of medical knowledge(s) and an obfuscation of broader social and ethical questions concerning the status of disabled people in society'.[61] The decisions amount to a further example of the position observed by Janet Read and Luke Clements of failure to recognise that the rights of caring parents and the children they care for may not always be coterminous.

Without seeking to defend the judicial decisions, which should have taken a more critical approach to the evidence before them, it is important to position the cases within the social context in which the decisions were made. In their analysis, Lee and Morgan placed the perceived need to sterilise young women with learning difficulties within the context of the policy of the then Government for community care aimed at placing limits upon the cost of healthcare,[62] reflecting the policy of 'redrawing the boundaries of State intervention'.[63] Under-resourced, community care which they describe as the 'residualisation of support' for people

---

58 *Re HG* (n 56) 592.
59 *Re F* (n 41).
60 Keywood (n 46) 129.
61 Kirsty Keywood, '"I'd rather keep him chaste": Retelling the Story of Sterilisation, Learning Difficulty and (Non)sexed Embodiment' (2001) 9 *Feminist Legal Studies* 185, 194.
62 Local authority social service departments were the lead agencies in the planning and assessment of the need for community care but had flexibility to arrange packages of care using private, voluntary, and statutory sectors, Christine Hallett, 'The Children Act 1989 and Community Care: comparisons and contrasts' (1991) 19 *Policy and Politics* 283, 284.
63 Carole Smith, 'Disabling Autonomy: The Role of Government, the Law and the Family' (1997) 24 *Journal of Law and Society* 421, 434.

with disabilities, had the effect of increasing devolution of responsibility to the family – the familiarisation of caring responsibilities –[64] explaining the perception of vulnerability to which sterilisation was felt, by families, to be a solution. As Felicity Scroggie suggested, the stress and worry which prompted parents to seek sterilisation in the welfare of their child arose in the context of lack of support in meeting the needs of the child within the family.[65] It is not, of course, for judges to comment on the social and political context, but it is important to recognise that their decisions are informed by an understanding of that context. It is, however, for judges to assess the evidence before them critically.

The context in which these decisions were taken started to change. It started to be recognised that the social environment contributed to the social exclusion of people living with disabilities. Furthermore, as Kirsty Keywood has argued, the needs of people with disabilities became understood as a matter of public concern requiring structural responses rather than a private tragedy.[66] Disability discrimination legislation was enacted in 1995. Reflecting changing attitudes, the Court of Appeal subsequently established a more cautious approach in *Re A* and *Re SL*.[67] As a consequence, the question has first to be asked whether contraception is necessary because the individual is engaging in consensual sexual activity, and then the question is whether less invasive methods have been attempted or are suitable. This should usually result in the conclusion that sterilisation of a child with learning difficulties is not in their best interests. The BMA, *Children and Young Persons Toolkit*, provides that sterilisation for contraceptive purposes should not normally be proposed for children, given that there are other options available but that if, in exceptional circumstances there is agreement that this is the best option, legal advice should be sought about getting a court order.[68] The Mental Capacity Act 2005 now applies to young people aged 16 or over who lack the capacity to make the decision. The Mental Capacity Act Code of Practice advises that proposals for non-therapeutic sterilisation should continue to be referred to the court.[69] Practice Guidance issued by Hayden J in January 2020 provides that when the procedure is primarily for the purpose of sterilisation, it is 'highly probable' that the decision will be that it is appropriate to apply to the Court of Protection.[70] I have been unable to find any reported cases since

---

64 Lee and Morgan (n 31).
65 Felicity Scroggie, 'Why Do Parents Want Their Children Sterilised - A Broader Approach to Sterilisation Requests' (1990) 2 *Journal of Child Law*, 35, 35.
66 Kirsty Keywood (n 52) 55.
67 *Re A* [2000] 1 FLR 549; *Re SL* [2000] 2 FLR 452.
68 BMA, *Children and Young People Ethics Toolkit*, 40, last updated March 2019, https://www.bma.org.uk/advice/employment/ethics/children-and-young-people/children-and-young-peoples-ethics-tool-kit, accessed 16 April 2020.
69 Department of Constitutional Affairs, *Mental Capacity Act Code of Practice*, 2007 last updated 2016, 8.22, https://www.gov.uk/government/publications/mental-capacity-act-code-of-practice accessed 27 March 2020 (under review).
70 Court of Protection, *Practice Guidance 9E: Applications Relating to Medical Treatment* [2020] EWCOP 2, [10], [11].

the early 1990s although, as the number of applications noted above at that time compared with the reported cases suggests, that does not mean they have not occurred, or, alternatively, that sterilisations have been performed and justified as therapeutic.

Marie Fox and Michael Thomson have argued that the judgement in *Re D*,

> respects the emerging right of the child to make embodied choices for herself and recognizes her emerging legal subjectivity. ... [T]his reasoning positions the integrity or autonomy of the child as ethically prior to the integrity or autonomy of the family and aligns with the core proposition of the open future principle that '"parental practices which close exits virtually forever are insufficiently attentive to the child as an end in herself".[71]

As an analysis of the first decided case, this indicates that this approach could have been adopted to the question whether sterilisation was in the best interests of a child in the cases that followed. Hopefully this view, which recognises the independent interests and rights of the disabled child, is reflected in current discussions about sterilisation and applications to court.

Withholding or Withdrawing of Life-sustaining Treatment from Children in Care

The respective responsibilities of the local authority, parents, doctors, and the court have also been addressed in relation to decisions to limit life-sustaining treatment of children in care. In *K (A Minor)*, the local authority had an ICO in respect of five-month-old K, who remained in hospital.[72] Sir Mark Potter described the proceedings as 'comparatively unusual', in that they were non-contentious as all parties agreed that artificial nutrition should be withdrawn to end K's suffering and enable her to die in peace.[73] This compared with the case law in the preceding years which had been dominated by different views between parents and doctors on life-sustaining treatment.[74] However, the Trust had sought a declaration from the court, as the local authority also had parental responsibility, by virtue of s.33, so that 'the parents could thus not themselves act alone in consenting to withdrawal of treatment'.[75] The implication was that when a child is in care so that parental responsibility is shared by parents and the local authority, they cannot together agree that life-sustaining treatment should

---

71 Marie Fox and Michael Thomson, 'Bodily Integrity, Embodiment, and the Regulation of Parental Choice' (2017) 44 *Journal of Law and Society* 501, 528, ending with a quote from D. Davies, 'Genetic Dilemmas and the Child's Right to an Open Future' (1997) 28 *Rutgers Law Journal* 547, 570.
72 [2006] EWHC 1007.
73 *K* (n 72) [42].
74 Examined in chapter six.
75 *K* (n 72) [9].

be withdrawn or withheld, but the issue must be referred to court, necessary to ensure the protection of the interests of a vulnerable child in the care of the state. This has been clarified in subsequent cases such that decisions about withholding or withdrawal of life-sustaining treatment from a child in care are an example of decisions to which all with parental responsibility must agree or a court order is required. Decisions about the life-sustaining treatment of a child need to be made in a public forum where the decision-maker can be held to account to ensure that decisions which result in the ending of a child's life are made according to socially acceptable standards. In order for the legal process to properly protect the interests of the vulnerable in such cases, it is necessary for there to be a critical examination of the medical evidence and also for the court to ensure that appropriate steps have been taken to secure the views of the parents as evidence which must be before the court.

In *Kirklees Council v RE and Others*,[76] the local authority made an application for a declaration that it was not in SE's best interests to receive further life-sustaining treatment and in his best interests to receive palliative care. SE had lung, heart, and kidney conditions. An ICO had been made soon after his birth. Although he had not been able to live with his foster carers as he had remained in hospital since his premature birth, they spent time with him daily at the hospital. The application was supported by the Trust and by SE's Guardian, and his mother accepted the medical opinion as she did not want him to suffer. Moor J expressed his disagreement with paragraph 2.5 of the 2004 edition of the guidance from the RCPCH, *Withholding or withdrawing life-sustaining treatment in children*[77] which said:

> If the local authority achieves a care order, it gains parental responsibility and the power to restrict the natural parents' authority or that of any other person who would normally carry such authority. Parents can appeal to the High Court and to the Court of Appeal.

Moor J agreed with Counsel for the local authority that this guidance was wrong and that an application had to be made to court '[i]f there is parental opposition, parental equivocation, or doubt as to parental capacity to decide'.[78] Whilst the local authority had parental responsibility for the child by virtue of the ICO, parental views were important no less in cases such as SE where the parent lacked the capacity to litigate. For the protection of the interests of the child as well as ensuring that the views of the parent were properly taken into consideration, it was necessary to bring the matter before the court.

---

76 [2014] EWHC 3182.
77 RCPCH, *Withholding or Withdrawing Life-Sustaining Treatment in Children: A Framework for Practice* (2004).
78 *Kirklees Council v RE and Others* (n 76) [20].

Whilst the 2004 RCPCH guidance reflected the terms of s.33(3)(b) of the Children Act, the current RCPCH guidance notes that non-parents may obtain parental responsibility by a court order, including, for example, 'a local authority, grandparents, foster carers etc'.[79] It advises, reflecting the position stated by Moor J above:

> where PR is shared, if there is parental or other opposition, parental equivocation, or doubt as to parental capacity or a disagreement as to what is in the child's or young person's best interests, an application should be made to court for determination as to best interests.[80]

Moor J went on to say that when there is a Care Order, the Guardian should be involved in the decision, and the court application should be made by the local authority or Trust.

In some of the 'non-contentious' cases, the parents have lacked the capacity to decide about life-limiting treatment, which requires a decision of the court given that consent cannot be provided by all with parental responsibility. In the 2008 case of *Re B*,[81] 22-month-old L had profound mental and physical disabilities from an inherited metabolic condition. Her mother, who was 15 1/2-years-old, had learning difficulties. From just a few days old, L had been in the care of foster carers, Mr and Mrs B. The case concerned plans for her longer-term medical care, the view of the Trust being that in a 'few years' her condition would have deteriorated so that she may require ventilation or cardio-pulmonary resuscitation and that it would be in her best interests for this to be withheld if she was severely unwell or her condition was deteriorating rapidly. Coleridge J thought the local authority, which had asked the Trust to make the application, was 'probably right' in the view that the parental responsibility which the local authority had by virtue of the care order did not confer the authority to consent to the withholding of life-sustaining treatment. If there were any uncertainty, given the gravity of the decision, local authorities should make an application to court.[82]

Describing it as a 'consensual approach to the court'[83] and making the declaration sought, Coleridge J noted the legal duty of the Trust to consult with L's

---

79 RCPCH, *Making Decisions to Limit Treatment in Life-Limiting and Life-Threatening Conditions in Children: A Framework for Practice* (2015), para 2.3.3.A https://adc.bmj.com/content/100/Suppl_2/s1.full.pdf+html accessed 16 April 2020.
80 RCPCH, 2015 (n 79) para 2.3.3.A.
81 [2008] EWHC 1996.
82 *Re B* (n 81), [7]. Serious medical treatment issues such as the withholding or withdrawal of life-sustaining treatment from a child are different, King LJ determined in *Re H (A Child) (Parental Responsibility: Vaccination)* [2020] EWCA Civ 664, from vaccination which in the light of the medical evidence should no longer be considered a grave issue. Local authorities can arrange for the vaccination of children in their care in the exercise of their parental responsibility under s.33.
83 *Re B* (n 81) [16].

mother and the local authority and included in the terms of the draft order that they must consult her foster parents who at the time of the hearing stressed that L had a quality of life that was 'certainly worth living'.[84] The effect of the judgment was that the decision could not be made by the local authority alone in the exercise of parental responsibility. The court order authorised the withholding of treatment in the future if, in the clinical judgement of those caring for L and following consultation with those with parental responsibility and caring for L, continued treatment was not in her best interests. To require the doctors to consult with L's foster carers ensured that the decision was informed by those who knew her best and were best placed to advocate for L, a vulnerable child in the care of the state. Although, given the application related to the withholding of ventilation in the event of a deterioration in the future, protection of L's welfare through an examination of the evidence and consideration of the views of those caring for her would have been more effectively achieved by requiring the question to be brought back before the court at the point when it was considered that this deterioration had started to occur.

In *Re Jake*,[85] Sir James Munby P stressed the importance of facilitating the involvement of parents who lack the capacity to make decisions about the child's future medical care. The local authority shared parental responsibility with the parents of ten-month-old Jake under an ICO. Both parents had a diagnosed learning disability. His father had the capacity to litigate whilst his mother did not.[86] Jake's parents and the local authority agreed with his doctors that, in the event of a deterioration in his condition, Jake should be given palliative care. The judge observed that the position of the father, that he could not make the decision, was nothing to do with his capacity but was a 'human and very understandable' position shared by many parents who were confronted with making decisions in such tragic circumstances. Still, the President stressed it was important that the parents were involved, told what was happening and what was being proposed.[87] The judge stressed the importance of ensuring that the views, wishes, and feelings of the parents, who were 'faced with this dreadful situation, [and who] very much understand the fundamental dilemmas and the fundamental problems', were taken into account by both doctors and lawyers.[88] In practice, this observation appears to have related more to good medical practice than it did to the legal process. The hearing was an urgent application, although given that it concerned the withholding of treatment in the event of continuing deterioration, the reasons for the extreme urgency are not clear from the judgement. Although the parents were represented, the hearing, which took place outside the court term, was heard by telephone and lasted about 90 minutes. The local authority

---

84 *Re B* (n 81) [6].
85 [2015] EWHC 2442.
86 *Re Jake* (n 85) [3].
87 *Re Jake* (n 85) [46].
88 *Re Jake* (n 85) [44].

accepted the recommendation of the medical team so did not put independent evidence before the court. The judge viewed this as acceptable given that the proceedings were 'non-contentious'. Although the judgment recorded the views of both Jake's mother and father, as presented by their Counsel, the judgment is dominated by the reports and witness statement of Dr W, Jake's consultant paediatric neurologist, including her account of the second opinion doctor. The aspiration to ensure that the interests of the vulnerable child and parents were protected through the judicial process appears not to have been fulfilled very effectively.

Although these were all cases in which the court was asked to authorise, as in the best interests of the child and consequently as lawful, the withholding or withdrawal of life-sustaining medical technology, the central issue was the protection of vulnerable children and in many cases vulnerable parents. Whilst neither parents, local authority, nor the court can require a doctor to treat contrary to their professional judgement, there must be an agreement of all with parental responsibility or the court to the withdrawal or withholding of life-sustaining treatment from a child in the care of the state. The local authority obtains parental responsibility to enable it to care for the child but not to authorise doctors to end life-sustaining treatment which will lead to the death of the child. This applies beyond cases where parents disagree or are uncertain as to their child's best interests to include cases in which parents lack the capacity to exercise their responsibility. However, for court review to be effective protection of the interests of these vulnerable children and their vulnerable parents, closer critical scrutiny needs to be given to the medical evidence and support given to the parents to ensure that their views are heard and given appropriate weight.

Parental Care Putting the Child at Risk of Significant Harm

The vast majority of cases in which doctors seek the advice of the designated doctor, safeguarding team, or local authority arise from concerns that the child's injuries or health are indicative of abuse or neglect.[89] However, it may also be the case that it is necessary for doctors to work together with local authority social services because the parental care of a child with a serious medical condition or complex needs is not what is it reasonable to expect and presents the risk of causing significant harm.

The issue of the relationship between an application to the court for it to exercise its inherent jurisdiction and care orders has only recently been considered by the court in a case concerning a child AB, who had a complex neuro-metabolic, neuro-developmental, neuro-degenerative disorder. The local authority and the

---

89 In *Westminster City Council v M and F and H* [2017] EWHC 518 Hayden J found that H's parents had caused him significant harm by misreporting and exaggerating his medical symptoms and tampering with medical equipment.

courts had been involved in AB's care for a number of years. Munby P observed that it was 'likely to be problematic and may well turn out to be ineffective' for the local authority to seek care orders in order to obtain parental responsibility so that it could make decisions about AB's medical treatment. The local authority, Munby P said, would be 'ill-advised' to seek to rely upon s.33(3)(a) to authorise medical treatment opposed by the child's parents.[90] Furthermore, the judge suggested that local authorities would need to give careful thought before 'embarking upon care proceedings against otherwise unimpeachable parents who may justifiably resent recourse to what they are likely to see as an unnecessarily adversarial and punitive remedy'.[91]

The relationship between care proceedings and the court's exercise of its inherent jurisdiction was considered by the Court of Appeal in *Re E*.[92] The question for the court was whether the parents of Alfie Evans were, following an application by Alder Hey for a declaration that it was no longer lawful or in Alfie's best interests to continue to provide mechanical ventilation, in an analogous position to parents in care proceedings. The argument presented on their behalf was that if they were, there should only be intervention by public authorities into their decisions with respect to his medical treatment if those decisions placed him at risk of significant harm. King LJ stated that it would be 'inappropriate' for a local authority to use s.33(3)(b) to consent to the withdrawal of treatment overriding the wishes of the parents who have refused to consent to treatment withdrawal'.[93] The judge continued to say that if, during care proceedings, an issue arose as to the child's medical treatment, the Trust would bring proceedings under the inherent jurisdiction and the two applications would be determined together. In her Ladyship's experience the circumstances which ordinarily led to care proceedings were very different from those which resulted in the application from the Trust for declarations about Alfie's future medical treatment:

> In my judgment care proceedings are part of the picture in medical treatment cases only in exceptional circumstances and as an adjunct of, or precursor to, an application under the inherent jurisdiction. The sort of devastating illness with which this court is concerned can and usually does come out of nowhere, regardless of whether the family is rich or poor, educated or uneducated, reasonable or unreasonable. The one thing these disparate families have in common is that it is 'not their fault', and in my experience, even

---

90 *In the Matter of AB* [2018] EWFC 3, [24], citing *Barnet London Borough Council v AL and others* [2017] EWHC 125, [32]. And if the local authority was seeking to remove the child from parental care, the practical issues of finding an appropriate placement and of ensuring contact with the child needed to be addressed.
91 *In the Matter of AB* (n 90) [24].
92 *In the Matter of E* [2018] EWCA Civ 550, [87]. The arguments based upon significant harm raised upon appeal in both the Charlie Gard and Alfie Evans cases are considered in chapter eight.
93 *In the Matter of E* (n 92) [87].

if their emotion is sometimes expressed inappropriately, they each and every one of them share a fierce devotion and protective instinct towards their vulnerable, often dying, child. These unhappy parents, finding themselves the victims of an appalling twist of fate, are not the type of parents who find themselves the subject of care proceedings.[94]

In *Re E*, King LJ referred to the judgment of Hedley J in *Re K (Children with Disabilities: Wardship)*, in which the judge distinguished between the risk of significant harm which arose from the 'inherent condition' of the children who had severe disabilities as opposed to the quality of care provided to them.[95] Care proceedings would only be initiated when parental care of their child presented 'significant additional issues of concern' distinct from the disagreement with doctors about the future treatment of a child with a serious medical condition.[96]

Applications for declarations or orders in respect of a specific medical issue are made by Trusts, whilst it is the responsibility of the local authority to seek care orders when parental care of their child is not what it is reasonable to expect and is putting the child at risk of significant harm. An example is *A Local Authority and An NHS Trust v MC & FC & C*.[97] C had multiple disabilities and had been cared for by his mother for much of his life with the support of specialist medical care and periods of hospitalisation including in intensive care. Upon a previous application by the Trust, Francis J had made a declaration permitting his doctors to insert a feeding tube. Concerned about his mother's inability to co-operate with C's treatment plans and medication, and specifically that his mother had removed his feeding tube as she would not accept the medical opinion that it was not safe for C to be fed orally, the local authority had issued care proceedings as a result of which an ICO was made. C's condition deteriorated, and the Trust applied for a declaration that it was lawful for life-sustaining treatment to be withheld and palliative care provided. The local authority accepted this treatment plan, but his mother wanted all treatment to be given that may prolong C's life. Ms Russell J considered that as the local authority had parental responsibility by virtue of a contested ICO, it was first necessary to review whether the statutory grounds for an ICO had been made out. The judge concluded that the threshold set by s.31(2) had been met on the evidence that C's mother had removed C's feeding tube which 'compromised his physical safety and the ability to provide C with sufficient nourishment' as well as further compromising his health by exposing him to further radiation as x-rays were required to re-position the tube.[98] Interim

---

94 *In the Matter of E* (n 92) [101].
95 *Re K* [2011] EWHC 4031 [24] the evidence was that it was beyond the capacity of the parents to meet the needs of their children alone. Hedley J gave the local authority leave to withdraw care proceedings but, given the history of the conflict over their care, with the consent of all parties, made the children wards of court.
96 *In the Matter of E* (n 92) [107].
97 [2017] EWHC 370, [37].
98 *A Local Authority and An NHS Trust v MC & FC & C* (n 97) [19].

declarations were made, authorising a 'ceiling of care' which redirected treatment from life-sustaining to palliative, pending a neurological assessment, with care proceedings postponed pending completion of proceedings with respect to C's future medical treatment although the ICO remained in place.

In a subsequent judgment a year later when C had been discharged from hospital into foster care, Russell J noted that in contrast to the 'discomfort, malnourishment, and distress' C had suffered in the care of his mother, he then showed enjoyment in his 'life, existence, and surroundings'.[99] The judge made final care orders and limited the contact which C was to have with his mother. Thus, decisions about C's medical treatment were made upon application by the Trust at the instigation of the medical team with responsibility for C's treatment. Decisions about his care were made upon application by the local authority to the court to determine first whether the threshold had been met and then C's welfare. Decisions about the treatment and care of a vulnerable child were made in the public forum of the court so that those decisions could be held to account, whilst anonymity protected the identity of C, his mother, and the professionals involved in his care.

Many of the cases in which care proceedings have been initiated, like *A Local Authority and An NHS Trust v MC & FC & C* have involved children with severe disabilities in relation to whom concerns have arisen about the ability of the child's parents, who have been their primary carer, to continue to meet their needs.[100] Concerns that parental care is putting the child at risk of significant harm may arise from lack of co-operation with, and aggression to, professionals involved in the provision of the child's care.[101] The threshold was crossed in *A Local Authority v J, S and R* in respect of the mother's care of 11-year-old R, who was profoundly disabled as a consequence of a life-limiting, incurable, and progressive condition. Her mother had not attended all medical appointments, did not always follow medical advice, and was considered to be 'chaotic' in her decision-making about R, decisions which were not always considered to be in R's best interests and were affected by her beliefs about R's quality of life.[102]

---

99 *A Local Authority v MC & FC & C* [2018] EWHC 1031 [25].
100 For example, see *County Durham & Darlington NHS Foundation Trust v SS & FS & MS* [2016] EWHC 535.
101 *In the Matter of AB* (n 90), the matter came back to the Family Division for a re-hearing following a successful appeal against a care order. By that time, the local authority sought to withdraw their application, satisfied that the parents were co-operating and working with professionals in his care, so the local authority no longer sought to establish the threshold criteria, considering the Child Protection Plan and ongoing support package to be sufficient to safeguard AB's welfare.
102 [2018] EWFC 28 [55].

Conclusions: Welfare, Support, Protect

Many of the early cases in the body of case law concerned with the medical treatment of children were brought to court by or upon the advice of the local authority. The respective duties and the balance of responsibilities between parents, doctors, Trusts, local authorities, and the courts were thus determined in relation to children in the care of the state or through the involvement of the state to protect the welfare of the child. When decisions are made about the future medical treatment of children in local authority care whose parents lack the capacity or have shown their inability to protect the welfare of the child, it is crucial that decisions can be justified and are made publicly and decision-makers are held to account. Even when it is recognised that parents are genuinely seeking to achieve what is best for their child, in the context of the medical treatment of a seriously ill child, parents are expected to comply with norms of reasonable parenting including co-operation with the professionals with expertise in their child's condition. Failure to do so justifies health professionals seeking the advice of the local authority or the court. This understanding of the issues requires us to think differently about children's healthcare law, recognising the protective duties of professionals, working alongside local authorities and the courts, to support parents and protect the welfare of children. Although all decisions have to be understood within the social and political context in which they were decided, the courts will only be effective in their protection of the interests of the vulnerable if they are critical in their examination of the evidence before them. Having considered in this chapter the particular issues concerning the withholding and withdrawal of life-sustaining treatment from vulnerable children in the care of the state, the next chapter considers the wider context for decisions to withhold or withdraw life-sustaining treatment from seriously ill children.

6 Professional Duties and Public Responsibilities in Limitation of Life-Sustaining Treatment Cases

Withholding or Withdrawing of Life-Sustaining Treatment

When parents and doctors are agreed that life-sustaining treatment is not in the best interests of a child, it is lawful to withhold or withdraw it and to provide palliative care with the aim of limiting pain and suffering and enabling a peaceful and dignified death. The focus upon determination of the child's best interests, in individual cases, professional guidance, and academic commentary has resulted in a failure to consider the legal and professional duties of doctors central to determination of these cases. Inevitably, each case is factually distinct, and each decision is a particularistic assessment of the best interests of the child. Yet, as the principles by which courts decide these cases have been established, so has the balance of responsibilities between parents, doctors, the Trust, and courts.

The context for these cases is of developments in medical science and technology which enable doctors to maintain the lives of children born prematurely or with disabilities or rare conditions. The study by Wilkinson et al of deaths in the neonatal intensive care unit of a quaternary referral centre for newborn infants with surgical conditions, complex malformations and syndromes, and severe respiratory failure, in the periods July 1985 to June 1987 and January 1999 to December 2001, found that in both periods, more than 75% of deaths followed after treatment had been withheld or withdrawn.[1] The authors observed that between the two periods of time there was a decrease in the admission rate for, and in the number of deaths attributable to, severe chromosomal disorders. The authors suggested that this may in part be the result of changes in patterns of referral but also partly resulted from the termination of pregnancies following prenatal diagnosis. Questions about the withholding or withdrawal of life-sustaining treatment were first brought before the courts at the time when there was a debate within the medical community and the public more generally about

---

1 Dominic Wilkinson and Others, 'Death in the Neonatal Intensive Care Unit: Changing Patterns of End of Life Treatment Over Two Decades' (2006) 91 *Archives of Disease in Childhood, Fetal and Neonatal Edition* F268.

the selective non-treatment of disabled babies[2] since which time societal attitudes to disability have changed. The case law considered in this chapter has also to be positioned in the context of greater recognition of the individuality and rights of the child. Furthermore, over this time the nature of the patient/parent and professional relationship has changed, and parents are able to access an increasing range of sources of information about their child's medical condition which may lead to requests for treatment not offered by the treating team.

This chapter sets the context in which the issue of limiting the treatment of a child first came before the courts and within which the approach adopted in the cases and their outcomes need to be understood. It then considers the initial cases concerned with children in the care of the state such that it was important that decisions made to limit their treatment were made in a public forum where the decision-maker could be held to account. It is argued that, given prevailing attitudes which considered that the quality of disabled lives was poor, judicial scrutiny was not sufficiently critical nor encouraged to be by debate surrounding the cases. The litigation about the medical treatment of Charlotte Wyatt and the case of *An NHS Trust v MB* are analysed, and it is argued that these two cases were followed by a change in practice in terms of the circumstances when decisions about life-sustaining treatment are referred to court. Consideration is then given to the cases which followed. It is argued that in these more recent cases, the matter is now usually only referred to court when the doctors consider that to continue to treat is not only not in the best interests of the child but is contrary or inimical to the interests of the child. In most of the recent cases, the multi-disciplinary treatment team, supported by second opinions, the view of independent experts, and with reference to the RCPCH guidance, have reached the conclusion there is no treatment which can improve the condition of the child who, in the majority of cases, cannot benefit from interaction with their parents and has no prospect of leaving intensive care. The recent litigation on the question of continued ventilation of Charlie Gard, Isaiah Haastrup, and Alfie Evans is considered in which the parents were not only unable to accept the professional judgement of their child's best interests but would not accept the decision of the courts. The parents unsuccessfully appealed to the law. In contrast, in the case of Tafida Raqeeb there was evidence before the court of a competent body of professional opinion prepared to care for her in the same way that children with similar conditions to Tafida were cared for elsewhere in this jurisdiction. It is argued that separate consideration of the medical evidence before best interests, with consideration of professional duties as well as parental responsibilities, would enable the issues to be better understood and ensure the court effectively fulfils its public responsibilities.

---

2 Janet Read and Luke Clements, 'Demonstrably Awful: The Right to Life and the Selective Non-Treatment of Disabled Babies and Young Children' (2004) 31 *Journal of Law and Society* 482, 489-494.

Bringing Private Decisions into the Public Domain

Although arriving in the courts a few years later than the sterilisation cases considered in chapter five, the case law concerning the withholding or withdrawal of life-sustaining treatment from children commenced within the same societal context and public attitudes to the quality of life of children with disabilities.[3] Janet Read and Luke Clements have detailed the social context in which people with disabilities were segregated, had no public voice and from the perspective of the non-disabled professional were viewed as not having 'lives worth living'.[4] The primary public provision was the large, long-stay institution where children lived in conditions described as 'inhumane and depriving',[5] whilst services for those who lived at home were virtually non-existent, requiring families to manage with their own personal and material resources. Consequently, living with disabilities was perceived as burdensome. Societal barriers prevented disabled people living ordinary lives. Disabled people were excluded from political and policy agendas. The result was that children with disabilities lived marginalised and segregated lives. Janet Read and Luke Clements conclude of the 1970s and 1980s:

> Taken together, the overwhelmingly negative and burdensome images of living with disability, the barriers which prevented disabled people living ordinary lives, the segregated and frequently dehumanizing service provision, the tendency to characterize disabled children and adults as falling outside majority definitions of personhood, and the exclusion of disabled people and disability issues from political and policy agendas may be seen as significant factors in a context where practices to curtail disabled children's lives were legitimated.[6]

Attitudes were starting to change. Janet Read and Luke Clements quoted David Plank, the Director of Social Services for Hammersmith and Fulham where *Re B, Baby Alexandra*, was born, who explained that the local authority had intervened because 'it was our legal responsibility as a social services authority to intervene on behalf of the child' to protect her right to life. He explained that whilst he could understand what her parents were going through, to have failed to intervene would have been to have failed to 'distinguish between the parents and the child and [to see] the child wholly as a possession of the parents'.[7]

---

3 Preceded by a debate about selective treatment of children with spina bifida, Helga Kuhse and Peter Singer, *Should the Baby Live? The Problem of Handicapped Infants* (Oxford University Press, 1985).
4 Read and Clements (n 2).
5 Read and Clements (n 2) 496, referring to the research by M. Oswin, 'An historical perspective' in C Robinson and K Stalker (eds), *Growing Up with Disability* (J Kingsley, 1998).
6 Read and Clements (n 2) 497.
7 Read and Clements (n 2) 501.

Helga Kuhse and Peter Singer, in *Should the Baby Live?*, noted the evidence for the defence in *R v Arthur* that managing the care of babies with disabilities that would end in their death was common practice.[8] Ian Kennedy quoted an editorial from *The Times* in November 1981, which challenged the view that this practice was acceptable,

> Parents' wishes in these tragic circumstances deserve every respect, but they must be set against the proposition that their child is not wholly at their disposal: every live-born baby enters civil society and by doing so acquires independent rights, of which the chief concerns life itself.[9]

Janet Reid and Luke Clements observed that the cases of *R v Arthur* and *Re B* resulted in unprecedented 'public interrogation' of medical practice and decisions which had previously been reached privately between parents and doctors.[10] Gradually, Janet Read and Luke Clements explained, attitudes were changed by research which presented a more positive account of disabilities, demands for better services, and the emergence of recognition of children's rights. There was a shift in policy away from long-stay institutions,[11] such that the majority of children with disabilities no longer lived in residential care. Professional practice started to recognise that parents of children with disabilities had expertise which needed to be recognised.

The Court of Appeal in *Re B* established the role of the court in decisions about a child's future medical treatment which had previously been seen as within the exclusive province of parents and doctors.[12] The case established that it was not lawful for parents and doctors to leave a child to die just because that child had disabilities. Importantly, the case established that doctors had duties to involve local authority social services and to ensure that questions about a child's medical treatment were brought before the court where it was the responsibility of the court to ensure that decisions were reached according to socially acceptable standards.

---

8 Kuhse and Singer (n 3) 8.
9 Ian Kennedy, '*R v Arthur, Re B*, and the Severely Disabled Newborn Baby' in Ian Kennedy, *Treat Me Rights: Essays in Medical Law and Ethics* (Clarendon Press, 1988) 154–174, 156 quoting *The Times* editorial (6 November 1981).
10 Read and Clements (n 2) 501.
11 Following a review of conditions in Ely hospital, Department for Health and Social Security, *Report of the Committee of Enquiry into the Allegations of Ill-treatment and Other Irregularities at Ely Hospital, Cardiff* (Cmnd. 3785, 1969) leading to Department for Health and Social Security, *Better Services for the Mentally Handicapped* (Cmnd 4683, 1971).
12 Jonathan Herring, '*Re B (A Minor) (Wardship: Medical Treatment)*; 'The Child Must Live': Disability, Parents and the Law in Jonathan Herring and Jesse Wall (eds), *Landmark Cases in Medical Law* (Hart, 2015) 63-81, 66.

Establishing the Balance of Responsibilities: An Unequal Partnership

The absence of, and need for guidance, on the law and ethics of withholding life-sustaining treatment requested in the first two cases considered by the courts, *Re C*[13] and *Re J (1991)*,[14] was considered in chapter three, and the central place of the latter in establishing the applicable legal principles and approach of the courts in all cases concerned with the medical treatment of children are explained in chapter four and will not be repeated here. This chapter is concerned with the balance of responsibilities between parents, doctors, the local authorities, and the courts for the decision to withhold or withdraw life-sustaining treatment and, as it is argued this is crucial for a critical understanding of the cases, to place them in the social context.

In *Re C*, Lord Donaldson quoted from Ward J in the court below who said that the unanimous medical opinion was that C, a ward of court, had severe permanent brain damage and there was no treatment that could alter that prognosis.[15] The court authorised Baby C to be treated according to the advice of the professor who gave a second opinion which included that, as C was terminally ill and seemed to be in distress, the provision of antibiotics, intravenous fusions, or nasogastric feeding were not in her best interests. But also that final decisions about C's treatment should be made by the nurses caring for her who knew her best.[16] The decision of the court was that it was lawful to withhold treatment from C, but that did not prevent those caring for her from providing any treatment they considered to be in her best interests. As Lord Donaldson MR observed, the public interest in cases which had the effect of authorising the limitation of treatment to a vulnerable child in the care of the state required the judge's decision and the reasons for it to be given in open court and subject to public scrutiny. The judge quoted extensively from the report of the professor in order to explain the medical facts upon which the decision had been made without compromising the privacy of those involved. Despite the appreciation of the significance of the decision and the need to explain and justify why it was in C's best interests for life-sustaining treatment to be limited, it is not clear from a reading of the judgment why C was considered to be terminally ill. The judgment portrays a child with severe brain damage, in pain, and without prospect of any improvement who, given the prevailing attitudes towards disabilities, was considered not to have a quality of life worth living. What it was about her condition that meant that C was dying may have been apparent to those with medical expertise but, given the emphasis placed upon the role of the judgment in ensuring that the public understood the reasons for the decision of the court, the failure to explain this is a crucial omission. The judgment uncritically accepted the

---

13 [1990] Fam 26.
14 [1991] Fam 33.
15 *Re C* (n 13) 34.
16 *Re C* (n 13) 33.

medical evidence about C's quality of life which led to the conclusion as to her best interests, rather than examining the medical evidence in the context of the professional duties to the child in their care and the public responsibility of the local authority and the court to ensure her best interests were protected.

In *Re J (1991)*, the unanimous view of the doctors was that J, who had irreversible brain damage due to oxygen deprivation at his premature birth, should not be ventilated if he stopped breathing. Ventilation would sustain J's life but would not affect his prognosis or improve his quality of life. As Lord Donaldson observed, there was 'no real difference of opinion' between his parents and doctors, but the decision was for the court as J had, for unrelated reasons, been made a ward of court.[17] Taylor LJ identified the three factors that had led Scott Baker J to conclude that ventilation was not in J's best interests: that J had severe brain damage; if ventilation were required then J would have deteriorated further; and, the invasive nature of ventilation. The judgment clearly involved an assessment of J's future quality of life and found it wanting. J was

> likely to develop serious spastic quadriplegia, that is to say, paralysis of both his arms and legs. It is debatable whether he will ever be able to sit up or to hold his head upright. J appears to be blind, although there is a possibility that some degree of sight may return. He is likely to be deaf. He may be able to make sounds which reflect his mood, but he is unlikely ever to be able to speak, even to the extent of saying 'Mum' or 'Dad'. It is highly unlikely that he will develop even limited intellectual abilities. Most unfortunately of all, there is a likelihood that he will be able to feel pain to the same extent as a normal baby, because pain is a very basic response. It is possible that he may achieve the ability to smile and to cry.'[18]

The prognosis for J was uncertain as was his life expectancy – between a few years and his late teens – during which, with appropriate care, he may have enjoyed some quality of life. The conclusion of the court was that it was lawful to withhold life-sustaining treatment from a child with uncertain capacities if in the view of his doctors it was in his best interests given their judgement of his future quality of life. A judgement made in the context of prevailing attitudes of the poor quality of lives of people with disabilities and a future for J, if he survived to leave hospital, of institutional care provided by the State.

Questions about where the responsibility lies for decisions about the provision of life-sustaining treatment to a child in care were soon back before the courts in the case of *Re J (1993)*, this time within the context of the changes to public and private law enacted by the Children Act 1989.[19] Sixteen-month-old J had sustained severe injuries in a fall when one month old, leaving him with profound

---

17 *Re J* (n14).
18 *Re J* (n 14) 39.
19 [1993] Fam 15.

physical and mental impairments. He had been discharged from hospital to the care of foster parents who had cared for him with dedication and skill. Parental responsibility was thus shared by his parents and the local authority, although not by his foster carers who cared for him. Prompted by a report from the consultant paediatrician responsible for his medical care and although J was not at that point in hospital, the local authority sought leave under s.100 of the Children Act 1989 to invoke the inherent jurisdiction of the court to determine whether artificial ventilation or other life-saving measures should be administered if J suffered a life-threatening event. The local authority social work team would have supported the view of the consultant that ventilation in the event of a life-threatening event was not in J's best interests but, in light of the seriousness of the issue, referred the question to a case review sub-committee. The sub-committee asked the court to require the health authority to continue to provide all available treatment to J including resuscitation, although they changed their position to support the health authority following the decision of the court.[20] On appeal by the health authority with the support of the Official Solicitor, J's mother supported continued treatment, whilst his father did not hold a firm view on the treatment that should be given to J.[21]

Lord Donaldson's judgment was structured around professional duties and respect for clinical judgement but did not extend the role of the court to a critical examination of either or the evidence upon which clinical judgement was based. He saw the issue as whether the court, exercising its inherent jurisdiction to protect the interests of the child, could require a doctor to treat contrary to his or her clinical judgement of the best interests of their patient.[22] The judge held that the court could not require doctors to act other than in fulfilment of their duty which was, subject to consent from someone authorised to give it, 'to treat the patient in accordance with his own best clinical judgment' even if other doctors have reached a different judgement or that the court, in light of the evidence before it, disagrees.[23] Whilst J's future medical treatment was considered by the court, as the issue of ventilation was not immediate, the effect of the court's judgment was to return questions about his future medical treatment to his doctors enabling them to treat according to their clinical judgement. The consent of the court to the withholding of ventilation made it clear to the doctors, J's parents, the local authority, and the public generally that the doctors would be acting lawfully if they withheld ventilation. It did not prevent the doctors from ventilating J if, in their professional judgement, they considered that to be in his best interests. As demonstrated in this chapter, it is medical practice, rather than this legal principle which has changed to ensure that the clinical judgement of the doctors treating

---

20 *Re J* (n 19) 23.
21 *Re J* (n 19) 23.
22 *Re J* (n 19) 26–7. Repeating as part of the ratio of the case the views he had expressed obiter in *Re J* (n 14) and *Re R* [1992] Fam 11, 26.
23 *Re J* (n 19) 27.

the child accords with a competent body of professional opinion, is supported by second opinions, independent experts, and conforms with professional guidance. Whilst Lord Donaldson MR in *Re J* separated out the legal duties of professionals from the best interests of the child, he then conflated them by making the professional judgement of the child's best interests the one that mattered, without critically examining the fulfilment of professional duties to the child, the medical evidence upon which it was based, or the duties of the state, the local authority, and the court, to the child in their care. The consequence was that the medical view of disability, of a life not worth living, was accepted rather than tested or challenged.

Janet Read and Luke Clements have explained that attitudes which had started to change by the early 1980s when *Re B* was decided were advancing by the time of *Re J* a decade later, although that change is not reflected in the professional judgement or judicial acceptance of it in *Re J*. They showed that, as a result of research, a more positive account was starting to be presented of living with disabilities. The disabled people's movement was developing, with the result that '[d]isability was beginning to be politicized in an effort to change its definition from one of a private misfortune to one of a matter of public responsibility'.[24] The Children Act 1989 placed the protection and welfare of all children at the centre of public and parental responsibilities. Peter Smith has observed that, by specifically including disabled children within its provisions, the Children Act ensured that disabled children were to be seen first as children, entitled to have their needs met in the same child-centred way.[25] It provided for the first time for services to support the families of children with disabilities to fulfil their primary responsibility. A child with disabilities is a child 'in need'[26] for the purposes of section 17 of the Children Act 1989. This places a duty upon the local authority to provide services to safeguard and promote the child's welfare and promote their upbringing within their families by providing a range of services for a child in need or for any member of his family. The responsibility of public services is to work in partnership with parents, supporting them to fulfil their responsibilities to the child, and to enable the disabled child to live as normal a life as possible within their family. However, the duty imposed upon local authorities to take reasonable steps to provide services for disabled children[27] is a general duty, not a specific duty to meet the assessed needs of an individual child enforceable by judicial review.[28] Research has found that these duties have consistently not been

---

24 Read and Clements (n 2) 504.
25 Peter Smith, 'Disabled children and the Children Act 1989' (2010) 5 *Journal of Children's Services* 61, 63.
26 CA 1989 s 17(10). Disability is defined in s 17(11).
27 CA 1989 Sch 2 para 6.
28 *R (G) v Barnet London Borough Council* [2003] UKHL 57; As Judith Masson explained, this is in effect a power which does not found a claim for a specific service or impose a duty to provide a specific service for a specific child, Judith Masson, 'The Climbié Inquiry – Context and Critique' (2006) 33 *Journal of Law and Society* 221, 236.

124 *Limiting Life-Sustaining Treatment Cases*

implemented and therefore failed to provide a 'reasonable level of support to families with disabled children'.[29] These societal changes were not immediately reflected in the case law which was dominated by the medical view of the quality of life for children with disabilities.

There were four reported cases concerned with the withholding or withdrawal of life-sustaining treatment from a child in the decade from *Re J (1993)* to the litigation concerning Charlotte Wyatt which, it is argued below, was followed by a change in practice in the circumstances in which decisions were referred to court. The balance of responsibilities of parents, doctors, and the courts were still being worked out in these cases. Sir Stephen Brown P gave a short judgment in *Re C (1996)* in order to relieve the parents of the responsibility when all were agreed that it was in C's best interests for ventilation to be withdrawn but did not critically examine the evidence for this view.[30] His judgment in *Re C (1998)* focused upon the parents religious objections to failing to re-intubate if C was unable to breathe independently, with little consideration of their evidence that she responded positively to them.[31] Bodey J authorised the withholding of ventilation from B, in an urgent out of hours application, in circumstances where it was thought that without ventilation, B might have died that afternoon.[32] Whilst the decision whether to ventilate B had to be made that afternoon, the hearing took place via telephone, hearing from B's mother and two doctors, but not the doctor who would consider ventilation or the doctor who was clinically responsible for B who was on leave until the following day. The judge spoke to the witnesses, took a note of their evidence and relayed it to Counsel for any submissions; no authorities were placed before the court. The submission made on behalf of B's mother that the doctor who was prepared to ventilate should take over her care was noted but not commented upon. The role of the court in such cases was raised by Counsel for the Official Solicitor, who submitted that the court should not make the declaration, rather it was a matter of clinical judgement. Bodey J thought that whilst that might normally be an 'appropriate course' and whilst the evidence was imperfect, it was in E's best interests to give those responsible for her medical care the confidence of a court ruling, given the disagreement about her treatment and the lack of trust. It is hard to see that her parents, having lost trust in her doctors, would have had trust in the legal proceedings which determined that, contrary to their views, it was lawful and in the best interests of their child not to be ventilated.

The personal context for the case of 19-month-old ID who had severe, chronic, irreversible, and worsening lung disease was of attentive, conscientious, devoted care at home by his parents working with a range of community professionals

---

29 Smith (n 25) 66; Jane Tunstill, Jane Aldgate and June Thoburn, 'Promoting and safeguarding the welfare of children: a bridge too far?' (2010) 5 *Journal of Children's Services* 14.
30 *Re C* [1996] 2 FLR 43.
31 *Re C* [1998] 1 FLR 384.
32 *Royal Wolverhampton Hospital NHS Trust v B* [2000] 1 FLR 953.

– paediatric therapist, occupational therapist, home visitor, lead nurse in neonatal home care, and speech and language therapist – who had maximised his capacities and the quality of life he was able to enjoy. The evidence of the speech and language therapist was that ID had become more alert and responsive, that he recognised familiar people, he was able to follow people and toys with his eyes, showed some signs of vocabulary, and a hand and arm movement to indicate goodbye.[33] Cazalet J made the declaration that it would be lawful to withhold ventilation in the event of a respiratory or cardiac failure or arrest. The expert instructed on behalf of ID's parents, Dr P, referred to guidance from the RCPCH on *Withholding or Withholding Life Saving Treatment in Children, a Framework for Practice* which had been published in 1997, setting out the clinical circumstances which justified withholding or withdrawal of treatment. Dr P considered that ID was within the category of 'no chance', defined in the guidance as a child who has such a 'severe disease that life-sustaining treatment simply delays death without significant alleviation of suffering'.[34] Cazalet J accepted the unanimous view of ID's treating consultant paediatricians, a second opinion consultant, and the expert instructed by the parents. Their evidence was that ventilation might achieve a short extension to his life but at the expense of having to anaesthetise and paralyse him in order to insert the tube, causing him pain and distress and inevitably leading to further periods of ventilation. Mechanical ventilation may have sustained ID's life, but the burdens involved and the detriment to his quality of life led to the conclusion that ventilation was not in his best interests. As drug treatment had proven successful on his previous admission with a fever, he would be provided with drug treatment, oxygen, and antibiotics if required. He would be assessed, and ventilation provided if clinically appropriate. But again, the court did not fulfil its public responsibility to examine critically the medical evidence, accepting the professional judgement that a short extension of ID's life was not worthwhile.

Challenging Decisions, Changing Practice?

The cases of Charlotte Wyatt and *An NHS Trust v MB*[35] appear to have resulted in a change in practice, rather than the approach of the courts, to decisions about the provision of life-sustaining treatment to children. Both cases involved strongly held differences of opinion between parents and the treating doctors about the provision, in Charlotte's case, and continuation in the case of MB, of life-sustaining treatment in the context of judgements about the child's quality of life. The place of the judgments in both cases in establishing the modern articulation of the legal principles applicable in cases concerning children's medical treatment generally are explained in chapter three and four are not repeated here.

---

33 *A National Health Service Trust v D* [2000] 2 FLR 677, 684.
34 *A National Health Service Trust* (n 33) 694.
35 [2006] EWHC 507.

Both cases, in different ways, addressed the balance of responsibilities between parents, doctors, and the courts.

Charlotte Wyatt had chronic respiratory and kidney problems and profound and irreversible brain damage as a consequence of her premature birth. The first application to court by the Trust on behalf of her treating doctors, was when Charlotte was a year old and had not yet left hospital. Charlotte had been ventilated for the first three months of her life and had suffered a severe infection for which she had to be transferred from Portsmouth to Southampton for intensive care and which caused a deterioration in her respiratory and neurological functioning. The view of her doctors was that she would never leave hospital but would suffer a fatal respiratory infection over the winter. The medical evidence before the court was unanimous that, should she have a respiratory infection, it was not in her best interests to provide ventilation. Her parents wanted ventilation to be initiated and an elective tracheostomy to be performed to prepare for this.

In his analysis of her best interests in his first judgment on her future medical treatment in October 2004,[36] and in the first case concerning the withholding of life-sustaining treatment from a child to be decided in open court, Hedley J referred to the responsibility of parents and the role of the judge when an application has been made to court, to the medical evidence, referenced 'fundamental principles that undergird our humanity',[37] considered sanctity of life, quality of life, the right to dignity, the desire for a good death, and emphasised that he was mindful that Charlotte was not merely a 'physical being but a body, mind, and spirit expressed in a human personality of unique worth who is profoundly precious to her parents'.[38] Hedley J considered the dispute, on the issue whether Charlotte should have an elective tracheostomy or initial ventilation, to fall into the third category of cases he identified, where the doctor advises against treatment which the parent wants but is able in conscience to give it.[39]

The medical evidence was that it was not in Charlotte's best interests to ventilate her in the event of a respiratory arrest. Whilst of that opinion, Dr G, instructed by the parents, was prepared to take that course of action.[40] Dr G's evidence was that he was prepared to do an elective tracheostomy or initial ventilation in order to accommodate her parents' views and to give them more time to come to terms with the advice they were being given. In other words, his willingness to provide initial treatment was to accommodate parental views as to their daughter's best interests rather than representing a different view from the other

---

36 *Re Wyatt* [2004] EWHC 2247.
37 *Re Wyatt* (n 36) [21].
38 *Re Wyatt* (n 36) [39].
39 *Re Wyatt* (n 36) [18]. The four categories are explained in chapter four. Although inconsistently, Hedley J also noted that the evidence was that in such cases the doctors would in such cases provide it.
40 *Re Wyatt* (n 36) [18].

doctors as to Charlotte's best interests.[41] Hedley J tried to avoid approaching the decision through consideration of Charlotte's quality of life, viewed by her doctors as terrible, or in terms of intolerability – the medical view was that to subject her to further aggressive treatment would be intolerable – given the subjectivity involved in assessments of quality of life and intolerability. Hedley J reached the conclusion that it was not in her best interests to be subjected to aggressive ventilation in the event that Charlotte developed a respiratory infection, given that whilst ventilation might restore her to her present condition, there was a strong possibility that an infection would in any event be fatal.[42] Making the declaration sought by the Trust, Hedley J emphasised that the effect of the declaration was permissive, her doctors remained under a duty to treat her in accordance with their professional judgement of her best interests in the circumstances.[43]

Against medical expectation, Charlotte survived the winter and her parents applied to court for the declarations to be discharged.[44] All of the medical opinion before the court, apart from that of Dr G, was that treatment should be provided up to but not including ventilation. Dr A recognised that Charlotte's survival was against expectations but that a respiratory crisis was still virtually inevitable. Aggressive treatment would not be justified in response to a crisis as Charlotte was unlikely to survive and, if she did, it was likely to cause her further damage so that a return to her current condition was unlikely.[45] Dr H considered that ventilation would prevent a peaceful death and Dr I thought transfer to an intensive care unit would be 'oppressive' and serve no purpose.[46] In contrast, Dr G considered that if she did have an infection, ventilation was justified and if Charlotte responded she might recover to her current condition, although if she did not respond, her quality of life would be awful. Hedley J noted Dr G's view that as ventilation was a reversible procedure, as long as terminal damage had not occurred it should be tried if that is what her parents wanted.[47] Dr G's view, shared by one of the experts, Ms K, was that it was 'neither right nor practicable to give or withhold treatment against the wishes of the parents'.[48] As Hedley J observed, whilst doctors may be prepared to accommodate parental wishes, when

---

41 Doctors providing treatment that is not in their professional judgement in the best interests of the child in response to parental wishes is considered in chapter four.
42 Although Hedley J did ask the treating clinicians to 'give further consideration to an elective tracheostomy', *Re Wyatt* (n 36) [41].
43 *Re Wyatt* (n 36) [41].
44 *Wyatt v Portsmouth NHS Trust and Wyatt (By her Guardian) (No 3)* [2005] EWHC 693. In January 2005, Hedley had declined to stay the orders in the absence of evidence that observed improvements amounted to improvements in her underlying condition, emphasising that even though the declarations remained in place, her doctors must treat according to their judgement of her best interests, *Portsmouth Hospitals NHS Trust v Wyatt and others* [2005] EWHC 117.
45 *Wyatt (No 3)* (n 44) [9].
46 *Wyatt (No 3)* (n 44) [11].
47 *Wyatt (No 3)* (n 44) [10].
48 *Wyatt (No 3)* (n 44) [12].

128 *Limiting Life-Sustaining Treatment Cases*

the decision is before the judge, the views of parents will be given profound respect but they are not decisive.[49] The preponderance of the medical evidence of Charlotte's best interests was that ventilation would serve no purpose and prevent a peaceful death, require sedation, and force her to become 'more an object to whom things are done, than a child'[50]:

> it would not be in Charlotte's best interests to die in the course of futile aggressive treatment. Dr H and Dr A came close to saying that such treatment would be inconsistent with professional conscience. Others, like Dr F and Dr I, did not go that far but expressed firm views that such treatment would not accord with her best interests.[51]

On this evidence, Hedley J refused to discharge the declarations.[52] In this judgment, in April 2005, Hedley J noted that decisions about Charlotte's medical treatment were being made in an environment in which relations between her parents and the hospital had become 'fragile'. When visiting, her father had to be accompanied by security staff. The judge noted the stress caused to the staff by the issues surrounding Charlotte's care, the 'volatility' of her parents, and hurtful comment which had followed the publicity surrounding the case.[53] The case had been heard in public to enable 'full and open debate' about the role of the courts when it was proposed to withhold life-sustaining treatment from a child but that had been at the expense of causing stress to the health professionals who were providing Charlotte with the highest possible quality of care.

A year after the initial hearing, in October 2005, the declaration was discharged following improvements in Charlotte's neurological functioning and a reduction in her need for oxygen.[54] On this occasion, Hedley J detailed the extent to which the relationship between her parents and doctors had broken down. Before the court proceedings, Charlotte's parents had complained to the police about the care provided to her. For much of the time, Charlotte's parents were required to be accompanied by security when they were on the ward.[55] Hedley J quoted Dr K, her consultant paediatrician, who was concerned that,

> the history of the case suggests that any clinician who refused to ventilate CW, without a court order authorising such a step, would face condemnation

---

49 *Wyatt (No 3)* (n 44) [12].
50 *Wyatt (No 3)* (n 44) [18].
51 *Wyatt (No 3)* (n 44) [16].
52 Upheld on appeal, *Re Wyatt (a child) (medical treatment: continuation of order)* [2005] EWCA Civ 1181.
53 *Wyatt (No 3)* (n 44) [18].
54 *Re Wyatt* [2005] EWHC 2293 (Oct 2005).
55 *Re Wyatt (Oct 2005)* (n 54) [18]-[21].

in the media, complaints to the police, a probable report to the General Medical Council, and civil litigation.[56]

The issue was back before the court in February 2006 when Hedley J again made the declaration upon application by the Trust when Charlotte's oxygen levels needed to be increased due to a viral infection.[57] Contrary to medical expectation, Charlotte was discharged from hospital, into foster care, in December 2006.[58]

The case concerning the future medical treatment of Charlotte Wyatt was thus unusual in the body of case law. As Charlotte survived against medical expectation in hospital for over two and a half years and the partnership between her doctors and parents had broken down, there were numerous court hearings, not confined to the primary issue of ventilation. In the glare of publicity, her parents shared their views, feelings, and experiences in a blog.[59] All hearings were in open court so that the evidence and judicial conclusions about life-sustaining treatment to a disabled child could be subjected to scrutiny. Louise Jackson and Richard Huxtable have argued that cases like that of Charlotte Wyatt and Luke Winston-Jones at the same time, suggested 'that the judges will never quite shake off the shackles of *Bolam*'.[60] That is, the unquestioning acceptance of the medical evidence prioritised clinical judgement over the duty of the court to protect the interests of the vulnerable child. Independent review was required, but they suggested it was arguable whether or not the court provided this.

Just days after the last judgment concerning the care of Charlotte Wyatt, following an application by the BBC, Holman J heard the case of *An NHS Trust v MB*[61] in public. The issue was whether ventilation that was keeping MB alive should be withdrawn. MB, 18 months old at the time of the hearing, had been diagnosed when seven weeks old with degenerative and progressive spinal muscular atrophy of the most severe form, since which time he had not left hospital. SMA is a progressive and degenerative condition which affects the voluntary muscles such as the respiratory muscles. As a consequence of his condition, MB was unable to breathe unaided so was assisted by positive pressure ventilation via an endo-tracheal tube. Medical opinion was that M had an intolerable quality of life. The evidence was that MB's treating doctors had over a long period increasingly felt that continued ventilation could not be justified.[62] Dr SN explained that he had 'felt for a considerable time that he is acting unethically in continuing

---

56 *Re Wyatt (Oct 2005)* (n 54) [15].
57 *Re Wyatt* [2006] EWHC 319.
58 Her parents' relationship had broken down and her father explained that social services were unable to provide the care package necessary for her to live with him, S Payne, 'Christmas with foster parents for right-to-life Charlotte' *Daily Telegraph* (21 December 2006).
59 http://charlottewyatt.blogspot.com [no longer accessible].
60 Louise Jackson and Richard Huxtable, 'The Doctor-Parent Relationship: as Fragile As Glass?' (2005) 27 *Journal of Social Welfare and Family Law* 369, 377.
61 *An NHS Trust v MB* (n 35).
62 *An NHS Trust v MB* (n 35) [25-26].

to subject MB to discomfort and pain and that he would personally find it very difficult to continue much longer to do so'.[63] Four expert witnesses, instructed by the Trust and by the parents, agreed with the treating doctors' opinions on diagnosis, prognosis, current and future pain and distress, and that ventilation should be withdrawn.[64]

Despite the unanimous medical evidence, that it was not in MB's best interests for ventilation to be continued,[65] Holman J declined to make the declaration sought by the Trust. Continuous positive pressure ventilation had been adjudged proper medical treatment for MB. The issue before the court was whether to continue to provide it was in MB's best interests, which the judge concluded, assessed in the widest possible sense, it was.[66] The case reveals different perspectives underpinning the conclusion as to MB's best interests given that ventilation was keeping MB alive but was not restoring his health,[67] and there was no treatment available that could improve MB's condition. His doctors focused upon the burdens to MB arising from uncertainty as to the extent to which he was in discomfort, distress, or pain, and his inability to communicate or seek help to relieve it.[68] The judge adopted the parental perspective which prioritised MB's relatedness, connectedness, and interaction with his family. Despite his physical inability, MB responded to his family, followed his mother with his eyes, showed 'pleasure to her by his eyebrows going up slightly' and the 'merest movement upwards of the side of his lips as if he is trying to smile'.[69] His mother's evidence was that MB responded to his siblings and demonstrated his likes and dislikes in television programmes and music. The evidence before the court was that MB interacted with the 'sights, sounds, experiences, people, and activity'[70] around him, had bonded with his family, taking pleasure in his relationship with them. Whilst a range of childhood 'experiences, pleasures, moods, and emotions'[71] were denied to MB by his condition, he was still able to enjoy 'a core of pleasure, including what is probably the single most important source of pleasure and emotion to a small child, his relationship with his parents and family'.[72] The judge considered that it was in MB's best interests for the current care he was receiving to be continued but not for treatment to be escalated. Applying the principle that a judge could not require doctors to treat contrary to their professional judgement,[73] Holman J

---

63 *An NHS Trust v MB* (n 35) [37].
64 *An NHS Trust v MB* (n 35) [29].
65 *An NHS Trust v MB* (n 35) [89].
66 *An NHS Trust v MB* (n 35) [90].
67 *An NHS Trust v MB* (n 35) [26].
68 *An NHS Trust v MB* (n 35) [70].
69 *An NHS Trust v MB* (n 35) [43].
70 *An NHS Trust v MB* (n 35) [63].
71 *An NHS Trust v MB* (n 35) [69].
72 *An NHS Trust v MB* (n 35) [69].
73 *An NHS Trust v MB* (n 35) [54].

stated his conclusion but that he could not make an order or declaration to that effect.[74]

Although there will inevitably be differences in their medical condition, the approach of Holman J in *Re MB* can be compared to the approach adopted in the judgment in the 1998 case of *Re C* who also had spinal muscular atrophy, type 1.[75] 16-month-old C had first received hospital treatment eight months before the court judgment at which time she had been in hospital receiving ventilation for about a month. C was conscious, could recognise her parents, smile, and had a small amount of movement in her hands and feet. Her doctors considered that ventilation should be removed to see whether she could breathe independently but that ventilation should not be restored if she could not. Sir Stephen Brown P noted that her parents loved their daughter and saw her react positively to them but their objection to withholding re-ventilation was presented primarily in terms of their religious beliefs. As Orthodox Jews, they could not agree to withholding ventilation as that was contrary to their religious beliefs that it was wrong to fail to intervene when that could prevent death. The medical evidence before the court was unanimous that C should be weaned off the ventilator as she may be able to breathe independently, but she should not be re-ventilated if she sustained a further respiratory arrest. The second opinion evidence was that she would almost certainly die within the next year, and the independent advice obtained by the parents was that 'ventilation is not in the best interests of these very unfortunate children'. The two judgments reflect changed medical practice about the extent of ventilation of children and changing assessments of quality of life that justifies continued treatment.

Whilst central in terms of establishing the applicable legal principles, the Wyatt litigation and *Re MB* represent a change not in the law, which is well-established, or the approach of the courts, but in terms of the circumstances in which Trusts will apply to court for authority to withhold or withdraw life-sustaining technology in cases of disagreement between parents and doctors. In November 2006, the Nuffield Council of Bioethics Report on *Critical care decisions in fetal and neonatal medicine* sought to provide an ethical framework for critical care decisions about the foetus and newborn with reference to the value of human life; the role of best interests; the deliberate ending of life; the withholding and withdrawing of treatment; and the weight that should be accorded to economic and social considerations. The Report emphasised the importance of a partnership of care and that every effort should be made to resolve differences of opinion without

---

74 *An NHS Trust v MB* (n 35) [90]. Anne Morris has argued that the effect of Holman J stating his conclusion that continued ventilation was in MB's best interests would be to require its provision given that where the judge has determined that continued treatment is in the child's best interests to withdraw it is a culpable omission, 'Selective Treatment of Irreversibly Impaired Infants: Decision-making at the Threshold' (2009) 17 *Medical Law Review* 347–376, 369. Given the unanimous evidence before court, it may not have been possible to find a clinician willing to treat to whom his care could be transferred.
75 *Re C* (n 31).

recourse to court.[76] Reflective of a change in attitudes to the quality of life of children with disabilities, it recommended that intolerability should be the test in such cases.[77] The UK ratified the United Nations Convention on the Rights of Persons with Disabilities in 2007, elaborating the rights of persons with disabilities and providing a code of implementation, committing to combatting stereotypes and prejudices, and to promote understanding of the capacities of people with disabilities in order to change perceptions. Discussions about and decisions to withhold or withdraw life-sustaining treatment from a child occur within the changing social and policy context with respect to disability, which shape professional duties and public responsibilities to disabled children.

Responsibilities Rebalanced?

Mr Lock QC, submitted to the Court of Appeal in *Wyatt*, that applications are only made to court by Trusts in the 'most unusual of circumstances', when the Trust 'cannot accede to the treatment plan proposed by the parents'.[78] The circumstances in which the professional judgement is reached by the child's treating doctors that they cannot accede to what the child's parents want occur within the prevailing medical and social context. Consequently, whilst the cases in which the legal principles were established remain authoritative as to the law, they are no longer representative of the circumstances that result in applications to court or of the judgements about the quality of life with disabilities which prompted them. One change over the period in which courts have been asked to make decisions about life-sustaining treatment for a child are developments in medical science and technology, which not only enable lives to be sustained but enable some children with life-limiting conditions to be cared for at home. Consequently, some of the recent cases involve older children with complex medical conditions who have been cared for at home. MacDonald J noted that seven-year-old Y, who had spinal muscular atrophy type 1, had enjoyed a very happy and engaged life with her family until the cardio-respiratory arrest which caused irreversible brain damage.[79] Without the 'care, love, devotion, and expertise' of her family, supporting her through 'technically demanding' treatments, Y would 'undoubtedly have died many years ago'.[80] Twelve year old AA, who had been born with a serious brain malformation causing hydrocephalus, severe epilepsy, visual impairment, significant developmental delay, and lack of mobility had been cared for at home by her mother and family, with love and devotion providing her 'in her own small closed world, [...] some modest quality of life'.[81]

---

76 Nuffield Council of Bioethics, *Critical care decisions in fetal and neonatal medicine: ethical issues* (2006) 2.53.
77 Nuffield Council of Bioethics (n 76) 2.11.
78 *Re Wyatt (continuation of order)* (n 52) [100].
79 *King's College Hospital NHS Foundation Trust v MH* [2015] EWHC 1966, [49].
80 *King's College Hospital NHS Foundation Trust* (n 79) [10].
81 *Re AA* [2014] EWHC 4861, [5].

Continued change in attitudes to disability accompanied by legislative change[82] and greater respect, reflected in the RCPCH guidance, for the rights of the child have also affected the social context in which children with disabilities and their families live. In the context of the medical treatment of children, the shift to greater respect for patient autonomy, reflecting the importance of individual beliefs and values to medical decision-making, has required greater weight to be given to parental decisions. Information about medical conditions and the treatments available for them is easier to access. These changes have not led to fewer cases being brought to court[83] but have led to changes in the circumstances in which decisions about a child's future medical treatment are referred to court, to the circumstances which prevail before doctors reach the point where they can no longer, in their professional judgement, accede to parental wishes. It has become ever more important for judges to address the legal and professional duties of doctors to children in their care within the context of public responsibilities, because it is in the fulfilment of their professional duties to the child that legal proceedings are brought.

Whilst, because it is the legal principle, the difference of opinion between doctors and parents is addressed in terms of the child's best interests and the focus of the court is upon the same, in many of the more recent cases, the medical evidence before the court is not that the doctors disagree that treatment is in the *best* interests of the child given the child's quality of life. Rather, the medical evidence is that to continue to treat the child, or to treat the child as the parents wish, would, in their professional judgement, be *contrary* to the interests of the child. This is not the same as a professional judgement that the treatment is not in the best interests of the child. It is far from a judgement that what the parents want is not in the *best* interests of the child but at the other extreme, that what the parents want, in their professional judgement, is *inimical* to the child's interests. Medical technology may enable the child to survive when, in the professional judgement of those caring for the child, there is no further treatment that can offer any chance of any improvement in the child's condition, and the prospect is a gradual deterioration from a low threshold in an intensive care unit. For example, in *An Hospital Trust v GM, DK, HK,* Baker J concluded that the evidence before the court showed that,

> There is manifestly no prospect of any recovery and indeed all the evidence points to his condition deteriorating further. Tragically, it seems this baby

---

82 Disability Discrimination Act 1995 repealed by the consolidating Equality Act 2010; the Equality and Human Rights Commission was established in 2007 to promote and enforce non-discrimination laws including against discrimination on the grounds of disability.
83 The Appendix shows there were 5 cases concerning the withholding or withdrawal of life-sustaining treatment from children between 1990-1999, 8 between 2000-2009, 14 between 2010 and 2015 and 15 from 2016 to end April 2020.

will not survive long. It is clear from the unanimous view of the doctors that there is nothing to be gained from any further neurosurgical intervention.[84]

As explained in chapter four, health professionals have duties to children in their care, and when they reach the limits of what is possible and permissible in their professional judgement, it is contrary to their duties to the child to continue. To make a professional judgement about treatment options is to make a value judgement about the risks, burdens, and benefits, but if there is *no* professional prepared, in the exercise of their professional judgement to provide a specific intervention, then the court cannot determine that it is in the child's best interests. The role of the judge when such cases are brought to court should be first to examine critically the evidence for this professional judgement and then the best interests of the child.

The majority of cases which have been brought to court since the case of Charlotte Wyatt are far removed from the quality of life judgement in that case or the earlier case of *Re J (1991)*. In the majority of cases since, the medical evidence before the court is that there is no further treatment which can improve the condition of the child, who demonstrates little or no awareness or ability to interact, form connections or attachments, and is expected always to be dependent upon intensive care. They involve a range of conditions including mitochondrial conditions,[85] neurodevelopmental disorders,[86] brain damage[87] including from deprivation of oxygen at birth,[88] heart conditions,[89] chronic lung disease,[90] accidental injury,[91] and undiagnosed conditions.[92]

Medical evidence before the court may detail the numerous procedures tried, such as the nine medications tried to control C's seizures[93] or the range of measures tried in the attempt to treat 11-year-old X's heart failure.[94] The Consultant Cardiothoracic Surgeon explained that they had 'left no stone unturned' in their search for treatment for X but had reached the point where there is 'nothing left to offer'.[95] As King J observed of AA, who screamed in pain and recently had been 'utterly inconsolable' for a 24-hour period: 'All the strategies, all the knowledge,

---

84 *An Hospital Trust v GM, DK, HK* [2017] EWHC 1710 [21].
85 For example, *An NHS Foundation Trust v R and Mr and Mrs R* [2013] EWHC 2340.
86 For example, *An NHS Foundation Trust v AB and CD and EF* [2014] EWHC 1031.
87 For example, *King's College Hospital NHS Foundation Trust v T, V, and ZT* [2014] EWHC 331.
88 For example, *King's College NHS Trust v Thomas & Haastrup* [2018] EWHC 127.
89 For example, *GOSH v NO& KK & MK* [2017] EWHC 241.
90 For example, *Kirklees Council v RE and Others* [2014] EWHC 3182.
91 For example, *Re A (A Child)* [2016] EWCA Civ 759.
92 For example, *Alder Hey Children's NHS Foundation Trust v Evans* [2018] EWHC 308.
93 *An NHS Trust v A & B & C* [2018] EWHC 2750 [16].
94 *An NHS Trust v W and X* [2015] EWHC 2778 [8].
95 *An NHS Trust v W and X* [2015] EWHC 2778 [16].

all the medical science available to the experts in both palliative care and in pharmacological medicine at GOSH have been unable to control her pain'.[96]

Frequently, the medical evidence is that whilst they can maintain life, they can only do so against the pain and suffering of the child's condition or by the infliction of further pain and suffering through medical intervention,[97] for example, that caused by suctioning.[98] The doctors treating 11-year-old X, the pain and suffering of whom was graphically conveyed in the judgment, expressed concern that 'we are lengthening X's suffering without any chance of success; this is as futile as it can get'.[99] Refusing permission to appeal, Jackson LJ concluded that X was 'beyond medical help. Life prolonging treatment will cause him intolerable suffering to no useful purpose'.[100]

In their evidence, doctors have also expressed concern that, as death is inevitable, medical intervention would merely prolong the dying process in intensive care in circumstances where the child cannot interact.[101] The doctors in *King's College Hospital NHS Foundation Trust v MH* expressed their concern that to intubate and provide artificial ventilation to seven-year-old Y, who had spinal muscular atrophy type 1 and showed no evidence of cognitive activity following cardio-respiratory arrest, would not 'alter her prognosis' but would lead to 'an unquantifiable period of time having her life artificially maintained on an intensive care unit' from which she would never leave.[102] Often the child's life has been maintained on a ventilator for a number of months whilst their condition and possible treatments have been investigated and tried. The possibility of withdrawing respiratory support was first discussed with A's mother within days of the accident which caused A to suffer irreversible brain damage, seven months before the decision of the court.[103] Seventeen-month-old ZT, born prematurely at 28 weeks gestation, had never left hospital after suffering acute cardio-respiratory deterioration resulting in severe irreversible brain damage including to his brain stem. He had been kept alive on a ventilator for ten months after his doctors concluded there was no prospect of recovery of brain function or of removal from ventilation.[104]

If the clinical judgement is that there are no treatment options that can improve the child's condition, where the child lacks awareness and does not respond to

---

96 *Re AA* [2014] EWHC 4861 [7].
97 *An NHS Trust v A & B & C* [2018] EWHC 2750 [44].
98 *Re OT* [2009] EWHC 633 [22] occurring between 4 and 30 times an hour, caused obvious distress, at best highly uncomfortable, at the worst probably very painful.
99 *An NHS Trust v W and X* [2015] EWHC 2778 [16].
100 *In the Matter of I (A Child)* [2015] EWCA Civ 1159 [91].
101 For example, *An NHS Trust v A & B & C* [2018] EWHC 2750 [44].
102 *King's College Hospital NHS Foundation Trust v MH* [2015] EWHC 1920 [22] urgent out of hours telephone hearing. Final orders were made the following week by which time the father was no longer opposed to the application but did not want to make the decision, *King's College Hospital NHS Foundation Trust v Y ND MH* [2015] EWHC 1966.
103 *Re A (A Child)* [2016] EWCA Civ 759.
104 *King's College Hospital NHS Foundation Trust v T, V, and ZT* [2014] EWHC 3315.

those caring for them, the conclusion will be reached that sustaining the child's life through long-term ventilation in an intensive care unit is not in the child's best interests and can lawfully be withdrawn.[105] One example is the judgment of Holman J in the case of 14-month-old identical twin boys who had been in hospital since the age of five months and were ventilated due to a progressive, incurable, untreatable, neuro-degenerative disorder. The evidence was that as a result of 'irreversible severely damaged, or atrophied and malfunctioning brains', they were 'merely artificially surviving'. To continue to prolong their lives 'lacks any purpose, confers no benefit at all apart from the fact of physical survival, and involves perpetuating the infliction of pain and discomfort for no gain or purpose'. Whilst the children could potentially survive for years on ventilation and with intensive care, their underlying condition would deteriorate, they would be subjected to increasingly painful and invasive interventions and be less able to express discomfort. There was no evidence of any pleasure or enjoyment of life; touch from their parents neither relaxed nor soothed them but led to muscle spasm.[106]

A further example is the case of 17-month-old ZT who had not left hospital since his premature birth. He had sustained severe irreversible damage to his brain, including to his brain stem which rendered him dependent on a ventilator. The evidence was that he was not generally in pain but that interventions such as suctioning and replacement of the nasogastric tube did cause him to suffer. The medical evidence was that he was extremely unlikely to survive off the ventilator but that if he did, he would have 'profound impairment of all neurological function with no prospect of meaningful movement, vision, communication, engagement with others or feeding', that he could not 'interpret anything of the outside world', and had 'no awareness of himself as a person and is unable to derive pleasure from any interactions with his environment or his family'. Given the severity of the damage to his brain there was no prospect of ZT recovering any of these functions.[107]

The judgments note the loving attentiveness of parents, their attempts to stimulate their child, and the care lavished upon the child, but, in the majority of the recent cases brought to court, the evidence is that the chid has no awareness[108]

---

105 For example, *NHS Trust v Baby X and others* [2012] EWHC 2188, cardiac arrest resulting in catastrophic brain damage, profoundly unconscious with no spontaneous purposeful movement, no prospect of regaining consciousness or awareness of self or environment, [20].
106 *Central Manchester University Hospitals NHS Foundation Trust v A and others* [2015] EWHC 2828 [25], [11], [13]. Holman J was careful to emphasise that, although they suffered from the same condition, he reached a decision about the best interests of each child as an individual.
107 *King's College Hospital NHS Foundation Trust v T, V, and ZT* [2014] EWHC 3315 [10], [13].
108 Or there may be minimal awareness, *Re OT* [2009] EWHC 633 [26] brief episodes of consciousness, rarely awake and when awake eyes not fully open or fix or follow objects.

or ability to respond.[109] For example, two-year-old A had suffered a devastating brain injury in a road traffic accident. The judge considered the possibility that he might improve, that there was a less than a 1% chance that he would be able to blink to communicate, he might draw comfort from touch, it was possible but unlikely that he would smile, but that any improvement would not extend to 'recognis[ing] his mother' or that it was her that sought to comfort him.[110] Balanced against this, was the evidence that the interventions caused him pain.[111] With evident distress, in his evidence the consultant paediatric intensivist treating A told the court,

> This is the first time in my twenty-seven years I'm coming here ... It was not an easy decision for the whole team to come here. I mean, we thought long and hard. It is not only the 8 paediatric intensive consultants, it is 80–100 odd nurses, it is the neurology team, the neurosurgery team, it is the physiotherapists. Everything together, we decided that it is not in A's best interest to continue this type of intensive care to keep him alive. He is not benefiting from any of this and that is why we're here, so that deferring it, and for us, we think that it is inhuman to keep A suffering like that. That's why we're here.[112]

This position was articulated on behalf of the Trust in *An NHS Trust v AB*:

> Miss Powell explained to the court that the medical team have now reached the stage where they would decline to treat AB as it would be unethical so to do. When asked by my Lord, McCombe LJ, whether that was the same as a best interest test, she said that it was not. What it represented, she told the court, was that we have now reached a state of affairs where the clinicians have come to the view that AB's clinical condition is such that life preserving treatment is so contrary to her best interest that it would be inimical to their respective Hippocratic oaths to treat her and would therefore be unethical.[113]

---

109 For example, *An NHS Foundation Trust v R and Mr and Mrs R* [2013] EWHC 2340. Some cases note limited awareness which enable, at a basic level, some comfort and reassurance from parents, *An NHS Trust v A & B & C* [2018] EWHC 2750 [32].
110 *Re A (A Child)* [2016] EWCA Civ 759 [26].
111 The judge's finding that A was in pain was one of the grounds for appeal, given that there was a difference of opinion on whether his brain injury meant that A was not able to feel pain. This was a matter upon which there was a 'reasonable range of professional opinion', *Re A* (n 110) [48].
112 *Re A* (n 110) [17] ventilation was keeping A alive, who had catastrophic injuries following an accident which meant he could not feel anything below his neck, did not respond to noise, had no sign of awareness of his surroundings, was minimally conscious, and had no spontaneous respiratory effort [6].
113 *An NHS Trust v AB* [2016] EWCA Civ 899, [23].

The benefits, burdens, and risks of any particular treatment option are not always clear cut, there may be uncertainty about the clinical effect of a treatment on an individual patient, or about the particular benefits, burdens, and risks for that patient. The decision that there is no further treatment which can benefit the child is a clinical judgement and a professional judgement, which as the RCPCH Guidance states includes value judgements:

> Deciding what outcomes or treatments are intolerable or unbearable, or what risks are acceptable, is an intrinsic part of the decision-making process. This is not confined to clinical considerations alone, and contextual factors relevant to the circumstances of the child and their family should be taken into account.[114]

Drawing on knowledge, expertise, and experience, professional judgements made in the face of medical uncertainty mean that other practitioners may reach a different conclusion. The judgments detail the good medical practice engaged in, in the recent cases, to test professional judgement. These include multi-disciplinary treatment team meetings to ensure that the decision is reached collectively and with insights from all disciplines, securing second opinions from experts from other hospitals with a range of relevant expertise, and independent expert opinion secured for the parents or jointly. Through these means, the treating doctors can satisfy themselves that their conclusions on diagnosis, prognosis, and whether there are any treatment options are reasonable. Frequently, in the evidence before the court, doctors have explained how their conclusion accords with the good practice guidance from the RCPCH. The guidance is primarily referenced to the four sets of circumstances when treatment limitation can be considered rather than the legal or ethical aspects: because it is no longer in the child's best interests to continue; because treatments cannot provide overall benefit; because life is limited in quantity or quality; or, where there is an informed refusal of treatment.[115] Judges have noted that the categories set out in the RCPCH Guidance have served as the 'backdrop against which multidisciplinary medical teams conduct their assessments'.[116] The judiciary have recognised that the RCPCH Guidance 'provides valuable direction for a court when it is required to grapple with the ethical and medical issues',[117] and as such, is 'entitled to the closest attention

---

114 RCPCH, *Making Decisions to Limit Treatment in Life-Limiting and Life-Threatening Conditions in Children: A Framework for Practice* (2015), 3.3.1, https://adc.bmj.com/content/100/Suppl_2/s1.full.pdf+html accessed 16 April 2020.
115 RCPCH (n 114) 4–5.
116 *Re A* (n 110) [40].
117 *County Durham and Darlington NHS Foundation Trust v SS, FS and MS* [2016] EWHC 535 [22]. Cobb J detailing those aspects of the guidance of particular relevance to the circumstances of the child in the case before him.

and respect'.[118] But they have stressed it is not 'authoritative as to the law'[119] nor will it 'bind the court',[120] but rather the guidance enables the judge making a welfare determination to 'understand the framework of thought of the witnesses'.[121] Good practice will involve holding a number of meetings with the parents to discuss the acceptable options during this time. However, a further notable development in the case law, is the refusal of parents in some of the recent high profile cases to accept the decision of the judge that withdrawal of life-sustaining treatment was in their child's best interests and to seek to overturn the decision by appealing through the appeal courts.

Unsuccessful Appeals to the Law

Consistent with the argument presented above, in the recent cases of Charlie Gard, Isaiah Haastrup, and Alfie Evans, the treating doctors had reached the conclusion that all treatment options had been exhausted but, in the face of parental opposition to withdrawal of ventilation, in fulfilment of their professional duties to the child they sought a decision of the court. What makes these cases stand out, are the exhaustive efforts of the parents of each child to try to secure the continued ventilation of their child by seeking alternative centres which would admit their child and pursuing their case through the courts.

In their individual interpretation of parental responsibility to ensure the welfare of their child, as noted in the majority speech of the Supreme Court in *Montgomery*, these parents were able to access other sources of information beyond that being conveyed to them by their child's treating doctors about 'symptoms, investigations, treatment options, risks, and side-effects',[122] informing the choices they sought to make about the future care of their child. The parents of Charlie Gard and Alfie Evans were able to identify institutions and practitioners abroad who were willing to take over the care of their child and raised the money necessary to fund transfer and care. However, parents do not have unconstrained liberty to find a hospital anywhere in the world which will accept their child and take them there. Not only will the courts not require a practitioner to treat contrary to their professional judgement, the limits to parental choice are set by professional judgement.

Charlie Gard's life had been sustained by mechanical ventilation whilst the doctors at Great Ormond Street Hospital (GOSH) explored all therapeutic options, including nucleoside bypass therapy for the treatment of the rare inherited mitochondrial condition from which he suffered, infantile onset encephalomyopathic mitochondrial DNA depletion syndrome (MDDS). MDDS is a

---

118 *King's College Hospital NHS Foundation Trust v Y ND MH* [2015] EWHC 1966 [51].
119 *An NHS Trust v MB* (n 35) [23].
120 *NHS Trust v Baby X and others* [2012] EWHC 2188 [19].
121 *NHS Trust v Baby X* (n 120) [19].
122 *Montgomery v Lanarkshire Health Board* [2015] UKSC 11, [76].

progressive condition which severely affected Charlie's brain, muscles, and ability to breathe. In evidence Dr B, Consultant Paediatric Intensivist on the Paediatric and Neonatal Intensive Care Unit at GOSH said that,

> there were no further treatments available to Charlie which could improve him from his current situation and that this was the opinion of the entire team – including those from whom a second opinion had been obtained – with the view of the entire team that Charlie is deteriorating, that he cannot get better, that he cannot understand anything or develop, that there is no prospect of this and that he should be allowed to slip away peacefully and with dignity.'[123]

The medical evidence of Charlie's treating team supported by second opinions was that Charlie had no spontaneous respiration, no purposeful response, was not capable of spontaneous movement, there was no treatment that could improve his condition, his condition was deteriorating, irreversible, and the invasive procedures necessary to sustain his life were, although they could not be certain, probably causing him pain and suffering,[124] such that to continue with those life-sustaining procedures was contrary to his interests.[125] Francis J said in his judgment that Charlie's parents agreed with the medical opinion that Charlie's 'current quality of life is not one that should be sustained without hope of improvement',[126] so that absent any treatment which might improve his condition it was in his best interests for ventilation to be withdrawn. As stated in the GOSH position paper, '[d]espite all the advances in medical science made by GOSH and the other hospitals around the world, there remain some conditions that we cannot cure and we cannot ameliorate'.[127] However, because there was a doctor in the United States who was prepared to try an innovative therapy, his parents sought to give him that chance. The central issue in the case was therefore whether nucleoside bypass therapy was a viable alternative therapeutic option,[128] an appropriate treatment option supported by a reasonable body of professional opinion. Francis J concluded that it was not, and thus it followed that it was in Charlie's best interests for ventilation to be withdrawn. Granting a further stay of the declarations, over two months after Francis J's determination of Charlie's best interests, to enable the European Court of Human Rights to consider the

---

123 *GOSH v Yates & Gard* [2017] EWHC 972, [88].
124 *GOSH v Yates* (n 123) [58], [88], [114].
125 *Judgment of the UK Supreme Court in the Case of Charlie Gard*, 19 June 2017, [17] https://www.supremecourt.uk/news/latest-judgment-in-the-matter-of-charlie-gard.html, accessed 29 February 2020.
126 *GOSH v Yates* (n 123) [126].
127 GOSH position statement of the 13th July, [13] https://www.serjeantsinn.com/news/charlie-gard-position-statements/ accessed 29 February 2020.
128 This was the phrase used in the Court of Appeal, *In the Matter of Charles Gard* [2017] EWCA Civ 410. This aspect of the case is considered in chapter seven.

parents' application, Lady Hale observed that it was lawful for his doctors to continue to provide ventilation and artificial nutrition and hydration. However, following the conclusion of Francis J that it was not in Charlie's best interests, his doctors felt that it was 'professionally wrong' to continue to act 'otherwise' and 'contrary' to his best interests.[129]

In the case that followed, MacDonald J noted the unanimous medical evidence, that Isaiah Haastrup had severe and irreversible brain damage which meant that he was unable to breathe for himself and thus dependent upon a ventilator, required regular suctioning of his airways, and nasogastric feeding.[130] The question of a move to palliative care had first been raised six days after his birth, but Isaiah's parents wanted intensive care to be continued; withdrawal of that intensive care was the issue before the court 11 months later. The Trust had made an application to court following a best interests meeting where there was consensus amongst those responsible for his clinical care that there was no evidence that Isaiah was able to interact in a way that brought him pleasure, that there had been no material change in his functioning since birth, that his brain damage was so severe he could not make any substantial improvement, and he could not be weaned off the ventilator.

MacDonald J concluded that Isaiah demonstrated no meaningful response and that he probably had a profoundly depressed level of awareness, but if he was aware then he was also experiencing pain.[131] The judge found that the evidence was that there was no prospect that Isaiah would recover or improve.[132] Ventilation would sustain life 'with no chance of restoring his health or providing benefit in terms of his prognosis' and without 'meaningful awareness of his surroundings'.[133] He would have to remain in intensive care for continued ventilation at risk of potentially fatal chest infections, would require surgery to fit a permanent feeding tube, and possibly further surgery to prevent reflux common in children who are chronically tube fed. It was also likely that his muscle spasticity would increase, resulting in scoliosis and hip dislocation.

MacDonald J's conclusion that continued ventilation was not in Isaiah's best interests was reached on the findings that there was no prospect of recovery or

---

129 *In the matter of Charlie Gard (Permission to Appeal Hearing)*, 19 June 2017, [15], [17] https://www.supremecourt.uk/news/latest-judgment-in-the-matter-of-charlie-gard.html accessed 29 February 2020. The Supreme Court noted that the ECtHR would treat any application with urgency, which it did, finding all complaints manifestly unfounded eight days later, *Charles Gard and Others v United Kingdom*. Application no. 39793/17, 28 June 2017 [85]-[98] http://hudoc.echr.coe.int/eng#{"documentcollectionid2":["DEC GRANDCHAMBER","ADMISSIBILITY","ADMISSIBILITYCOM"],"itemid":["001-175359"]} accessed 29 February 2020.
130 *King's College NHS Trust v Thomas & Haastrup* [2018] EWHC 127, [87].
131 *King's College NHS Trust v Thomas & Haastrup* (n 130) [94], [95].
132 The BBC news website reported that his parents wanted him to have hyperbaric therapy, 'Isaiah Haastrup: Parents make appeal to European Court', 2 March 2018, www.bbc.co.uk/news/uk-england-london-43245813 accessed 5 March 2018.
133 *King's College NHS Trust v Thomas & Haastrup* (n 130) [97].

142 *Limiting Life-Sustaining Treatment Cases*

any improvement. Continued ventilation would sustain his life, putting him at risk of complications which would increase the pain he suffered, if his awareness was sufficient for him to experience pain. But importantly, MacDonald J's conclusion captures something of the human life that Isaiah's condition had deprived him of. His condition meant that he would never be able to engage in meaningful interaction, to see, to move independently, he may have some hearing, but there was no evidence he could make sense of anything he might hear, no evidence that he was aware of what was going on around him, or of an ability to experience enjoyment, pleasure, or comfort, to develop emotional attachment to his family, or to benefit from the experiences of love, human connection, a sense of identity and belonging. His condition would confine Isaiah to being kept alive for his entire life in an ICU sustained by machines.[134] The judicial analysis of best interests was thus based upon the evidence that there was no prospect that Isaiah could improve from a condition which prevented him from interacting, or forming connections or attachments. Whilst this was a judgment about his quality of life, it is far removed from the quality of life which justified the withholding or withdrawal of life-sustaining treatment in the early reported cases.

In the first hearing of the numerous judicial considerations of the future medical treatment of Alfie Evans,[135] Hayden J considered at length the medical evidence of those responsible for the care of Alfie at Alder Hey, the second opinions secured by the Trust and from the parents' expert, and the views of the doctors from Rome and Munich who were prepared to accept him as a patient. Although at that time he had no diagnosis,[136] 15 months after he had first been admitted to hospital, the evidence from the independent expert was that his brain had been irrecoverably devastated by a progressive, untreatable, ultimately fatal, neurodegenerative condition, most likely mitochondrial in origin. His respiratory effort would not sustain life so that he was dependent upon ventilation but that his condition would continue to deteriorate.[137] The conclusion that it was in Alfie's best interests for ventilation to be withdrawn was thus reached upon the evidence that there was no prospect of any improvement, that he could not hear, see, smell, or respond to touch,[138] and although it was unlikely that he could feel pain, it was not possible to know as he did not react.

As Lord Donaldson MR had commented in *Re J*, where another professional is prepared to treat, a transfer should be arranged if it is safe to do so.[139] The clinicians in Rome and Munich who were prepared to take over his care did not have

---

134 *King's College NHS Trust v Thomas & Haastrup* (n 130) [107].
135 *Alder Hey Children's NHS Foundation Trust v Evans* [2018] EWHC 308.
136 His condition was identified after his death as a rare brain condition GABA-transaminase deficiency, BBC News, 'Alfie Evans parents 'feared' they would resent new baby' (3 September 2018) https://www.bbc.co.uk/news/uk-england-merseyside-45402094 accessed 24 February 2020.
137 *Alder Hey Children's NHS Foundation Trust v Evans* (n135) [16]-[17].
138 *Alder Hey Children's NHS Foundation Trust v Evans* (n135) [57].
139 *Re J* (n 19) 28.

a different opinion about Alfie's condition, prognosis, or treatment options but upon the management of his end of life care. The hospital in Rome was prepared to offer long-term ventilation and feeding by nasogastric tube, the German doctor to provide home ventilation and training for his parents in his care. The judge concluded that a transfer would be burdensome for Alfie. It would have put him at risk of infection and there was a risk that his anti-convulsive regime would be compromised. The risk of sudden and undignified death during transfer was not worth taking, given that there was no prospect of any treatment. King LJ in the Court of Appeal quoted from one of his treating doctors who said that, 'we cannot in good conscience agree that by simply transferring Alfie to another hospital (to continue prolonged treatment which is of no benefit to Alfie) that we are acting first and foremost in Alfie's best interests'.[140]

As MacDonald J had said in *Haastrup*,

> It would be extremely unfortunate if the standard response to applications of this nature was to become one of scouring the world for medical experts who simply take the view that the medical, moral, or ethical approach to these issues in their jurisdiction, or in their own practice is preferable to the medical, moral, or ethical approach in this jurisdiction. This is particularly so where parents in the situation these parents find themselves in are understandably desperate to grasp any apparent life raft in the storm that is engulfing them.[141]

Notably, the issue in the cases of Isaiah Haastrup and Alfie Evans was not about the future medical treatment for the child as all the medial evidence was that there were no treatments available that could improve their condition. As Hayden J said in his third judgment in the Alfie Evans case, some two months after his conclusion on Alfie's best interests, the issue before the court had always been, 'what is the appropriate end of life plan for Alfie?'[142]

Over the course of three and a half months, the case of Charlie Gard went through the domestic appeal courts and to the ECtHR before being referred back to Francis J in the High Court. The case of Alfie Evans took the same path twice, with a third hearing before the High Court and appeal against its decision expedited over two months. As these cases progressed through the courts, the parents clutched on to the hope promised by the offer of care elsewhere and the willingness of the courts, out of respect for their desperate situation, to hear the cases. Faced with an insurmountable challenge they fought with all they had to overcome it, in what they genuinely believed was their child's best interests. Had the court first addressed the question whether the therapy being offered to Charlie Gard was an appropriate treatment option supported by a reasonable

---

140 *In the Matter of E (A Child)* [2018] EWCA Civ 550, [22].
141 *King's College NHS Trust v Thomas & Haastrup* (n 130) [83].
142 *Alder Hey Children's NHS Foundation Trust v Evans* [2018] EWHC 953, [3].

body of professional opinion, or in Alfie's case whether there was any treatment which could have improved his condition enabling him to interact with his parents and experience the love surrounding him, the options from which to determine the course that was in the best interests of each child would have been clearly understood.

An Appropriate Treatment Option?

Although it was an Italian hospital and doctors who were prepared to take over the care of Tafida Raqeeb, the court was not concerned with different values about the ethical approach to care at the end of life, as it had been with Isaiah Haastrup and Alfie Evans. MacDonald J was asked to make an SIO and declarations under the courts' inherent jurisdiction that it was lawful to withdraw ventilation from Tafida Raqeeb and to determine a judicial review of the decision of the Trust not to permit her to be transferred to Italy for continued treatment pending the determination of the court of the best interests proceedings.[143] Eight months before the court hearing, five-year-old Tafida suffered catastrophic and irreversible brain damage from a rare and undetected asymptomatic genetic condition, ruptured arteriovenous malformation.[144] Tafida's treating team had reached the conclusion that continued treatment was futile and not in her best interests. Her parents had located a team at the Gaslini Paediatric Hospital in Genoa, Italy, which was prepared to accept her, subject to her parents being responsible for all costs of transfer and treatment. The evidence before the court was that whilst the Italian team thought it was highly unlikely they could improve her condition, they considered that they could ensure her comfort through the provision of palliative care and would explore whether it was appropriate to undertake a tracheotomy to permit home ventilation and through these measures sustain her life in her current condition.[145] The Italian team were prepared to give her more time until a clearer prognosis could be reached, given uncertainties around the outcomes for children with prolonged disorders of consciousness. MacDonald J referred to the situation as one in which 'different teams of reputable clinicians take contrasting views as to the appropriate way forward'.[146]

At the time of the hearing, the evidence before the court was that Tafida was unable to breathe independently and consequently was ventilator dependent, and she was receiving medication for epilepsy but was otherwise medically stable. MacDonald J concluded that the consensus of medical opinion was that it was

---

143 *Tafida Raqeeb (by her Litigation Friend) v Barts NHS Foundation Trust* [2019] EWHC 2531 (Admin); *Barts NHS Foundation Trust v Shalina Begum and Muhhamed Raqeeb & Tafida Raqeeb (by her Children's Guardian)* [2019] EWHC 2530 (Fam). Judicial Review proceedings are considered in chapter three.
144 *Tafida Raqeeb* (n 143) [9].
145 *Tafida Raqeeb* (n 143) [15].
146 *Tafida Raqeeb* (n 143) [25], [113].

Limiting Life-Sustaining Treatment Cases 145

not possible to exclude some level of conscious awareness,[147] and in her resting state she did not perceive pain.[148] The evidence was that medical treatment was unlikely to change her profound cognitive impairment,[149] and the prospect was of developing further debilitating conditions.[150] However, there was also medical evidence that the prognosis for children with prolonged disorders of consciousness was uncertain but that the prognosis for Tafida should become clearer over time.[151] Transfer to Italy carried minimal risk.

The care plan proposed by the Italian team was advanced by a 'competent body of professional opinion', but there was also some evidence that it was consistent with the domestic approach in other areas to children in a similar position to that of Tafida.[152] That care plan was that she should be maintained on life support with a view to her being cared for at home on ventilation where she would benefit from being at home, in the care of her loving and dedicated family, and, if she did have some minimal awareness, benefitting from awareness of both.[153] MacDonald J did not make the declarations sought by the Trust. For Tafida to be treated as her parents wished would not require her doctors to treat contrary to their professional judgment, as there was a competent body of professional opinion, supported by independent experts, willing to accept her as a patient to continue ventilation, giving Tafida more time and the prospect of returning home to her family.

The contrast with the cases with which this chapter started is the development of technology which makes possible the care of children with complex conditions at home and a shift in perceptions of the quality of life that can be enjoyed through the loving care of children who may have severe disabilities but have awareness of what is going on around them, responsiveness to their carers, and the ability to interact with others. What Tafida, and the children in *Re C*, *Re J (1991)*, and *Re J (1993)* could benefit from, but what Charlie Gard, Alfie Evans, Isaiah Haastrup, and many of the children in the recent cases could not, was the ability to form attachments, to experience love, to respond to their families and carers. The more recent cases demonstrate a different appreciation to the early

---

147 *Tafida Raqeeb* (n 143) [161].
148 *Tafida Raqeeb* (n 143) [162].
149 *Tafida Raqeeb* (n 143) [175].
150 *Tafida Raqeeb* (n 143) [168].
151 *Tafida Raqeeb* (n 143) [174].
152 *Tafida Raqeeb* (n 143) [179]. Ms Gollop QC for the Trust submitted that the court did not have before it cogent evidence on this point, [73]. In their commentary on the case, Emma Cave, Joe Brierley and David Archard, observed that the number of children being cared for on long term ventilation is increasing and that inconsistent practice may have arisen as a result of a lack of guidance as to the circumstances in which this is in the best interests of the child, 'Making Decisions for Children – Accommodating Parental Choice in Best Interests Determinations: *Barts Health NHS Trust v Raqeeb* [2019] EWHC 2530 (Fam); *Raqeeb and Barts Health NHS Trust* [2019] EWHC 2531 (Admin)' (2020) 28 Medical Law Review 183.
153 *Tafida Raqeeb* (n 143) [173].

cases, that life with disability can have a quality worth living, particularly if that involves living at home, surrounded by the love of, and interacting with, family. The cases show that there is now greater accommodation of parental wishes with regard to their child's treatment, consistent with the shift in medical law to greater respect for patient autonomy and for the responsibility of the patient for decisions about their treatment. The question is whether there is any appropriate treatment, supported by a competent body of professional opinion, that may improve the condition of the child. If not, and life can be sustained in the current condition, the question is whether the child is aware, responsive, and able to gain pleasure in life through experiencing love of their families and interacting with them.

Professional Judgement, the Limits of the Possible and Duties of Care

The review of the case law concerned with the withholding or withdrawal of life-sustaining treatment from children demonstrates that the legal framework of principles for determining such cases, originating in the early cases of *Re J* in which the Official Solicitor asked for guidance, set out as 'intellectual milestones' by the Court of Appeal in *Wyatt*,[154] and as ten propositions by Holman J in *Re MB*[155] as to how the judge should determine the best interests of the child, is clear and firmly established. It is the circumstances in which cases are referred to court by the child's doctors, having reached the view that the child's quality of life is such that it is not in the best interests of the child for life-sustaining intervention to be provided or continued, that have changed. The circumstances in which the court is asked to undertake a best interests analysis have changed due to a change to medical practice which reflects societal change and the approach within medical law more generally.

A review of the case law charts the shifting landscape of advancing medical technology, medical attitudes to quality of life, societal attitudes to disability,[156] and the parent/doctor relationship. This is evident in the case concerning Midrar Namiq.[157] Born at full term, Midrar was deprived of oxygen due to a cord prolapse

---

154 *Re Wyatt (continuation of order)* (n 52) [87], approving Hedley J in the court below *Re Wyatt* (n 36).
155 *An NHS Trust v MB* (n 35) [16].
156 Although legal challenge was planned to the NICE, *COVID-19 rapid guideline: critical care in adults* (2020), that the 'clinical frailty scale' to assist in the decision-making process did not fully respect the rights of the disabled, particularly healthy adults with autism or learning difficulties and those with stable conditions such as cerebral palsy. NICE revised its advice to make it clear that it should not be used in younger people, people with stable long-term disabilities (e.g., cerebral palsy), learning disabilities, or autism.
157 *Manchester University NHS Foundation Trust v Namiq, Ali, Namiq* [2020] EWHC 180, with reference to *Re A (A Child)* [2015] EWHC 443 in which the court determined the application two days after 19-month-old A had been declared dead four days after choking on a piece of fruit.

and was ventilated. The Trust applied to court two months after two brain stem death tests were carried out, which led his doctors to conclude that Midrar was brain stem dead. The question before the court was whether Midrar was dead according to clinical guidance.[158] Lieven J concluded that Midrar met the criteria for brain stem death, noting that Midrar was believed to have spent the longest time on a ventilator after being found brain stem dead of any person in the UK. The judge's conclusion was that Midrar had died four months earlier when the test confirmed brain stem death.[159]

If the medical evidence is that treatment is unethical or inimical to the doctor's duty to the child, and if there are no appropriate treatment options that might improve the child's condition and no doctor prepared to treat, the conclusion of the court will inevitably be that the provision of treatment or continued treatment is not in the best interests of the child. Submissions to the court and the judgment, because that is the legal and ethical principle, will be articulated in terms of the best interests of the child. When the conclusion is that life-sustaining treatment should be withheld or withdrawn with the consequence that the child will die, parental judgement about the best interests of their child appears to be overridden and replaced by judicial determination which supports clinical judgement. This gives the impression that the state has given up on the child and the parental view of their child's interests judged as misguided or misinformed. However, Trusts, on behalf of doctors who have legal duties to the children in their care, have an obligation to bring before the courts those cases in which parents want their child's life to be continued, but the doctors in the exercise of their professional judgement, supported by second opinions and in compliance with professional guidance, cannot continue. Currently, the majority of cases are now brought before the court only at the point when the treating doctors have reached the conclusion that to continue to maintain life is contrary to their professional and legal duties to the child. It is for the court to assess the medical evidence, to ascertain whether the conclusion of the treating doctors it is supported by a competent body of professional opinion and stands up to logical analysis, and further, whether there is any professional willing to provide the treatment to whom care of the child could be transferred. The role of the court, to protect the interests of the child, parents, doctors, and the public, is to determine whether the decisions about withholding or withdrawing of life-sustaining treatment are reasonable, logical, and socially acceptable conforming to norms of the care of children.

---

158 Academy of Medical Royal Colleges, *A Code of Practice for the Diagnosis and Confirmation of Death* (2008) which does not apply to babies under two months of age and has been supplemented by guidance from RCPCH, *The diagnosis of death by neurological criteria in infants less than two months old* (2015).
159 *Manchester University NHS Foundation Trust v Namiq* (n 157) [52]. The Court of Appeal refused permission to appeal, *Re M (Declaration of Death of Child)* [2020] EWCA Civ 164, confirming that the judge had determined as a matter of fact on the basis of the current clinical guidance that Midrar was dead, so that there could be no best interests analysis.

7 At the Frontiers of Medicine

Introduction: Leaving No Stone Unturned

The exclusive focus upon the best interests analysis in cases concerning the medical treatment of children has resulted in an understanding of such applications as a challenge to the decision of the parents by the Trust and a challenge to parental authority or family autonomy by the state. However, if alongside parental responsibilities the duties which professionals owe to children in their care are recognised, the issue can be understood to be that of determining what is best for the child from the appropriate treatment options. Recognition of professional duties to children in their care separates out the two questions. First, is the treatment the parents want for their child appropriate treatment according to a reasonable body of professional opinion. Second, is that treatment option in the best interests of the child or, if there are treatment options, which of those options is in the best interests of the child. It will be generally accepted and understood that parents will wish to seek all possible, and the best possible, treatment for a seriously ill child, leaving no stone unturned. However, limits have to be placed upon the pursuit of that which is unproven, experimental, innovative, or novel. Normally, fulfilment of parental responsibility and professional duties ensures that, working together, children are treated within reasonable bounds. Where they cannot agree, court intervention is required to ensure that the treatment of the child is according to socially acceptable norms.

The majority of reported cases are about the treatment of seriously ill children or children with complex conditions who have received the highest quality of care, and it is not uncommon for the issue under dispute to concern the provision of innovative treatment. The liver transplant operation at issue in *Re T* was described by Butler-Sloss LJ as 'experimental'[1] and by Waite LJ as 'relatively novel treatment, still unavailable in many countries'.[2] Likewise, Holman J acknowledged in *An NHS Trust v A* that the bone marrow transplant recommended by A's doctors was 'pioneering and evolving' but not 'so experimental as

---

1 *Re T* [1997] 1 WLR 242, 251.
2 *Re T* (n 1), 253.

to be treating A as a proverbial "guinea pig"'.[3] The primary concern of the parents of both children was the pain and distress that had been caused to their child by previous treatment and that which may be caused by the proposed treatment, rather than an objection to the novel nature of the transplant. In both cases the medical evidence from the child's treating doctors and the independent experts was that the transplant was in the child's best interests, demonstrating through the best interests analysis that there was a reasonable body of opinion in support of the transplant.

In the majority of cases, it has been the parent who has wanted something novel to be tried, all conventional treatment options having been exhausted. This chapter considers disputes between parents and doctors about the provision of innovative treatment, therapy, or procedures to a child from the perspectives of both professional duties and the best interests of the child. First, cases in which parents have pursued innovative therapies for their child are considered. Then, the legal and professional duties of doctors in the context of the administration of innovative therapy are explained. The legal and professional duties of doctors and the best interests of the child in the dispute over the administration of innovative therapy to Charlie Gard is then considered. It is argued that, when the issue of the administration of an innovative therapy is before the court, consideration should first be given to the medical evidence that the therapy is an appropriate option supported by a reasonable body of professional opinion. Only if it is, can the court decide whether to try it is in the best interests of the child. To do so recognises professional duties, alongside parental responsibilities, and enables the court to fulfil its public responsibilities to children.

Parental Pursuit of Innovative Therapy

Parental pursuit of innovative therapy, when the treating doctors have advised them that further treatment is not in their child's best interests because the risks and burdens outweigh the possible benefits, is not a new phenomenon. Neither is resort to the courts to resolve the issue. Although the case was not formulated in such terms, the issue in *R v Cambridge Health Authority ex p B* could be understood to be whether the treatment, identified by Jaymee Bowen's father and being offered to her in the private sector by a specialist in adult leukaemia for which the health authority had refused to fund an extra-contractual referral, was an appropriate treatment option supported by a reasonable body of professional opinion and in her best interests.[4]

In January 1995, Jaymee suffered a relapse after a period in remission following treatment for acute myeloid leukaemia as a secondary cancer following

---

3 [2007] EWHC 1696, [55].
4 [1995] 1 FLR 1055. Before the court in judicial review proceedings, considered in chapter three.

treatment for non-Hodgkin's lymphoma.[5] Her father, David Bowen, was told by the doctors treating Jaymee at Addenbrooke's, with whom doctors at the Royal Marsden where Jaymee had earlier undergone a bone marrow transplant agreed, that no further treatment was available and that she only had a few weeks to live.[6] Their professional judgement was that it was in Jaymee's best interests to be given palliative care. Using the library at the Royal Society of Medicine, David Bowen researched leukaemia and its treatment, locating doctors in California who were prepared to perform a second bone marrow transplant.[7] He did not have the funds to pay for this treatment. Further research led him to a specialist in adult leukaemia, Professor Goldman, who was prepared to treat, but his ward, at the Hammersmith Hospital, had no available beds. Professor Goldman recommended Dr Gravett at the private Portland Clinic. He was prepared to administer a further course of chemotherapy and bone marrow transplant, a course described in the judgment as at the 'frontier of medical science'.[8]

A UK specialist in adult treatment was offering innovative and as yet unproven therapy privately as the only hope of prolonging Jaymee's life.[9] In contrast, the paediatricians who had been caring for Jaymee, following evidence-based treatment protocols in the NHS, could only offer palliative care based upon a holistic analysis of her best interests.[10] In their analysis of the case, Chris Ham and Susan Pickard contrasted the differing philosophies informing the views of the paediatricians who had been responsible for her care and those of the specialists in adult cancer prepared to try further therapy. The former, they argued, believed that treatment should be protocol driven, provided within the framework set by the United Kingdom Children's Cancer Study Group, using treatments of proven effectiveness. Where conventional options had been exhausted, experimental treatment should be provided within clinical trials or developmental treatment provided by specialist NHS units.[11] In their judgement, the therapy her father wanted her to have was experimental and neither clinically appropriate nor effective. They considered that it was clinically wrong to submit her to further therapy causing unnecessary suffering with little prospect of cure, a view reached in light of both clinical experience and lack of published data. As the experimental therapy was in their professional judgement not clinically appropriate, it followed that administration of it was not in her best interests.[12] The Court of Appeal allowed

---

5 *Ex parte B* (n 4).
6 *Ex parte B* (n 4). Jaymee was first diagnosed at the age of 6 and had already undergone two courses of chemotherapy, total body irradiation and a bone marrow transplant. Her younger sister, Charlotte, was the donor, raising questions about the duties of parents in balancing the best interests of their children.
7 Chris Ham and Susan Pickard, *Tragic Choices in Health Care: The case of Child B* (King's Fund, 1998) 2–3.
8 *Ex parte B* (n 4).
9 Ham and Pickard (n 7) 71–2.
10 Ham and Pickard (n 7).
11 Ham and Pickard (n 7) 70, 73.
12 Ham and Pickard (n 7).

the health authority's appeal against the decision of the judge to quash the decision not to fund the course of therapy, but it was not necessary for the court, in judicial review proceedings, to examine whether there was a competent body of professional opinion which supported the therapy her father wanted her to have.

The evidence base for the therapy his mother wanted seven-year-old Neon Roberts to have was explored in the court proceedings. Following surgery to remove a malignant brain tumour, his mother wanted him to receive complementary or alternative therapies rather than the 'gold standard' post-operative radiotherapy and chemotherapy which his doctors sought to administer in accordance with guidance from the Childhood Cancer Leukaemia Group. Before the court, the mother relied upon the view of an 'internationally acclaimed expert in agricultural, environmental, and health sustainability'. Dr A, Neon's consultant paediatric oncologist, explained that the therapies recommended by the expert were either experimental, used by patients in relapse, or by patients who could not be treated with standard doses of chemotherapy or radiotherapy. They had not been subjected to the clinical trials necessary before approval for use in the treatment of a child.[13] In contrast Bodey J observed, Dr A, experienced in the treatment of children, was highly impressive in knowledge and experience, worked at the cutting edge of the discipline, kept up with developing techniques, had gone beyond the call of duty in his dedication to the case and, the judge considered, would provide credible alternative therapies.[14] Bodey J invited the mother to identify the two pieces from the published research upon which she relied which best supported her case. The judge considered that neither supported the mother's claim that there were 'Chinese or Russian or other reports which speak to thousands of children surviving cancers without mainstream treatment'.[15] The mother had been unable to provide the court with the evidence required to enable the judge to determine that there was an alternative to conventional treatment which was accepted by a competent body of professional opinion from which the judge could then determine which was in Neon's best interests. Bodey J stated that before a court could authorise an alternative to the standard mainstream treatment it would require more than evidence of 'research and experimentation', of 'ideas and possibilities', or reports of 'success stories'. Bodey J set out the evidence which would need to be provided before a judge could determine that an alternative to conventional treatment was in the best interests of a child. This included,

> the identification of a clinician experienced in treating children aged about seven having this kind of brain cancer, a clinician with access to the necessary equipment and infrastructure to put the suggested treatment into effect and able and willing to take over the medical care of and responsibility for N. [...]

---

13 *An NHS Trust v SR* [2012] EWHC 3842 [13].
14 *An NHS Trust v SR* (n 13) [20].
15 *An NHS Trust v SR* (n 13) [14].

The treatment proposed by any such clinician would have to be (or should preferably be) properly studied, tested, reported on, and peer-reviewed. To have any realistic prospect of becoming selected by the court [...] the proposed plan would have to have a prognosis as to probable survival rate not much less than (and preferably equal to) the sort of survival rate achievable through the use of the orthodox treatment universally applied at present by oncologists in this country.[16]

Whilst approached through a best interests analysis, as only to be expected, here Bodey J was in effect saying that Neon's mother had an alternative view about his medical treatment, but it was not one that was supported by a competent body of medical opinion and thus not one the court could consider to be in the child's best interests.[17]

In contrast, the treatment which the parents of five-year-old Ashya King wanted him to have, Proton Beam Therapy rather than conventional radiotherapy, as post-operative treatment following surgery to remove a malignant brain tumour, medulloblastoma, was supported by a competent body of professional opinion. His treating doctors could not administer it to him as, at the time, Proton Beam Therapy was not available in the UK.[18] His parents believed that Proton Beam Therapy, which they had discovered from a search of the internet, offered the chance of fewer long-term detrimental effects upon his future quality of life than conventional radiotherapy, as post-operative treatment necessary to ensure all cancerous cells were eradicated. Brain surgery had caused Ashya an acquired brain injury, paralysis, he was unable to communicate or swallow, and thus was fed by nasogastric tube.[19] Radiotherapy risks serious side-effects including intellectual and cognitive impairment, effects upon growth, thyroid (which may cause lethargy or weight gain] and sub- or infertility, and risks secondary cancers in later life.[20] Proton Beam Therapy results in a lower dose of

---

16 *An NHS Trust v SR* (n 13) [25].
17 Bodey J also noted that his doctors could have provided the treatment given that Neon's father had given consent but that he understood the decision to apply to court given the serious nature of the treatment in question and the vehement objection of the mother.
18 *In the Matter of Ashya King* [2014] EWHC 2964. Except low energy proton therapy for patients with eye tumours at The Clatterbridge Cancer Centre NHS Foundation Trust. The Christie NHS Proton Beam Therapy Centre, Manchester, opened in 2018 and a centre is due to open at University College London Hospital in 2020, https://www.england.nhs.uk/commissioning/spec-services/highly-spec-services/pbt/ accessed 24 February 2020. Upon application by the consultant individual cases are reviewed by a national panel of clinical experts. If the panel determines that the patient is suitable for proton beam therapy in line with NHS England clinical commissioning policies, a referral is made to either the NHS centre in Manchester or, until both NHS proton beam therapy centres are fully operational, one of the NHS commissioned overseas centres in Germany, the USA or Switzerland.
19 *In the Matter of Ashya King* (n 18) [7].
20 *An NHS Trust v SR* (n 13) [18]-[19].

radiotherapy to the tissues around the tumour than occurs with x-ray techniques potentially lessening the damaging effects.

Although an appropriate treatment for certain forms of cancer, Proton Beam Therapy was not available at the time in the UK. Patients who met the criteria stated in National Specialist Commissioning Team guidance were funded by NHS England for treatment abroad. Ashya's consultant at Southampton General referred his case to the NHS England Proton Clinical Reference Panel. The guidance on referrals stated that funding would only be approved for 'prioritised diagnostic categories and sites' after consideration of other factors affecting whether proton therapy offers advantages over conventional therapy.[21] Medulloblastoma was not then on the list. Funding was thus declined. His doctors could, therefore, only offer conventional, clinically tested, post-operative chemotherapy, and radiotherapy. His parents asked Southampton for a private referral to the Proton Therapy Centre in Prague which had treated cases of medulloblastoma and was willing to treat Ashya, but they did not, at that time, have the funds to pay for his treatment. The Trust maintained that, whilst the benefits were unproven in the treatment of medulloblastoma, they did not oppose the family's decision to obtain Proton Therapy. They could not provide it but would support it being provided to Ashya elsewhere, if the necessary arrangements could be made.[22] Thus, although Ashya was being offered treatment that was 'gold standard' within the NHS, his parents' concern was that, due to lack of funding within the NHS, Ashya was not being offered the best possible treatment. In his parents' opinion, that was only available through private treatment abroad.

His parents removed Ashya from Southampton General, without the knowledge of his treating doctors, taking him to Spain where they intended to sell their house in order to raise the money to pay for his private treatment at the Centre in Prague. By the time Baker J decided upon his treatment in wardship proceedings, a week after the family were located, there was no dispute. Southampton General did not oppose the provision of Proton Therapy given that the necessary arrangements were then in place. The doctors responsible for his treatment in Southampton were satisfied that it was an appropriate treatment option and there was a competent body of professional opinion prepared to administer it. Persuaded that there was a 'reasonable and coherent alternative treatment plan' for the provision of the post-operative care that Ashya now urgently needed, with funding and transport arrangements not opposed by the local authority, CAFCASS, or the hospital trust, Baker J authorised his treatment in Prague.[23]

---

21 National Specialised Commissioning Team, *Guidance for the Referral of Patients Abroad for NHS Proton Treatment,* July 2011 www.england.nhs.uk/commissioning/spec-services/npc-crg/group-b/b01/ accessed 19 January 2015, 2.5, 3.
22 *In the Matter of Ashya King* (n 18) [20].
23 *In the Matter of Ashya King* (n 18). Wardship was then discharged. NHS England subsequently funded the court-authorised treatment, Sarah Boseley, 'NHS to pay for Ashya King's Proton Therapy Treatment', *The Guardian* (26 September 2014) 8.

154 *At the Frontiers of Medicine*

These cases arose from parental concerns about the treatment options offered to their child within the NHS and their determination to secure treatment for their child which offered the only hope of prolonging life or which minimised the serious side-effects of treatment necessary for a life-changing illness. The therapies the parents wanted for their child could be considered 'novel', 'innovative', 'experimental', 'alternative', or 'unproven'. Over the forty years in which the courts have been asked to resolve issues about children's medical treatment, there have been radical developments in medical science and technology and hence, the range of treatments available. Innovative therapies may become appropriate treatment options, as did the donor lymphocyte infusion administered to Jaymee Bowen,[24] or the Proton Beam Therapy administered to Ashya King in the treatment of medulloblastoma.[25] But, as Joe Brierley and Vic Larcher have observed, rare and unique diseases create the need for compassionate use of novel therapies which have a 'theoretical basis' but which 'lack research or experimental justification'.[26] It is the role of the law to ensure that the interests of seriously ill children for whom conventional treatment options have been exhausted are protected, and that the concern of their parents who desperately want to find something to improve their child's quality or quantity of life and doctors whose primary goal is to use their knowledge and expertise to cure, improve health, and alleviate suffering are kept within acceptable limits. The role of the law is to ensure that the desires of parents and professionals to benefit the child are not pursued to the extent of risking causing the child harm. The next section explains the law within which the compassionate use of innovative therapies occurs, placing it within parental and professional duties to the child within acceptable norms for the care of children.[27]

Innovative Therapy: Definitions and Regulation

Various terminology is used in the case law in which parents have refused to consent to the administration of conventional treatment, preferring instead therapy

---

24 Panorama, *The Story of Child B* (26 October 1995) reviewed in Editorial, 'Rational Rationing', *The Times* (27 October 1995) a different course of treatment to that considered by the court.
25 *Clinical Commissioning Policy: Proton Beam Therapy for Children, Teenagers and Young Adults in the treatment of malignant and non-malignant tumours* (2018) https://www.england.nhs.uk/commissioning/wp-content/uploads/sites/12/2019/07/Interim-Policy-PBT-for-CTYA-for-malignant-and-non-malignant-tumours.pdf accessed 24 February 2020.
26 Joe Brierley and Vic Larcher, 'Compassionate and innovative treatments in children: a proposal for an ethical framework' (2009) 94 *Archives of Disease in Childhood* 651, 652. They propose an ethical framework which directs the decision-maker to scientific rationale, clinical judgement, best interests, informed consent from the competent child or the child's family and just allocation of resources.
27 An overview of the ethical issues is provided in Nuffield Council on Bioethics, *Briefing Note: Patient access to experimental treatment* (2018).

that is pioneering, innovative, experimental, or at the frontier of medicine. The term 'innovative therapy' will be used in this chapter, defined by Joe Brierley and Vic Larcher as 'any newly introduced treatment, or a new modification to an existing therapy with unproven efficacy and side effect profile, which is being used in the best interests of a patient, often on an experimental and/or compassionate basis'.[28] The juxtaposition of innovative and therapy is designed to indicate that, whilst it is of unproven benefit, it is administered with therapeutic intent.[29] Although the therapies considered in this chapter are requested for individual children rather than within a programme of clinical research,[30] it is hoped but not known if the therapy will be of benefit to the child.[31] It is likely that questions about innovative therapies will most often arise in relation to children with rare and severe or potentially fatal conditions, when all appropriate treatment options have been exhausted so that something new and unproven offers the last remaining hope.

In comparison with the regulation of clinical research trials, there is no single regulatory framework applicable to the use of innovative therapies.[32] As has been stressed throughout this book, doctors have legal duties to children in their care, at the most basic, the duty to act in accordance with a competent body of professional opinion which stands up to logical scrutiny in diagnosis, identification of treatment options, and provision of treatment. However, as was recognised in *Simms*,[33] when other options have been exhausted and an innovative therapy is considered for a seriously ill child, there may not be a competent body of professional opinion with the knowledge and experience to support its use. In such circumstances, as Butler-Sloss P stated in *Simms*, the *Bolam* test must not stifle innovation. In *Simms*, upon applications by their parents, the judge was asked to approve the administration of unlicensed therapy to two teenagers, one 18 and one 16 years old, both of whom had been rendered incompetent and entirely dependent by probable variant Creutzfeldt-Jakob disease (vCJD). Told there was no cure for vCJD, the father of the 18 year old, later identified as Jonathan Simms, through his research on the internet, found details of Japanese research

---

28 Brierley and Larcher (n 26).
29 Sara Fovargue preferred the term 'procedure' because it covers a range of interventions including medicines, surgery, therapies, devices, and implants, and also because, unlike the terms treatment and therapy, it does not suggest that the intervention is of proven benefit, 'The (Ab)use of Those with No Other Hope? Ethical and Legal Safeguards for Recipients of Experimental Procedures' (2013) 22 *Cambridge Quarterly of Healthcare Ethics* 181.
30 Which are subject to different regulatory regimes, see Hazel Biggs, *Healthcare Research Ethics and Law: Regulation, Review and Responsibility* (Routledge, 2009).
31 Sara Fovargue, 'Preserving the Therapeutic Alliance: Court Intervention and Experimental Treatment Requests', in Imogen Goold, Jonathan Herring and Cressida Auckland (eds), *Parental Rights, Best Interests and Significant Harms: Medical Decision-Making on Behalf of Children Post-Great Ormond Street Hospital v Gard*, (Hart, 2019) 153–176, 162.
32 Fovargue (n 31).
33 *Donald Simms and Jonathan Simms v An NHS Trust and Secretary of State for Health; PA and JA v An NHS Trust and Secretary of State for Health* [2002] EWHC 2734.

into unlicensed therapy, described at various points in the judgment as 'innovative', 'experimental', and 'pioneering', in which Pentosan Polysulphate infusions would be administered, following a surgical procedure, directly into the brain. There was research of its use in mice, but it was not known whether it would work in humans or on vCJD.[34] Butler-Sloss P first addressed the question as to whether there was a competent body of professional opinion within the United Kingdom which supported the therapy, subject to the risks and benefits of the therapy. The judge, concerned that the *Bolam* test should not 'inhibit medical progress', observed that if *Bolam* had to be 'complied with to its fullest extent' then no innovative treatment or procedures could be tried, giving as examples the use of penicillin and heart transplant surgery.[35] The evidence provided by three English doctors and the research of the Japanese neuropathologist led her to the conclusion that there was a responsible body of relevant professional opinion in support of administration of the therapy.[36] On the question as to whether this was a reasonable and logical opinion, as required by *Bolitho*, Butler-Sloss P explained that she considered benefit to a patient who will not recover to include improvement from their current condition, continuation in their current condition without deterioration for longer than may have been the case, and prolongation of life for longer than might otherwise have been.[37] Assessment of risks and benefits led the judge to the conclusion that the responsible body of medical opinion was a reasonable or logical one, as required by *Bolitho*. There was no alternative treatment, and although the benefits and risks of the innovative therapy were unknown, the evidence was that the therapy would not increase suffering and may benefit them and that it was reasonable to try it.[38] As John Harrington has observed,[39] Butler-Sloss P applied a 'fairly weak' version of the *Bolam* test based on the absence of negative opinions from the three English medical experts and the research of the Japanese neuropathologist. Margaret Brazier and Sara Fovargue have suggested that as long as there is evidence of a benefit to the particular patient such an interpretation of *Bolam* and *Bolitho* allows 'responsible innovation'.[40]

In addition to securing an evidence base for the potential benefits of the therapy and reassuring themselves about their professional judgement by consulting with colleagues, doctors will inform their practice by good practice guidelines. Recognising that there may be an urgent need where conventional treatments are producing no benefit, the Declaration of Helsinki, the World Medical Association

---

34 *Simms* (n 33) [22].
35 *Simms* (n 33) [48].
36 *Simms* (n 33) [51].
37 *Simms* (n 33) [57].
38 *Simms* (n 33) [57].
39 John Harrington, 'Deciding Best Interests: Medical Progress, Clinical Judgment and the "Good Family"' [2003] 3 *Web Journal of Current Legal Issues*.
40 Margaret Brazier and Sara Fovargue, 'Transforming wrong into right: What is "proper medical treatment"?' in Sara Fovargue and Alexandra Mullock (eds), *The Legitimacy of Medical Treatment: What Role for the Medical Exception?* (Routledge, 2015), 12–31, 29.

statement of ethical principles for research, provides on the use of 'unproven interventions in clinical practice', that,

> In the treatment of an individual patient, where proven interventions do not exist or other known interventions have been ineffective, the physician, after seeking expert advice, with informed consent from the patient or a legally authorised representative, may use an unproven intervention, if in the physician's judgement it offers hope of saving life, re-establishing health, or alleviating suffering. This intervention should subsequently be made the object of research, designed to evaluate its safety and efficacy.'[41]

In the UK, Regulation 167 of the Human Medicines Regulations 2012[42] permits the use of unlicensed medicine, that is, medicine used outside the terms of the UK licence or which have no licence for use in the UK. Guidance provided by the Medicines and Healthcare Products Regulatory Agency[43] states that doctors are allowed to prescribe unlicensed therapies without reference to the licensing authority, subject to demonstrating the patients' special clinical needs and the doctor's acceptance of responsibility for delivery of the therapy and follow up care. This is reflected in GMC guidance on the prescription of medicines and

---

41 World Medical Association, *Declaration of Helsinki – Ethical Principles for Medical Research Involving Human Subjects* (2013) para.37 https://www.wma.net/policies-post/wma-declaration-of-helsinki-ethical-principles-for-medical-research-involving-human-subjects/ accessed 8 March 2020. The Access to Medical Treatments (Innovation) Act 2016 is intended to promote access to innovative medical treatment by the establishment of a database of use of off-label and unlicensed medicines. Provisions which would have required a record of the results of any ad hoc use of innovative treatments for the benefit of subsequent patients, including both beneficial and harmful effects and failures to respond, were dropped. Whilst the Act has been passed, the regulations required for introduction of the database have not yet been. When originally introduced by Lord Saatchi as the Medical Innovation Bill in 2014, it was concerned with the law relating to negligence, claiming that a fear of litigation was discouraging medical innovation, for critical examination see José Miola, 'Bye-bye Bolitho? The curious case of the Medical Innovation Bill' (2015) 15 *Medical Law International* 124; José Miola, 'Postscript to the Medical Innovation Bill: clearing up loose ends' (2019) 11 *Law, Innovation and Technology* 17.
42 Human Medicines Regulations 2012, SI 2012/1916, consolidating the Medicines Act 1968, statutory instruments and amending instruments and EU enactments, notably Directive 2001/83/EC of the European Parliament and of the Council on the Community Code relating to Medicinal Products for Human Use (2001), https://ec.europa.eu/health//sites/health/files/files/eudralex/vol-1/dir_2001_83_cons2009/2001_83_cons2009_en.pdf accessed 8 March 2020, *Explanatory Memorandum to the Human Medicines Regulations 2012*, No. 1916, http://www.legislation.gov.uk/uksi/2012/1916/pdfs/uksiem_20121916_en.pdf accessed 8 March 2020.
43 MHRA, *The supply of unlicensed medicinal products ('specials') Guidance Note 14* (2014) https://www.gov.uk/government/publications/supply-unlicensed-medicinal-products-specials accessed 8 March 2020; MHRA, *Off-label or Unlicensed Use of Medicines: Prescribers' Responsibilities* (2014) https://www.gov.uk/drug-safety-update/off-label-or-unlicensed-use-of-medicines-prescribers-responsibilities accessed 8 March 2020.

devices, which provides that unlicensed medicines may be prescribed where, on the assessment of the individual patient, it is necessary for medical reasons to meet the specific needs of the patient.[44] The guidance requires that the doctor must be satisfied that the evidence demonstrates the safety and efficacy of the medicine, must take responsibility for prescribing the medicine, overseeing the patient's care, monitoring, and any follow up treatment, or ensure that arrangements are made for another suitable doctor to do so. They must also keep records of the medicines prescribed and the reasons for prescribing an unlicensed medicine.[45] Vic Larcher, Helen Turnham and Joe Brierley have suggested that clinical ethics committees have a role in cases of children with life-threatening or seriously debilitating conditions for which there are no comparable or satisfactory alternative therapies or appropriate clinical trial in which they could enrol, or where there is resistance to, or an inability to tolerate, conventional therapy.[46] They argued that consideration by a clinical ethics committee could provide a 'principled, consistent, fair, and transparent response'[47] that balances the need for those with serious illnesses to be protected from harm whilst responding to demands for 'early use of innovative or experimental treatment on a compassionate basis'.[48]

Beyond fulfilling the standard of reasonable care, doctors should work in partnership with parents to determine the best interests of the child. In order for parents to make decisions on behalf of their child, they need to be provided with information about the treatment options from which, ideally together with doctors, they can determine which is best for the chid. As the judgment of the Supreme Court in *Montgomery* made clear, doctors must make information about the treatment options available to patients and presumably the parents of child patients, including why the doctor considers one option is medically preferable.[49] When conventional treatment options have been exhausted and a doctor is considering an innovative therapy, parents need to be informed of the innovative nature of the procedure and the potential risks and benefits. Where the parent has identified an innovative therapy, doctors will likewise need to discuss with the parents its innovative nature and potential risks and benefits. If the doctor, in the exercise of their professional judgement, considers that the therapy identified by a parent is not medically acceptable, they would have to explain why they did not consider the procedure to be an appropriate option. Whether it be the use of

---

44 GMC, *Good practice in prescribing and managing medicines and devices* (2013) paras 67-71, file:///D:/Research%202018%20Book/materials%20read/GMC%20prescribing.pdf accessed 8 March 2020, providing more detailed advice on fulfilling *Good Medical Practice* (2013) paras 12, 14, 16, 18, 19, 21.
45 GMC (n 44) para 70.
46 Vic Larcher, Helen Turnham and Joe Brierley, 'Medical Innovation in a Children's Hospital: "Diseases desperate grown by desperate appliance are relieved, or not at all"' (2018) 32 *Bioethics* 36, 38-9.
47 Larcher, Turnham and Brierley (n 46) 42.
48 Larcher, Turnham and Brierley (n 46) 36.
49 *Montgomery v Lanarkshire Health Board* [2015] UKSC 11, [95].

mechanical devices, the post-operative administration of Proton Beam Therapy, or 'alternative' therapies, it is necessary to establish that the innovative therapy is an appropriate option, trial of which was supported by a reasonable body of professional opinion, without limiting reasonable innovation for compassionate use. That what is proposed is an appropriate option, albeit without the information about risks and benefits which supports conventional treatment, is necessary before it is an option to be considered as in the best interests of the child.

Having concluded that the therapy was supported by a reasonable body of professional opinion capable of withstanding logical analysis, the next question in *Simms* was whether it was in the best interests of the teenagers. Butler-Sloss P considered that trial of therapy was in the best interests of the patients assessed in the 'widest possible way', 'to include the medical and non-medical benefits and disadvantages, the broader welfare issues of the two patients, their abilities, their future with or without treatment, the views of the families, and the impact of refusal of the applications'.[50] Whilst there were risks involved in the therapy and its administration, it offered the chance of a slightly longer life within their devoted and caring families.[51] Butler-Sloss P gave much weight to the views of the parents, recognising the 'agony' they had gone through in witnessing the deterioration of their children and their deep commitment to the therapy, whilst considering that they recognised the risks and the uncertainty of benefit and would not prolong life if their child was suffering.[52] Whether innovative therapy was in the best interests of the child was the issue in the case of Charlie Gard.

Charlie Gard, the Courts, and Innovative Therapy

Parental responsibility, professional duties, the public interest, and the role of the state in the protection of the welfare of the child were all raised in the dispute in 2017 whether it was lawful and in Charlie Gard's best interests to have a trial of an innovative therapy. GOSH applied for a declaration under the inherent jurisdiction and a SIO that continued ventilation of Charlie Gard was not in his best interests and it was therefore lawful to withdraw it. Francis J also had to determine whether the provision of innovative nucleoside bypass therapy was in Charlie's best interests.[53] This was because, although neither Charlie's parents nor the court could require his doctors to treat contrary to their professional judgement, there was a doctor in the US who was prepared to try the therapy, and, through crowdfunding, his parents had raised the money to take him to America for a trial of the therapy. His parents agreed with his doctors that Charlie's 'quality of life was not one that should be sustained without hope of

---

50 *Simms* (n 33) [60].
51 *Simms* (n 33) [61].
52 *Simms* (n 33) [64].
53 *GOSH v Yates & Gard* [2017] EWHC 972 [27].

improvement'.[54] Consequently, as McFarlane LJ observed upon appeal, 'the sole issue in the hearing before the judge turned upon the evaluation of the viability of the only alternative treatment option, namely, nucleoside therapy'.[55]

Charlie Gard appeared to be a healthy baby when he was born in August 2016. At eight weeks old, he was admitted to hospital and transferred to the care of GOSH where he remained on a ventilator and was fed by nasogastric tube for the rest of his short life. Charlie was diagnosed with an extremely rare, inherited, progressive condition, infantile onset encephalomyopathic mitochondrial DNA depletion syndrome, MDDS. Mitochondrial conditions affect the generation of the energy supply of cells,[56] and in Charlie's case, affected his ability to move, breathe, neurological functioning, and hearing.

Following what was described by one of the GOSH consultants as a 'parent-driven exploration of all alternatives internationally', Charlie's parents were in contact with parents of children who had received nucleoside therapy for a similar mitochondrial condition, TK2, and whose quality of life had improved. There was no prospect of a cure, but his parents believed it offered a chance of improving the length and quality of his life.[57] Charlie's parents were thus determined that he should have this 'one shot, one chance of life'. The doctors responsible for Charlie's medical treatment at GOSH had initially been prepared to try the therapy. As it had not been tested or used in patients with Charlie's condition, his clinical team started to prepare an application to the GOSH Rapid Response Clinical Ethics Committee to seek approval for a trial of the therapy as a safeguard to the rights and interests of the child. In January 2017, before the application could be made, Charlie had seizures which his doctors considered caused severe and irreversible brain damage. This deterioration in his condition led his doctors to the conclusion that it was no longer in Charlie's best interests to try the therapy; it was, in their opinion, by then too late to present a chance of having a positive effect on his quality of life. As a consequence, his doctors concluded that the burdens of everyday living outweighed the benefits and that it was not in his interests to be maintained on a ventilator, with associated pain and suffering, for the administration of therapy which was of uncertain benefit. The views of the US doctor, Professor Hirano, were considered by the multidisciplinary treating team. They secured second opinions from St. Mary's, Southampton, Newcastle Upon Tyne NHS Foundation Trust, and the independent expert for the parents from Southampton General to test whether there was a reasonable basis for trial of the therapy informed by the practice of colleagues. Second opinions from 'world leading authorities' supported their conclusion that withdrawal of life-sustaining

---

54 *GOSH v Yates & Gard* (n 53) [126], the question of withdrawal of life-sustaining treatment is considered in chapter six.
55 *In the Matter of Charles Gard* [2017] EWCA Civ 410, [19].
56 Department of Health, *Mitochondrial Donation: A consultation on draft regulations to permit the use of new treatment techniques to prevent the transmission of a serious mitochondrial disease from mother to child* (2014) 1.4.
57 *GOSH v Yates & Gard* (n 53) [107]–[112].

treatment was reasonable and in accordance with RCPCH guidelines.[58] There was then a competent body of professional opinion held by the treating team at GOSH, supported by second opinions and the expert on behalf of the parents, that there was no further treatment which could improve Charlie's condition.[59] His parents rejected his doctors' assessment of the severity of his brain damage, refused their consent to the withdrawal of ventilation, and maintained the view that he should be given the chance of benefitting from nucleoside therapy which Professor Hirano was prepared to administer.

The evidence before the High Court in April 2017 was that nucleoside bypass therapy had never been administered to a child with the form of mitochondrial depletion syndrome which Charlie had, nor had it been tested on mice with this mutation.[60] The therapy was being administered to children with a different mitochondrial condition, the TK2 mutation. Whilst there was scientific rationale that it was theoretically possible that it would be effective, there was no clinical evidence. A key difference between the two conditions was that to be beneficial with the RRM2B mutation which Charlie had, the drugs would have to cross the blood/brain barrier enabling it to work on the brain in the same way as the rest of the body,[61] of which there was 'theoretical and anecdotal', but no direct, evidence.[62]

Charlie's parents could not understand why they were prevented from accepting the offer of treatment from an expert made in the exercise of his professional judgement. As Francis J observed in April, at that time Professor Hirano, a recognised expert in a highly specialised field, was a 'lone voice' in his willingness to try the therapy.[63] Francis J noted that although Professor Hirano had been given access to Charlie's medical records and had seen the latest EEG, he had not examined Charlie.[64] On the basis of the then most recent EEG, Professor Hirano told the court that the damage to Charlie's brain was more severe than he had thought and agreed with Charlie's treatment team that the therapy was 'unlikely' to 'help Charlie's severe neurological disease'.[65] However, the probability was low but it was not zero, and he was prepared to try as it was the only option; without it Charlie's condition was fatal.[66] It was agreed that the administration of the therapy itself, a powder mixed into food, presented little risk.

---

58 *GOSH v Yates & Gard* (n 53) [60] referring to the RCPCH framework for good medical practice, *Making decisions to limit treatment in life-limiting and life-threatening conditions in children: a framework for practice* (2015) Archives of Disease in Childhood 1.
59 *GOSH v Yates & Gard* (n 53) [88].
60 Francis J explained that as a consequence, he viewed the therapy to be experimental rather than pioneering, *GOSH v Yates & Gard* (n 53) [49].
61 *GOSH v Yates & Gard* (n 53) [73].
62 *GOSH v Yates & Gard* (n 53) [76], [101].
63 *GOSH v Yates & Gard* (n 53) [16].
64 *GOSH v Yates & Gard* (n 53) [94], [98].
65 *GOSH v Yates & Gard* (n 53) [75].
66 *GOSH v Yates & Gard* (n 53) [127], [104].

In April, whilst the parents had identified an expert who was willing to try the therapy, at that time, the weight of evidence before the judge from the GOSH clinicians, second opinions, and the consultant instructed by the family was that, given the deterioration in Charlie's condition caused by the seizures he had suffered from January, the therapy was futile. It would be of 'no effective benefit' but would prolong his suffering.[67] At the first hearing, whilst there was an expert in the United States who was willing to try the therapy, there was not the evidence that the innovative therapy that the parents wished Charlie to have was an appropriate option, supported by a reasonable body of professional opinion, from which the parents, and then the judge, could choose according to their judgement of his best interests. The judge made the declarations sought by the Trust, having concluded that it was not in Charlie's best interests to undergo a trial of the therapy and consequently not in his best interests for ventilation to be continued, a view shared by the Guardian who was appointed by the court to provide independent representation of Charlie's interests.

The appeal process exhausted,[68] in July 2017, at the request of Charlie's parents, GOSH returned to the High Court for evaluation of what his parents hoped amounted to new evidence that the therapy offered a chance of improving the length and quality of their son's life. Whilst the evidence had not been before the court in April, Counsel for Charlie's parents, Grant Armstrong, submitted in July that they had new evidence about the therapy which meant there was a competent body of professional opinion which supported its provision. The parents' position statement submitted that they had research evidence of prospects of muscle recovery, reduction in artificial ventilation, NBT crossing the Brain Blood Barrier, and a small but significant chance of ameliorating Charlie's brain function. They had a team of 'independent international experts' who had met with his treating team and examined Charlie, and having analysed his most recent EEG and brain MRI, remained willing to support provision of the therapy or were offering to provide it.[69]

However, as the GOSH position statement explained, Professor Hirano stated in his evidence that he had not examined Charlie, read Charlie's contemporaneous medical records, viewed Charlie's brain imaging, read the second opinions, or the April judgment.[70] As Francis J explained in his July judgment,

[i]t seems to me to be a remarkably simple proposition that if a doctor is to give evidence to this court about the prospect of effective treatment in

---

67 *GOSH v Yates & Gard* (n 53) [93].
68 See the Appendix for the progression of the case though the appeals process.
69 Position statement on behalf of the parents, 24 & 25 July, [6], https://www.serjeantsinn.com/news/charlie-gard-position-statements/ accessed 29 February 2020.
70 Position statement on behalf of GOSH, 24 July, [10], https://www.serjeantsinn.com/news/charlie-gard-position-statements/ accessed 29 February 2020.

respect of a child whose future is being considered by the court, that doctor should see the patient before the court can sensibly rely upon his evidence.[71]

The conclusions of his treating team at GOSH were tested in multidisciplinary team meetings, informed by second opinions, the views of independent experts, and professional guidance. The conclusions of Professor Hirano were not tested in the same way and, as Jonathan Montgomery has suggested, it was questionable whether the position of Professor Hirano amounted to 'responsible professional practice' that would have fulfilled the standard of care owed to his patient.[72]

Consequently, at the invitation of Francis J, Professor Hirano came to London to examine Charlie and participated in a multidisciplinary meeting to discuss his condition and any viable therapy with his treating team. It was agreed that Charlie would undergo further tests. An MRI body scan, which had not previously been carried out, revealed the extent to which he had suffered irreversible muscle atrophy. Charlie's parents then agreed with his treating team that the therapy 'no longer offer[ed] a chance of a meaningful recovery to Charlie'[73] and that '[f]or Charlie, it is now too late'.[74] Consequently, the further evidence which Charlie's parents had amassed was not presented to, or evaluated by, the judge. His parents position statement explained that, 'when on the verge of being able to satisfy this Court (by new evidence and/or a new appreciation of existing evidence) that treatment was in Charlie's best interests, the parents [...], consistent with the proper exercise of their parental rights to protect their son's best interests'[75] withdrew their opposition to the orders.[76] Charlie's parents fought through the courts whilst they believed that he was being offered a viable alternative therapeutic option which gave him the chance of a better quality of life.[77] The initial difference of opinion between his treating team and Professor Hirano was not a difference in evaluation of risks and benefits, or different values informing their practice, but a question of medical knowledge of the patient.[78] The application of the *Bolam* test to innovative therapies, concerned not to stifle innovation, still

---

71 *GOSH v Gard, Yates and Gard* [2017] EWHC 1909, [9].
72 Jonathan Montgomery, 'The 'tragedy' of Charlie Gard: a case study for regulation of innovation?' (2019) 11 *Law, Innovation and Technology* 155, 170.
73 Position statement on behalf of the parents (n 69) [19].
74 Position statement on behalf of the parents (n 69) [31], [18].
75 Position statement on behalf of the parents (n69) [31].
76 *GOSH v Gard, Yates and Gard* (n 71).
77 The ECtHR found the parents' complaint that their Article 2 right to life had been infringed to be manifestly unfounded. Article 2 did not require access to experimental treatment to be regulated in any particular way and the UK had a regulatory framework in place which was derived from the relevant European Directives, *Charles Gard and Others v United Kingdom*. Application no. 39793/17, 28 June 2017, http://hudoc.echr.coe.int/eng#{"document collectionid2":["DECGRANDCHAMBER","ADMISSIBILITY","ADMISSIBILITYCOM"],"itemid":["001-175359"]} accessed 29 February 2020 [55], [86]-[87], [101-103].
78 *Montgomery* (n 49) [84].

requires an evidence base for the decision to try a novel therapy when all conventional treatment options have been exhausted.

Whilst there was scope for a difference of opinion as to whether it was in the best interests of a child with a progressive fatal condition to undergo an innovative therapy which offered a very small chance of improving quality of life, whether what the parents wanted amounted to an appropriate option according to a reasonable body of professional opinion had to be established before the court could determine whether it was in the Charlie's best interests to receive it. If there had been a reasonable body of professional opinion supporting the trial of the therapy, that may have led Charlie's treating team to have reassessed their professional judgement and to try the therapy, as they had initially been prepared to do. If, in their professional judgement, they could not do so, the best interests analysis would also have to assess the risks of transfer to the care of the doctor who was prepared to try the therapy. However, had consideration first been given to the evidence that the therapy was an appropriate option, supported by a reasonable body of professional opinion, from which the parents or court could then choose, the issue in the case and the evidence required to resolve it would have been clear. It would have been clear that the evidence that the parents sought to bring before the court in July was required before the therapy could be considered an appropriate option which they, or the judge, could choose.

Parents will be concerned to secure treatment for their children which offers the hope of a chance of life, and doctors will provide innovative therapy to seriously ill children or children with complex conditions for whom all conventional treatment has been exhausted, complying with their legal and professional duties to children in their care. As Emma Cave and Emma Nottingham observed in their commentary on the case of Charlie Gard, 'controls over access to innovative medicine are important to protect patients vulnerable to unsubstantiated promises of hope'.[79] In the majority of cases, these controls are provided by parents and doctors together making decisions, fulfilling their parental responsibilities and professional duties to the child. When there is doubt or disagreement, review by the court is necessary to ensure that decisions to provide innovative therapy to individual children meet socially acceptable standards depending upon the potential benefits, burdens, and risks. To establish that there is a reasonable body of opinion which considers the therapy appropriate for compassionate use, the court will need evidence of opinions from other practitioners, which might be from other disciplines within the multidisciplinary treatment team, second opinions, or independent experts. Compliance with professional guidance could also provide evidence that the professional judgement was supported by colleagues. An exclusive focus upon best interests meant that the initial set of legal proceedings failed to make clear that the doctor who was offering the hope of an alternative to the parents of Charlie Gard had insufficient knowledge of the medical evidence

---

[79] Emma Cave and Emma Nottingham, 'Who Knows Best (Interests)? The Case of Charlie Gard' (2018) 26 *Medical Law Review* 500, 503.

for it to amount to an appropriate option from which the decision could then be made as to best interests. This contrasted with the good practice evident on the part of the treating team at GOSH through which they satisfied themselves that their professional judgement was a reasonable one. This good practice included discussions in the multidisciplinary treatment team, securing second opinions, the opinions from independent experts, and compliance with professional guidance. Such good practice serves to protect the interests of the child, parents, and doctors in cases where there is no disagreement, as well as providing evidence for the court when there is a dispute. Separate consideration should be given to the evidence upon which the doctors, in their professional judgement and fulfilment of their legal duties to the child, have reached the conclusion that an innovative therapy is an appropriate option. Only then can it be decided if trial of that is an option that can be in the best interests of the child.

Conclusions

Jaymee Bowen's father lost his judicial review of the health authority's refusal to fund further treatment. Newspapers established appeals to raise money to pay for her treatment,[80] which was funded by an anonymous benefactor. Jaymee was one of the first children to have the experimental treatment, donor lymphocyte infusion, using blood cells donated by the original bone marrow donor, her younger sister, Charlotte. Jaymee went into remission and the NHS took over her routine care.[81] Jaymee died just over a year after the treatment commenced. Neon Roberts was treated, in accordance with the declarations of the court, with conventional treatment, whilst Ashya King received Proton Beam Therapy in the Prague clinic. Following declarations of the court on Charlie Gard's end of life care, his parents and doctors having been unable to agree, ventilation was withdrawn and Charlie died.

The public sympathy for the pursuit by the parents of Charlie Gard of the last hope for their seriously ill child was evident in the public reaction as the case progressed through the courts. The public interest in the case was, however, more than an understanding of the concern of loving parents to ensure that their child received any treatment that offered a chance of improving his condition. The public have an interest in ensuring that the concern of parents and doctors to provide innovative treatment to a child with a rare condition is balanced by protection of the child from harm. The protracted legal process, confined to consideration of Charlie's best interests, did not serve Charlie, his parents, or his doctors well. Examination of the evidence for the option his parents wanted him to have, in the context of the professional duties owed by those responsible for his medical care, before consideration of whether it was in his best interests, would

---

80 Vikki Entwistle, Ian Watt, Richard Bradbury and Lesley Pehl, 'Media coverage of the Child B case' (1996) 312 *British Medical Journal* 1587, 1588.
81 Sarah Barclay, *Jaymee; The Story of Child B*, 1996.

have clarified the issue upon which his doctors and parents were disagreed and the evidence the court required to determine that issue. To recognise professional duties separately from parental responsibilities enables the court to fulfil its public responsibility to protect the welfare of children and ensure that decisions about the provision of innovative therapies to them are reasonable and within socially acceptable boundaries.

The public interest in the case, and the concern that the current law is not effectively protecting the interests of children, is demonstrated by the support that the parents of Charlie Gard have secured for their endeavours to secure Charlie's legacy through Charlie's law, which, as explained in the concluding chapter, seeks to limit state intervention in family life to those cases where parental decisions about a child's medical treatment present a risk of causing significant harm. A critical examination of his case demonstrates that rather than change the threshold for intervention, separate consideration needs to be given to the professional judgement of treating doctors on the appropriate treatment options, before it can be determined which of the options is in the best interests of the child.

8 Professional Duties, Public Responsibilities, and State Intervention into Family Life

Introduction: Is Law Reform Necessary?

This concluding chapter considers arguments for reform of the law analysed in the preceding chapters, in which best interests is unassailable as the 'lodestar'[1] or 'gold standard'[2] for decisions about children's medical treatment. Consideration is first given to a reasonableness standard, then to a significant harm threshold, both of which have been addressed in the case law. Proposals for legislative reform which seek to alter the balance of responsibilities between parents, doctors, and the courts are then reviewed. The argument presented in this chapter is that it is not a different threshold for intervention that is required, but that the exclusive focus upon best interests has resulted in a failure to recognise that in addition to parents having responsibilities to their children, doctors have legal duties to children in their care, which bring public responsibilities into decisions for the welfare of children.

Alternatives to Best Interests: Reasonableness?

Writing in 1993, Andrew Grubb argued that there should be a presumption in favour of the immediate family making a decision on behalf of an incompetent patient; in the case of children who do not have the capacity to decide for themselves, this decision would be made by their parents. The court, he argued, should have a legislative function of establishing the criteria by which parents determine their child's best interests, establishing the 'outer limits of lawful decision-making'.[3] With the relevant criteria clearly established in the law,[4] the role of the court in individual cases would then be to review the parental decision

---

1 *NHS Trust v Baby X and others* [2012] EWHC 2188, [6]; *Alder Hey Children's NHS Foundation Trust v Evans* [2018] EWHC 308, [47].
2 *In the Matter of Alfie Evans,* 20 March 2018, https://www.supremecourt.uk/news/permission-to-appeal-determination-in-the-matter-of-alfie-evans.html accessed 3 March 2020.
3 Andrew Grubb, 'Treatment decisions: keeping it in the family' in Andrew Grubb (ed), *Choices and Decisions in Health Care* (John Wiley & Sons, Chichester, 1993) 37–96, 52.
4 Grubb (n 3) 52.

according to the legal standard. Andrew Grubb suggested that the court should only override the parental decision if the child's parents have not applied the correct criteria or had done so in a 'manifestly absurd or unreasonable way'.[5]

The question whether the court should review the reasonableness of the parental decision was the issue before the Court of Appeal in *Re T*. The Court of Appeal allowed the appeal of T's mother against the decision of Connell J to give consent to a liver transplant for 18-month-old T which his parents had refused. Considering that the mother had been unable to accept the medical advice that without the transplant T would soon die, Connell J had concluded that her refusal to accept the unanimous medical advice was not the 'conduct of a reasonable parent'.[6] On behalf of the parents, Mr Francis QC submitted that 'where the welfare of a child required a family decision, that decision if reasonable ought to be respected'.[7] The parents' decision, he submitted, came within the 'band of reasonable decisions' with which the court should not interfere.[8] Butler-Sloss LJ held that the approach the court must adopt, in the exercise of its inherent jurisdiction, to decisions about a child's medical treatment had been clearly established in the case law since *Re B* in 1981. It was the responsibility of the judge to reach an independent decision as to the welfare of the child. Her Ladyship stated that even if the court were minded to accept the argument that they should not interfere with the reasonable decision of the parent, they could not do so.[9] Furthermore, the decision of the parents and then the court was not confined to consideration of the clinical evidence, as had that of Connell J, but took account of all the relevant facts.[10] Roch LJ identified the difference that it would make to apply a test of reasonableness rather than a best interests analysis. A test of reasonableness would shift the focus from the best interests of the child to the qualities of his or her parents.

> Parents who are responsible and devoted will almost certainly reach a decision which falls within the range of decisions which can be classed as reasonable. If the decision falls outside the range of permissible decisions, it is unlikely that the parents are responsible and devoted parents who have sought only to decide in the best interests of their child.[11]

In his commentary on the case, Andrew Grubb applied the framework he had earlier suggested to argue that judicial review of the reasonableness of parental

---

5 Grubb (n 3) 53.
6 *Re T* [1997] 1 WLR 242, 247.
7 *Re T* (n 6) 248.
8 *Re T* (n 6) 248.
9 *Re T* was noted in the proceedings concerning the future care of Charlie Gard as a case in which an alternative approach to best interests had been advanced, *In the Matter of Charles Gard* [2017] EWCA Civ 410.
10 *Re T* (n 6) 250.
11 *Re T* (n 6) 255.

decisions could be compatible with the court's determination of the child's best interests. That would be the case, he argued, if the court set out the criteria for the exercise of legitimate parental discretion and then determined whether those criteria had been applied to reach a reasonable decision.[12]

To limit the role of the court to a judicial review of the reasonableness of the parental decision would be to hand to parents a zone of discretion reinforcing notions of parental authority which have been eroded by recognition of the interests of the child.[13] The current practice of referring cases to court when it is not possible, in the exercise of professional judgement, to accede to parental wishes, may mean that a reasonableness standard would make very little difference to the outcomes of cases. However, not only would such an approach be inconsistent with contemporary understandings of the child as an individual and the concern of parents of seriously ill children or children with complex needs to do all they can for their child, but it would be inconsistent with the legal and ethical duties which doctors owe to the children in their care. A better alternative to altering the standard from best interests to reasonableness would be to position best interests within the professional duties and public responsibilities arising in such cases.

Alternatives to Best Interests: A Threshold of Significant Harm?

A more recent challenge to best interests was presented to the appeal courts in the 2017 case of Charlie Gard[14] and the case of Alfie Evans[15] the following year. In both cases, submissions to the Court of Appeal and the application for permission to appeal to the Supreme Court presented the legal argument for a significant harm threshold.

The 'Threshold' Argument

The first ground of appeal on behalf of the parents of Charlie Gard, the 'threshold argument', was that where both parents in the joint exercise of their parental responsibility are agreed to the administration of a viable alternative therapeutic option offered by a doctor, in the exercise of his or her professional opinion, parental preference should be followed except in those cases where it risked

---

12 Andrew Grubb, 'Medical Treatment (Child): Parental Refusal and the Role of the Court' (1996) 4 *Medical Law Review* 315, 317.
13 Baker J may have appeared to have applied a reasonableness test in *In the Matter of Ashya King* [2014] EWHC 2964. The judge expressed the view that the treatment his parents wanted Ashya to have was 'entirely reasonable'. Given that both treatment alternatives were reasonable, the court should not interfere with their decision, [34]. This case is considered further below.
14 *In the Matter of Charles Gard* (n 9).
15 *In the Matter of E (A Child)* [2018] EWCA Civ 550.

causing the child significant harm. In his submissions to the Court of Appeal on behalf of the parents, Richard Gordon QC sought to bracket Charlie's case along with that of *King*, interpreting that as a case in which parental preference prevailed. In that case, Baker J, in wardship proceedings, had approved of the parental plan for their son, Ashya, following surgery to remove a malignant brain tumour, to be given Proton Beam Therapy in Prague rather than the conventional radiotherapy his doctors in Southampton were able to administer. The submission drew on the words of Baker J who had said that it is a

> fundamental principle of family law in this jurisdiction that responsibility for making decisions about a child rest with his parents. In most cases, the parents are the best people to make decisions about a child, and the State – whether it be the court, or any other public authority – has no business interfering with the exercise of parental responsibility *unless the child is suffering or is likely to suffer significant harm as a result of the care given to the child not being what it would be reasonable to expect a parent to give*.[16]

As McFarlane LJ observed in *Gard*, the reference of Baker J to significant harm in *King*, as is apparent from the following paragraphs of his judgment, referred to the actions of the local authority in the attempt to locate Ashya and his family, given concerns that he was at risk of significant harm. As McFarlane LJ noted, there is nothing in the judgment of Baker J to indicate that a significant harm threshold applied to the decision as to the choice of treatment.[17] Baker J did not address whether the treatment preference of Ashya's parents would cause him to suffer significant harm. As Baker J observed in his judgment, by the time the issue of Ashya's medical treatment was before the court in wardship proceedings, the situation had changed. There was no opposition from any of the parties to the treatment plan proposed by the parents and which the Prague Clinic had agreed to provide to him.[18] As McFarlane LJ observed, as the two forms of radiotherapy offered similar benefits and burdens, the judge could approve of the choice of the parents.[19] *King* did not provide a legal basis for the argument of a threshold of significant harm in medical treatment cases but had the judge so intended, McFarlane LJ explained, that position had 'no foundation as a matter of law, is contrary to established authority and is therefore plainly in error'.[20]

Counsel in *Gard* submitted that a legal test of significant harm for medical treatment cases would be consistent with the statutory scheme for care orders under s.31 of the Children Act 1989, which sets a threshold of significant harm

---

16 *In the Matter of Ashya King* (n 13) [31], emphasis added. The highlighted words paraphrase CA 1989 s 31(2).
17 *In the Matter of Charles Gard* (n 9) [102]. As noted above, if there was an alternative threshold implied by the judgment, it was reasonableness.
18 *In the Matter of Ashya King* (n 13) [33], [34].
19 *In the Matter of Charles Gard* (n 9) [96].
20 *In the Matter of Charles Gard* (n 9) [105].

upon local authority applications for the court to consider the welfare of the child in the exercise of their public law child protection powers.[21] Dismissing the appeal, McFarlane LJ concluded that the authorities demonstrated that the court does not evaluate the reasonableness of the parents' decision, nor is there any 'factor or filter' before the court evaluates the best interests of the child in medical treatment cases.[22] That was equally so when the child's parents presented an alternative course of treatment when the court would carefully consider that option in assessing the best interests of the child but would not prefer an option simply on the basis of who proposed it. McFarlane LJ explained that, in contrast to the limitations imposed upon local authorities by s.31 in child protection proceedings and by s.100 when the court is asked to exercise its inherent jurisdiction, there is no threshold of significant harm in cases where the Trust refers to court disagreements about a child's medical treatment. There is, he stressed, 'no statutory requirement for a hospital to go through the Section 100 hoop'.[23] Beyond the local authority, where a party with interest in the welfare of the child asks the court to exercise its inherent jurisdiction, it will do so as long as there is an issue between those with responsibility for the child's health, holders of parental responsibility, and the Trust.[24] Beyond *King*, the other cases cited by Mr Gordon QC in support of his submission, *Barnet* and *Re C*, were applications by the local authority which required leave of the court and not, as in *Gard*, an application by an NHS Trust with respect to a child in its care, which did not require leave of the court.[25]

Further, McFarlane LJ considered that had Francis J in the court below been invited to find whether Charlie was currently suffering significant harm, he would have so concluded,[26] and, it followed, significant harm would result to him from the continuation of ventilation in order to administer nucleoside therapy.[27] Thus, the judge concluded that not only did the submissions have no foundation in law as being contrary to established principle, but they could not be supported on the facts. The argument thus dismissed, there was no consideration by the Court of Appeal as to how a threshold of significant harm would apply in the context of the medical treatment of a child generally or specifically of a terminally ill child requiring artificial ventilation to sustain life, whose parents wished him to receive

---

21 Explained in chapter two.
22 *In the Matter of Charles Gard* (n 9) [94].
23 *In the Matter of Charles Gard* (n 9) [109]. Andrew Bainham has suggested that there is an argument for a threshold where the dispute is not between parents but between parents and another party, such as an NHS Trust, although he did not suggest what that should be, 'Private and public children law: an under-explored relationship' (2013) 25 *Child and Family Law Quarterly* 138, 158.
24 *LA v SB & AB & MB* [2010] EWHC 1744.
25 *In the Matter of Charles Gard* (n 9) [106], *Barnett London Borough Council v AL* [2017] EWHC 125; *Re C (Children) (Child in Care: Choice of forename)* [2016] EWCA Civ 374.
26 *In the Matter of Charles Gard* (n 9) [114].
27 *In the Matter of Charles Gard* (n 9) [115].

innovative therapy. Permission to appeal to the Supreme Court was refused. Lady Hale explained that although there was a significant harm threshold before the court could determine the child's welfare in child protection proceedings, the 'significant harm requirement does not apply to hospitals asking for guidance as to what treatment is and is not in the best interests of their patients'.[28]

Before the ECtHR,[29] the complaints of Charlie's parents based on significant harm were first that the decisions of the court amounted to a disproportionate interference with their Article 8 right to respect for private and family life, as the court made decisions on the basis of Charlie's best interests when they should have considered whether there was a likelihood of significant harm to Charlie. Second, that contrary to their Article 6 right, the Court of Appeal had concluded, without hearing any evidence, that the parents' decision would cause their child significant harm.[30] Viewing the complaint under Article 6 as supplemental to the complaint under Article 8 and thus examining it under Article 8 alone, the ECtHR concluded that there had been an interference with private and family life but one that was in accordance with the law and pursued the legitimate aim of protecting the 'health or morals' and 'rights and freedoms' of Charlie. On the question whether the interference was necessary in a democratic society, framed in terms of the argument that the appropriate test before the courts was one of risk of significant harm rather than best interests, the ECtHR noted the broad consensus within domestic and international law placing the best interests of the child as paramount. Whilst the facts of the case were exceptional and there was a lack of ECtHR guidance on the point, the Court noted that the domestic courts had concluded there was a risk to Charlie of significant harm,[31] in doing so not directly addressing the complaint of Charlie's parents that the courts had done so without hearing any evidence on the point. The ECtHR considered that the legal framework was not disproportionate, rather it was

> meticulous and thorough; ensured that all those concerned were represented throughout; heard extensive and high-quality expert evidence; accorded weight to all the arguments raised; and were reviewed at three levels of

---

28 *In the matter of Charlie Gard (Permission to Appeal Hearing)*, 8 June 2017, https://www.supremecourt.uk/news/permission-to-appeal-hearing-in-the-matter-of-charlie-gard.html accessed 29 February 2020.
29 Their complaints that by preventing Charlie from receiving life-sustaining treatment, GOSH had violated their and Charlie's Article 2 right to life, and that the consequence of the order of the court was to violate their and Charlie's Article 5 right by depriving him of his liberty, were manifestly inadmissible, *Charles Gard and Others v United Kingdom*, Application no. 39793/17 (28 June 2017), http://hudoc.echr.coe.int/eng#{"documentcollectionid2":["DECGRANDCHAMBER","ADMISSIBILITY","ADMISSIBILITYCOM"],"itemid":["001-175359"]} accessed 29 February 2020.
30 *Charles Gard and Others v United Kingdom* (n 29) [56].
31 *Charles Gard and Others v United Kingdom* (n 29) [119].

jurisdiction with clear and extensive reasoning giving relevant and sufficient support for their conclusions at all three levels.[32]

Respecting the state's margin of appreciation, the existing principles and processes of English law were compatible with Convention Rights. The decision made much reference to the earlier judgment in *Glass,* most notably that the violation there had arisen because of the failure to refer the question to the court, whereas here the decision had been made by the court applying the established procedure and upheld throughout the appeal stages.

The Court of Appeal, on the first occasion it considered the appeal against the decision of Hayden J that it was lawful and in the best interests of Alfie Evans to withdraw ventilation and provide palliative care, gave permission to appeal on the ground that to override his parents' decision in the exercise of the court's inherent jurisdiction was in the absence of proof of *significant harm*, discriminatory and consequently incompatible with Article 14 read with Article 8.[33] As King LJ observed, this was a 'bold submission', given that Baroness Hale in the Supreme Court in *Gard* could be considered to have 'laid such a proposition to rest'.[34]

The submission was based upon a comparison of the public law powers of the local authority with the duties of doctors and Trusts to children in their care. The argument was that there was no justification for the different treatment, whereby a local authority application for care proceedings first depended upon a finding of significant harm, whilst the best interests test was applied in proceedings brought by the Trust for the court to exercise its inherent jurisdiction in relation to a child's medical treatment. The submission was that both involved intervention into family life with the aim of safeguarding or promoting the welfare of the child by caring for the child contrary to the wishes of the parents.[35] The argument that the Children Act was discriminatory because it treated parents more favourably in care proceedings than under the inherent jurisdiction was rejected on the basis that they are not analogous. Any risk of significant harm to a child with a severe medical condition was inherent to that condition and not, as in s.31 cases, a consequence of parental care.[36] King LJ continued to hold that, if she were wrong in her conclusion that care proceedings and the inherent jurisdiction of the court were not analogous, the parents had not been discriminated against as justification for any distinction lay in the paramountcy of the welfare of the child over the wishes of parents.[37]

---

32 *Charles Gard and Others v United Kingdom* (n 29) [124].
33 *In the Matter of E* (n 15) [49].
34 *In the Matter of E* (n 15) [64].
35 *In the Matter of E* (n 15) [75].
36 CA 1989 s 31(2)(b)(i). As Hedley J observed, of 'entirely organic' cause, *Re Wyatt* [2004] EWHC 2247, [33].
37 *In the Matter of E* (n 15) [127]. The Supreme Court refused permission to appeal on the grounds that argument that the application of best interests rather than significant harm was discriminatory was unarguable, *In the Matter of Alfie Evans* (20 March 2018), https://ww

The 'jurisdiction' argument

The second ground for appeal in *Gard*, the 'jurisdiction' argument, also dismissed, was that the application by GOSH to prevent another doctor from administering treatment in the reasonable exercise of their professional judgement was beyond the powers of the hospital as a public authority, and, in the absence of significant harm, it was outside the court's jurisdiction to uphold the hospital's position.[38] The submission was that whilst the Trust could apply to the court and the court could make a declaration that it was lawful for the hospital not to provide nucleoside therapy, in the absence of significant harm it could not seek by way of a court order to prevent the parents from taking up the offer of treatment elsewhere. The Court of Appeal preferred the submission of Ms Gollop QC for GOSH that the issue had arisen between Charlie's parents and doctors, which the Trust had properly brought before the court for a judge to decide according to the best interests of the child.[39]

Significant Harm, Parental Authority?

There has been much consideration in the ethics literature of the application of a harm threshold before practitioners, or the courts should interfere with parental decisions about their child's medical treatment.[40] As an alternative to best interests, it has received less attention in the legal literature. In *The Best Interests of the Child in Healthcare*,[41] Sarah Elliston argued that the threshold for court intervention in parental decisions about their child's medical treatment should be a 'significant risk of serious harm'. A similar argument was advanced by Cressida Auckland and Imogen Goold in their article considering the cases of Charlie Gard and Alfie Evans. They argued that parental decisions should only be subject to court determination where the threshold of serious risk of significant harm had

---

w.supremecourt.uk/news/permission-to-appeal-determination-in-the-matter-of-alfie-evans.html accessed 3 March 2020. In the light of the ECtHR's conclusions in *Gard*, it was inevitable that the applications to the court concerning the domestic court's resolution of the care of Alfie Evans would be deemed inadmissible, ECHR declares application by parents of Alfie Evans inadmissible, 28 March 2018, https://hudoc.echr.coe.int/eng-press#{"fulltext":["Alfie Evans"]}, accessed 3 March 2020.

38 *In the Matter of Charles Gard* (n 9) [84].
39 *In the Matter of Charles Gard* (n 9) [88], [117].
40 The Bioethics literature is examined by Dominic Wilkinson, 'In Defence of a Conditional Harm Threshold Test for Paediatric Decision-making' in Imogen Goold, Jonathan Herring and Cressida Auckland (eds), *Parental Rights, Best Interests and Significant Harms: Medical Decision-Making on Behalf of Children Post-Great Ormond Street Hospital v Gard* (Hart, 2019), 85-105 and Giles Birchley, 'The Harm Threshold: A View from the Clinic' in the same volume 107-135.
41 Sarah Elliston, *The Best Interests of the Child in Healthcare* (Routledge, 2007).

been met, at which point the court should determine the child's best interests.[42] This threshold, they argued, 'better reflects the boundaries between our private lives and those areas into which the state can rightly intervene, is the most ethically justified, and strikes the most appropriate balance between parental authority and protecting the vulnerable'.[43] Parents are given much freedom to raise their children according to their own values, beliefs, and preferences. However, in the specific instance of the medical treatment of a child, parents have responsibilities to their child and treatment is provided by doctors who have duties to children in their care, which can require them to inform the local authority or refer questions about a child's treatment to the court. The view that a significant harm test is most ethically justified is premised on giving 'priority and protection to the autonomy of parents'[44] and, as such, could be viewed as consistent with the developments in the law relating to competent adult patients, which protect their autonomous choices. In daily life, parents won't always place the best interests of their child as the paramount consideration; that is neither feasible nor in the child's overall interests. However, when a child is seriously ill or requiring intensive medical intervention due to their complex condition, parents seek to do what they genuinely believe to be best for their child, not simply that which does not cause significant harm. Placing the best interests of a seriously ill child as the paramount consideration accords with generally accepted standards of the care of children. Where the balance is appropriately struck between parental authority and protection of the child is a matter of judgement. However, it would be a retrograde step to return to prioritisation of parental authority over their child rather than giving recognition to the rights of the child as an individual. To do so would be contrary to the approach of the Children Act that the upbringing of children is a 'collaborative responsibility in which parents take the leading role'[45] but in which the public and the state also have both interests and responsibilities.

The RCPCH Framework for Good Practice, cited in *Gard* and to which doctors refer in reaching a decision that it is necessary to apply to the court for a ruling on a child's continued life-sustaining treatment, states that '[p]arental decisions are generally respected in law, unless they appear to risk substantial harm to the child or are not in the child's best interests'.[46] Risk of substantial

---

42 Cressida Auckland and Imogen Goold, 'Parental Rights, Best Interests and Significant Harms: Who should have the final say over a child's medical care?' (2019) 78 *Cambridge Law Journal* 287.
43 Auckland and Goold (n 42) 288-289.
44 *In the Matter of Charles Gard* (n 9) [60].
45 Rachel Taylor, 'Parental Decisions and Court Jurisdiction: Best Interests or Significant Harm?' in Imogen Goold, Jonathan Herring and Cressida Auckland (eds), *Parental Rights, Best Interests and Significant Harms: Medical Decision-Making on Behalf of Children Post-Great Ormond Street Hospital v Gard* (Hart, 2019), 49-65, 65.
46 RCPCH, *Making Decisions to Limit Treatment in Life-Limiting and Life-Threatening Conditions in Children: A Framework for Practice* (2015) 2.4.3.

harm and not in the child's best interests are not the same, although as the analysis of the law in the previous chapters demonstrated, something may not be in the child's *best* interests, whilst being an acceptable treatment option, or it may be *contrary* to the child's interests, or *inimical* to the interests of the child. As has been demonstrated in the analysis of the case law in this book, the practice has altered to give weight to parental decisions until they are contrary to the duties of doctors to children in their care. This does not require a change to the principle applicable to the decisions of parents and then the court with regard to children's medical treatment. To replace best interests with a legal threshold of significant harm would be to revert to parental authority, through claims to parental autonomy, placing parental choice over the protection of the interests and rights of the child. What is required is a recognition of parental responsibilities balanced with a recognition of the duties of doctors and public responsibilities to children.

Argument through the appeal courts in the cases of Charlie Gard and Alfie Evans resulted in a clear restatement of established law that, in all cases, the duty of the court is to determine the best interests of the child. The best interests analysis arises from the long-established responsibility of the courts to protect the interests of the vulnerable in wardship or in the exercise of its inherent jurisdiction and is of wider reach than medical treatment of children cases. Any reform would have to be secured through legislation.

Legislative Reform?

The legislative reform proposals made following *R v Arthur* in 1981 compared with those made following the Charlie Gard case in 2017 reflect the changed context for decisions concerning children's medical treatment. The earlier measure was a Limitation of Treatment Bill. It proposed that no criminal offence would be committed when a doctor withheld or withdrew treatment from a child, and

(a) the child's parents had given written consent, and
(b) two doctors, both of at least seven years' standing, one a paediatrician, certified in writing that the infant suffered from severe physical or mental 'handicap' that was either irreversible or of such gravity that after receiving all reasonably available treatment, the child would enjoy no worthwhile quality of life.

In assessing the child's prospective quality of life, doctors would be directed to consider a number of factors including anticipated pain and suffering, the child's potential to communicate, and, reflecting the facts in *R v Arthur*, the willingness of his or her parents to care for the child. The terms of the Bill, which did not pass into law, reflected the concerns of the time, the potential criminal liability of doctors, that children with disabilities may not have a worthwhile quality of life, and that the care of disabled children, given attitudes to disability and lack of support, was burdensome.

More recently, and in contrast, the parents of Charlie Gard, and Tafida Raqeeb[47] have each responded to their experience of legal proceedings concerning the future medical treatment of their child by expressing the view that the law needs to change, as did an MEP supporter in response to the Alfie Evans case.[48] Most active have been the efforts of Connie Yates and Chris Gard to secure a legacy for Charlie through Charlie's Law. They have worked with NHS professionals, ethicists, and lawyers to develop Charlie's Law in the light of their experiences, seeking to change processes to prevent cases reaching court,[49] to improve the advice and support provided to families,[50] and to better protect parental rights. Reflecting their argument on appeal, they seek to change the law to restrict the involvement of courts to cases where the child is at risk of significant harm. They have expressed the view that the best interests analysis provides a 'broad platform for the overruling of parent's wishes' and consider that there was insufficient evidence that providing nucleoside therapy to Charlie would have caused him significant harm so that this threshold would have prevented the judge from deciding his case.

The first attempt to introduce legislative reform focused upon procedural changes. Lord Mackay introduced amendments to the Mental Capacity (Amendment) Bill to make provision for access to a clinical ethics committee and for medical mediation to be made available when a dispute has arisen.[51] As an amendment to the Mental Capacity Act 2005 it would only have applied to patients aged 16 or over. Lord Mackay explained that this provision, aimed at preventing cases reaching court unnecessarily, was a 'proportionate and long-overdue measure' which he hoped would be the first step to enactment of Charlie's Law'.[52] These amendments were not in the Act when it was passed in 2019.

The Access to Palliative Care and Treatment of Children Bill was introduced to the Lords in October 2019 by Baroness Finlay with specific reference to the cases of Charlie Gard and Alfie Evans. It would have applied in cases where there is a difference of opinion between parents and doctors responsible for a child with a life-limiting illness on the nature or extent of specialist palliative care or the extent

---

47 That the Children Act needed to be revised so that parental rights weren't taken away, 'Parents of Tafida Raqeeb: Our victory shows need for law change', *Sky News* (5 October 2019) https://www.youtube.com/watch?v=FNOykm02IV4 accessed 26 March 2020.
48 Steven Woolfe, 'The Alfie Evans case has proven that we need to change the law in favour of parents' *The Independent* (27 April 2020), proposing a panel from which to select legal representation, access to legal aid, and a right to choose a second opinion independent from the NHS.
49 Proposing access to clinical ethics committees, medical mediation, and medical reports.
50 On ethics and rights, to independent second opinions, and access to legal aid.
51 https://publications.parliament.uk/pa/bills/lbill/2017-2019/0117/18117-I(a).pdf accessed 31 January 2020.
52 Xavier Symons, 'Charlie Gard amendment introduced into British parliament' *Bioedge* (15 September 2018) https://www.bioedge.org/bioethics/charlie-gard-amendment-introduced-into-british-parliament/12811 accessed 31 January 2020.

to which palliative care should be accompanied by 'disease-modifying treatment'. In such cases, it provided that reasonable steps should be taken to ensure that the views of the parent are taken into account and to make any relevant medical data relating to the child available to the parent. Further, that reasonable steps must be taken to refer the matter to a clinical ethics committee of the hospital for advice and to provide and pay for a mediation process acceptable to both parties. When the difference of opinion is before a court, the Bill would have prevented court orders being made to prevent parents seeking disease-modifying treatment when that treatment was not harmful and when another reputable hospital was willing to provide it.[53] The progress of the Bill ended with the dissolution of Parliament.

Baroness Finlay introduced a further Access to Palliative Care and Treatment of Children Bill to the Lords as a private members Bill in January 2020. The provisions of the Bill would apply where consideration is being given to an application to the High Court under the Children Act 1989 or under the inherent jurisdiction of the High Court for an order which has the effect of approving the giving or withdrawal of any form of medical treatment for a child. With the exception of urgent cases, it would prevent an application being made unless an attempt had been made to resolve the differences, between the hospital and persons with parental responsibility or interest in the welfare of the child, by mediation with an independent mediator.[54] The Bill would introduce a presumption that medical treatment proposals put forward by any person holding parental responsibility for the child are in the child's best interests unless clearly shown to the contrary. It would have changed the law, from that where a doctor cannot be required to treat contrary to his or her professional judgement, to the position that doctors cannot be required to provide specific medical treatment to a child which a doctor refuses on reasonable grounds to provide to a child.[55] The Bill progressed through the readings in the House of Lords, but, at the time of writing, the Committee stage was yet to be scheduled, Parliamentary business having been disrupted by the COVID-19 pandemic.

The 2019 and 2020 Bills adopt a slightly different approach to the argument presented on appeal in the Charlie Gard case, although both were clearly informed

---

53 https://services.parliament.uk/bills/2019-19/accesstopalliativecareandtreatmentofchildren.html accessed 31 January 2020.
54 Louise Austin undertook a review of the literature on further discussions, second opinions, clinical ethics committees, and mediation for the Nuffield Council on Bioethics, *UK processes for resolution of disagreements about the care of critically ill children* (2018). Both the Nuffield Council on Bioethics, *Bioethics Briefing Note: Disagreements in the Care of Critically Ill Children* (2019) and RCPCH, *Achieving consensus advice for paediatricians and other health professionals: on prevention, recognition and management of conflict in paediatric practice* (2019) https://www.rcpch.ac.uk/resources/achieving-consensus accessed 16 April 2020, issued in response to these cases refer practitioners to the support available to prevent and manage conflict including second opinions, clinical ethics committees, and mediation.
55 https://services.parliament.uk/Bills/2019-20/accesstopalliativecareandtreatmentofchildren.html accessed 31 January 2020.

by the issues raised in that case and the terms of Charlie's Law. The 2019 Bill would have enshrined in legislation the liberty of parents to secure treatment at another reputable hospital as long as that treatment was not harmful to the child. The 2020 Bill would create a presumption that treatment proposed by anyone holding parental responsibility is in the best interests of the child. If the parental proposal for treatment were not to be administered this presumption would have to be rebutted. The burden would be upon the doctor to demonstrate reasonable grounds to refuse to provide that treatment. Presumably this would be, as with current practice, through the evidence of the treating team, second opinions, and independent experts. As Jonathan Herring has argued, the answer to the criticisms of the welfare principle is not to 'replace it with an approach that gives greater weight to the interests of the powerful'[56] which reasonableness and significant harm, as minimal rather than aspirational standards,[57] would do. Rather than introducing a new 'reasonable refusal' test, the legal and professional duties which doctors owe to children and the public responsibilities to children need to be recognised.

In his critique of the welfare principle, Jonathan Herring suggested that there is likely to be little dissent from the view that the welfare of the child should be paramount in determining disputes about the care of children, and it is important that the law is consistent with 'expectations and understandings of the general public'.[58] The parents of Charlie Gard and Alfie Evans, in order to challenge the conclusion of the judge, that it was in their child's best interests for ventilation to be withdrawn and palliative care provided and with which they disagreed, had to present arguments that the decision of the lower court was wrong or unjust because of a serious procedural, or other, irregularity in the proceedings.[59] Although in both cases the grounds for appeal included that the judge had erred in making the best interests analysis, inevitably, it was the legal argument based on significant harm which the Court of Appeal considered. Neither parents were seeking to establish their right to cause their child harm, as long as it was not significant, rather they believed that they were best placed to know what was best for their child and should be entitled to make decisions about their child's best interests. The sympathy of the public was with the parental pursuit of an alternative course that would sustain the child's life and not with the argument that parents should be entitled to harm their child as long as it was not significant.

In response to the criticism that judicial decisions about the best interests of children have subsequently been viewed as wrong, as a result of changing

---

56 Jonathan Herring, 'Farewell Welfare?' (2005) 27 *Journal of Social Welfare and Family Law* 159, 169.
57 Giles Birchley, 'The Harm Principle and the Best Interests Standard: Are Aspirational or Minimal Standards the Key?' (2018) 18 *American Journal of Bioethics* 32.
58 Herring (n 56).
59 Civil Procedure Rules r 52.21(3).

social norms, Jonathan Herring suggested that any other principle or rule would equally be vulnerable to the same criticism. Much of the academic criticism of the welfare principle has been made in response to its application in disputes between parents on issues of post-separation upbringing such as relocation and contact (now child arrangements).[60] On issues of a child's education, religious upbringing, where a child should live, or the arrangements for spending time with the non-resident parent, there is plenty of scope for disagreement about what are the best outcomes for children. In comparison, cases concerning children's medical treatment are less uncertain or unpredictable, and rather than reflect judicial prejudices or moral values, are determined within the context of widely accepted norms[61] which are more established in relation to the provision of medical treatment than with respect to issues of parenting more generally. As the analysis of the case law demonstrates, judicial decisions about the best interests of children in relation to their medical treatment do reflect the social norms of the time and so may subsequently be considered wrong. Yet approaches based on alternatives such as reasonableness or significant harm would similarly be determined according to existing norms as they are equally dependent upon value judgements informed by culture, beliefs, and social context and therefore are equally vulnerable to subsequently being viewed as wrong.[62]

Whilst taking the view that the best interests analysis is appropriate for decisions concerning the medical treatment of children, the critique advanced here is of the exclusive focus upon best interests in judgments, professional guidance, and academic commentary. Neither a move to a presumption that parental decisions are in the best interests of children, thereby placing the burden upon doctors to demonstrate that their refusal is reasonable, nor the introduction of a threshold of significant harm would address the failure to position the cases within the legal and professional duties of doctors to children in their care and framed by public responsibilities to protect the welfare of children as understood within the prevailing social, economic, and political context.

Charlie Gard's parents argued that it is too easy for disagreements between parents and doctors to become costly and protracted legal battles.[63] The analysis of the recent cases shows that disagreements do not easily become legal battles. The analysis of the cases shows that, in current practice, parental knowledge of their child and wishes for their child's treatment are given much respect in the partnership of care. The analysis shows that doctors will provide treatment to a

---

60 Helen Reece, 'The Paramountcy Principle: Consensus or Construct?' (1996) 49 *Current Legal Problems* 267; John Eekelaar, 'Beyond the welfare principle' (2002) 14 *Child and Family Law Quarterly* 237–49; Herring (n 56).
61 Herring (n 56) 161–2.
62 As Auckland and Goold acknowledged in their article which argued for a significant harm threshold (n 42) 315.
63 Charlie Gard Foundation, https://www.thecharliegardfoundation.org/charlies-law/ accessed 26 March 2020.

child that they consider is not clinically best in order to accommodate parental beliefs. However, legal and professional duties which doctors owe to children in their care mean that they cannot provide a child with treatment that, in their professional judgement, is not an appropriate treatment. Where they cannot persuade the parents of this view, they will test their judgement through consultation with other members of the multi-disciplinary team. If the disagreement continues, they may seek second opinions or the view of the clinical ethics committee. Seeking legal advice and referring the matter to court is a last resort. In the majority of recent cases, this has only occurred where the treatment the child's parents want is not only not in the *best* interests of the child, but, in the professional judgement of the doctors responsible for the child's medical treatment, *contrary* to or *inimical* to the best interests of the child.

The Balance of Responsibilities for Children's Medical Treatment

What needs to be recognised in the courts, academic debate, and professional guidance, is that whilst parents have responsibilities to their child, doctors have legal and professional duties to children in their care which bring in public responsibilities, the content of which is determined within the specific cultural, social, and political context of the time. A comparison of the terms of the 1981 Limitation of Treatment Bill and the proposed Charlie's Law shows that legislation in response to specific issues at specific times would soon become outdated.

Public responsibility, through local authority responsibilities, was formative in the early cases and continues to be important today in cases concerning vulnerable children in the care of the state who do not have parents advocating for them as did Charlie, Isaiah, Alfie, and Tafida. The shared responsibility for the support, protection, and welfare of children means that cases concerning vulnerable children in care need to be determined in the public forum of the court. And, when those with parental responsibility and professional duties cannot agree on the best interests of the child, those same shared responsibilities justify public intervention in family life. The significance for the understanding of the law governing children's medical treatment is a reorientation away from the sole preoccupation with best interests, clarification of the medical evidence of the treatment options available, and recognition of the social, political, economic, and cultural context in which decisions about the medical treatment of children are reached. The common law has the proven ability to develop in order to reflect changing social norms and expectations of parenting, professional duties, and public responsibilities to children. Whilst what is in the best interests of a child is informed by values, beliefs, and experiences, when the issue of the medical treatment that is in the best interests of a child is before the court, it must be determined according to the evidence and must be reflective of general standards of parenting and expectations of society of the treatment and care of children. The law needs to be informed by this understanding, or an understanding of what as a society we consider to be socially acceptable with regard to the treatment of children and not through individual crusades in reaction to personal experience. Cases about a child's medical treatment are not only concerned with the best interests of the child, they are also concerned with fundamental questions about the allocation and enforcement of parental, professional, and public responsibilities understood within their legal, political, economic, and social context.

Appendix

Reported Cases Concerning the Medical Treatment of Children (up to 30/4/20)

Case	Age and Medical condition	Treatment	Procedure by which brought to court	Issues	Decision
Re D (a minor) (wardship:sterilisation) [1976] Fam 185, Sept 1975, Heilbron J	11 years, Sotos Syndrome	Sterilisation	Application by the local authority for the child to be made a ward of court, for court to decide whether operation should be prevented		Wardship continued; sterilisation not in best interests
Re B (a minor) (wardship: medical treatment) [1981] 1 WLR 1421, Aug 1981, Templeman, Dunn LJJ; appeal from order of Ewbank J	1 week, Down's Syndrome and intestinal blockage	Operation to remove intestinal blockage	Application by the local authority for the child to be made ward of court, local authority given care and control; court gave authority to direct that operation be carried out. Surgeon refused to perform contrary to parental wishes, local authority brought back to judge who revoked the order, local authority appealed	Duty of judge to determine whether in best interests for operation to be performed Referenced in GMC, *Treatment and care towards the end of life*, 2010; Referenced in RCPCH, *Making Decisions to Limit Treatment in Life-Limiting and Life-Threatening Conditions in Children*, 2015	Authorised operation
Re P (A Minor) [1986] 1 FLR 272, Oct 1981, Butler-Sloss J	15 years, pregnant	Termination to which P consented but father opposed	In care of local authority following conviction for theft, application made by local authority for P to be made ward, originating summons in wardship proceedings		Best interests to have termination in accordance with wishes and lawful under terms of Abortion Act 1967
R v Arthur [1981] 12 BMLR 1, Nov 1981, Farquharson J	Died 3 days old, John Pearson	Whether to provide nursing care only, and whether prescription of dihydrocodeine following which the child died amounted to a criminal offence	Prosecution for murder, changed to attempted murder following post-mortem	Direction to the jury	Jury found Dr Arthur not guilty

(*Continued*)

Appendix 185

(Continued)

Case	Age and Medical condition	Treatment	Procedure by which brought to court	Issues	Decision
Re G-U (A Minor) (Wardship) [1984] FLR 811, April 1984, Balcombe J	16 years, pregnant	Termination of pregnancy arranged by local authority	Ward in local authority care under interim care order; ward for 5 years; brought before court upon direction of Registrar		Court order ratifying; satisfied in best interests but leave of court should have been sought prior to termination
Gillick v West Norfolk and Wisbech Area Health Authority and another [1986] AC 112, Oct 1985, Lords Fraser, Bridge, Scarman, Brandon, Templeman; appeal against decision of Eveleigh, Fox, Parker L.JJ; appeal against decision of Woolf J	Hypothetical issue of provision of contraceptive advice & treatment to a child under 16 without parental knowledge or consent	Whether DHSS Guidance, Health Notice (HN (80) 46) revising section G of Memorandum of Guidance on family planning services was unlawful	Woolf J held not entitled to the relief sought, Court of Appeal by majority (Parker and Fox LJJ) determined guidance unlawful (Eveleigh LJ dissented)	Majority Lords Fraser, Bridge; Lords Brandon and Templeman dissented. Referred to in BMA, *Children and Young People Ethics Toolkit*, 2019; GMC, *0-18 years*, 2018; GMC, *Protecting Children and Young People*, July 2012; RCPCH, *Making Decisions to Limit Treatment in Life-Limiting and Life-Threatening Conditions in Children*, 2015	House of Lords allowed appeal; in exceptional cases doctor who could not persuade child to inform her parents could provide contraceptive advice & treatment as long as she had sufficient understanding and intelligence to understand fully what is involved
Re B (a minor) (wardship: sterilisation) [1988] AC 199, April 1987, Lords Hailsham, Bridge, Brandon Templeman, Oliver affirming decision of Dillon, Stephen Brown, Nicholls L.JJ; upholding decision of Bush J	17 years, learning disabilities	Sterilisation	In local authority care under a care order; local authority applied for originating summons to be made ward & for leave to be given to perform operation, opposed by mother, supported by Official Solicitor		Bush J sterilisation in best interests; upheld by CA; appeal against CA dismissed

(Continued)

(Continued)

Case	Age and Medical condition	Treatment	Procedure by which brought to court	Issues	Decision
R v Central Birmingham Health Authority, ex parte Walker 3 BMLR 32, Nov 1987, Sir John Donaldson, Nicholls, Caulfield LJJ; appeal from Macpherson J	2 months, heart surgery	Allocation of resources resulting in delay to surgery	Application by parents for leave to apply for judicial review of decision of health authority		Application for leave refused, not justiciable, upheld by CA
Re M [1988] 2 FLR 497, Dec 1987, Bush J	17 years, Fragile X	Sterilisation	Application for leave by local authority in respect of ward		Leave given in best interests
R v Central Birmingham Health Authority ex parte Collier [1988] 1 WLUK 690 Jan 1988, Stephen Brown, Neill, Ralph Gibson LJJ; appeal from Kennedy J	4 years, heart surgery	Allocation of resources resulting in delay to surgery	Application by parents for leave to apply for judicial review of decision of health authority		Application for leave refused, not justiciable, upheld by CA
Re C (a minor) (wardship: medical treatment) [1990] Fam 26, April 1989, Lord Donaldson MR, Balcombe, Nicholls LJJ; appeal from Ward J	16 weeks, born prematurely, hydrocephalus	Withhold treatment	Ward of court at birth; decisions about medical treatment made by court	Balcombe LJ noted lack of guidance from legislature for courts or others tasked with making such decisions Referenced in GMC, *Treatment and care towards the end of life*, 2010; Referenced in RCPCH, *Making Decisions to Limit Treatment in Life-Limiting and Life-Threatening Conditions in Children*, 2015	Authority to withhold antibiotics, intravenous fluid, nasal-gastric feed, although determined by nurses judgement of her best interests

(Continued)

(Continued)

Case	Age and Medical condition	Treatment	Procedure by which brought to court	Issues	Decision
Re E (A Minor) (Wardship: Medical Treatment) [1993] 1 FLR 386, Sept 1990, Ward J	15 years, leukaemia	Administration of blood/blood products refused by E due to his faith as a Jehovah's Witness	Health authority applied ex parte for E to be made a ward of court; health authority application for leave to treat E with blood despite his refusal; continuation of wardship; order for care and control	Referenced in GMC Guidance, *0-18 years*, 2018	Leave for doctors to treat as necessary with administration of blood/blood products; wardship continued, order for care and control not necessary
Re J (A Minor) (Wardship: Medical Treatment) [1991] Fam 33, Oct 1990, Lord Donaldson MR, Balcombe, Taylor LJJ; appeal from Scott Baker J	5 months, severe brain damage due to prematurity	Withhold ventilation	Ward of court at birth; decisions about medical treatment made by court; application by local authority	OS sought guidance of the court; CA rejected absolutist position that court is never justified in withholding consent to treatment which may enable a child to survive a life-threatening event, and alternative that it may only do so if the child's quality of life is intolerable; Applied best interests test; Set out duties of doctors, parents & court & partnership in provision of treatment. Order made meant lawful to withhold ventilation but lawful to provide if appropriate in clinical judgement of those caring for J. Referenced in GMC, *Treatment and care towards the end of life*, 2010; RCPCH, *Making Decisions to Limit Treatment in Life-Limiting and Life-Threatening Conditions in Children*, 2015	Application by local authority to direct health authority to treat in accordance with opinions of Dr W to withhold ventilation; clarify neither local authority nor court can direct doctors to treat; treatment at all times according to clinical judgement of those caring

(Continued)

(Continued)

Case	Age and Medical condition	Treatment	Procedure by which brought to court	Issues	Decision
Re E (A Minor) (Medical Treatment) [1991] 2 FLR.585, Feb 1991, Sir Stephen Brown P	17 years, learning difficulties, serious menorrhagia	hysterectomy	Application by Official Solicitor in wardship proceedings	Sterilisation not the purpose but the effect of the surgery	Consent of the court not required; operation therapeutic; parents can give consent; had consent of the court been necessary would have given it on basis in best interests
Re B (Wardship: Abortion) [1991] 2 FLR 426, May 1991, Hollis J	12 years, pregnant	Termination, B consented, opposed by mother, supported by grandparents who cared for her & putative father	GP informed social services having diagnosed pregnancy; local authority applied for her to be made a ward of court & for leave to have termination; represented by the Official Solicitor	Decision of court in relation to ward did not have to determine whether competent but took into account her age & wishes & views of mother	Termination in best interests
Re R (A Minor) (Wardship: Medical Treatment) [1992] 1 FLR 190, July 1991; Lord Donaldson, Staughton, Farquharson LJJ, appeal from Waite J	15 years, psychotic state	Administration of anti-psychotic medication	In local authority care under ICO; local authority applied for R to be made ward of court	Referenced in GMC Guidance, 0-18 years, 2018	Lacked capacity to decide; as ward court had power to override refusal & give consent; administration of medication in her best interests

(Continued)

Appendix 189

(Continued)

Case	Age and Medical condition	Treatment	Procedure by which brought to court	Issues	Decision
Re J (A Minor) (Child in Care: Medical Treatment) [1993] Fam 15, June 1992, Lord Donaldson, Balcombe, Leggatt LJJ; appeal from order Waite J, March 1992 which CA had stayed May 1992	15 months, severe mental & physical handicap at 1 month, microcephalic, severe form of cerebral palsy, severe epilepsy, blindness.	Whether lawful to withhold life-sustaining treatment in event suffered a life-threatening event	J in care; local authority applied for leave under s.100(3) CA; Waite J made interim order that treatment should be provided pending full hearing	Whether court in exercise of inherent jurisdiction should ever require clinician to adopt a course of treatment which is contra-indicated as not in the best interests of the patient; considerations where there is a practitioner prepared to treat Referenced in GMC, *Treatment and care towards the end of life*, 2010	CA stayed order, appeal allowed; doctors must treat according to clinical judgment, including to withhold life-sustaining in event of life-threatening event
Re W (A Minor) (Medical Treatment: Court's Jurisdiction) [1993] Fam 64, July 1992, Lord Donaldson, Balcombe, Nolan LJJ; appeal from Thorpe J	16 years, anorexia	Whether it was lawful to move W to a named treatment unit without her consent	W in care; local authority applied for leave under s.100(3) CA for court to exercise inherent jurisdiction; granted	Obiter, holders of parental responsibility & court can give consent where refused by a child whether or not they have *Gillick* competence; obiter, court in exercise of inherent jurisdiction can refuse consent where given Referenced in GMC Guidance, *0-18 years*, 2018; RCPCH, *Making Decisions to Limit Treatment in Life-Limiting and Life-Threatening Conditions in Children*, 2015	Accepted conclusion of Thorpe J that W had capacity; court could give consent where refused; in best interests
Re S (A Minor) (Medical Treatment) [1993] 1 FLR 376, July 1992, Thorpe J	4 years, T-cell leukaemia	Administration of blood, parents refused given faith as Jehovah's Witnesses, otherwise agreeing to treatment	Local authority sought leave under s.100 CA; Parents sought PSO		Authorised administration of blood; PSO refused

(Continued)

Appendix

(Continued)

Case	Age and Medical condition	Treatment	Procedure by which brought to court	Issues	Decision
Re K, W and H (Minors) (Medical Treatment) [1993] 1 FLR 854, Sept 1992, Thorpe J	Application related to three young people aged 14, 15, 15	Treatment programme in secure unit	Applications made by independent Trust for leave for s.8 orders	Parents had given consent	S.8 orders not made as applications 'misconceived and unnecessary' given parental consent
Re HG (Specific Issue Order: Sterilisation) [1993] 1 FLR 587, Nov 1992, Peter Singer QC	17, learning disability	sterilisation	Application by child herself with father as next friend for SIO (so eligible for legal aid); Official Solicitor joined as ex officio respondent; local authority joined as non-statutorily, discharged as did not want to participate	OS argued could not seek SIO as could not in exercise of parental responsibility make decision about sterilisation	SIO made, was a question to be answered did not need to be disagreement upon it
Re O (A Minor) (Medical Treatment) [1993] 2 FLR 149, March 1993, Johnson J	2 months at judgment but decided when 7/10 days old, respiratory distress syndrome, due to prematurity	Administration of blood, parents refused given faith as Jehovah's Witnesses, otherwise agreeing to treatment	Doctor sought guidance from local authority; Emergency Protection Order made by local family court, without notice to parents; local authority applied to family proceedings court for a Care Order	Court held Interim Care Order and Emergency Protection Order inappropriate; SIO cannot be 'determined' on an ex parte application; Inherent Jurisdiction the preferred procedure	Authorised administration of blood
Re R (minor) (Blood Transfusion) [1993] 2 FLR 757, May 1993, Booth J	10 months, B-cell lymphoblastic leukaemia	Administration of blood, parents refused given faith as Jehovah's Witnesses, otherwise agreeing to treatment	Local authority applied for leave to apply for SIO	SIO the most appropriate procedure.	Authorised the administration of blood in a life-threatening emergency, if the situation was not imminently life-threatening to first consult with the parents about alternatives

(Continued)

(Continued)

Case	Age and Medical condition	Treatment	Procedure by which brought to court	Issues	Decision
Re S (A Minor) (Medical Treatment) [1994] 2 FLR 1065, June 1994, Johnson J	15 years, beta minor thalasssemia	Administration of regular blood transfusion	Local authority applied to court for leave to ask court to exercise inherent jurisdiction	Social services had been involved 5 years earlier when S's mother started to attend meetings of Jehovah's Witnesses due to concerns about impact upon her treatment; father prepared to consent and continued to receive transfusions; involved again when missed transfusions & S made it clear that she did not want any more blood; case concerned long term treatment for a chronic condition rather than acute	In best interests, authority for treatment to be carried out
R v Cambridge District Health Authority, ex parte B [1995] 1 FLR 1055, March 1995, Sir Thomas Bingham MR, Sir Stephen Brown P, Simon Brown LJ; appeal against decision of Laws J	Jaymee Bowen, 10 years, relapse of acute myeloid leukaemia following treatment for non-Hodgkin's lymphoma	donor lymphocyte infusion, 'at the frontier of science'	Appeal by health authority against decision of Laws J on application by father for judicial review of decision of health authority not to fund an extra-contractual referral	Innovative treatment, judicial review of allocation of funds so no judicial consideration of whether treatment was in child's best interests R v Cambridge District Health Authority ex p B (No 2) [1996] 1 FLR 375, anonymity order discharged	CA allowed appeal against decision of Laws J to issue certiorari quashing the respondent's decision treatment funded by anonymous donor; died a year later from side-effects

(Continued)

Appendix 191

192 *Appendix*

(Continued)

Case	Age and Medical condition	Treatment	Procedure by which brought to court	Issues	Decision
Re C (a Baby) [1996] 2 FLR 43, April 1996, Sir Stephen Brown P	3 months, premature then meningitis, serious brain damage, cerebral blindness, convulsions, condition described as 'almost a living death', no prospect of amelioration, no prospect of recovery, no independent life as unable to breathe without ventilation	Withdrawal of ventilation & provide palliative care	Ward of court, application by health authority for leave to exercise inherent jurisdiction	Parents, doctors, nurses, second opinions agreed; court take responsibility; judge asked to but thought not appropriate to comment on circumstances in which leave of court should be sought	Leave to withdraw ventilation
Re T (a minor) (wardship: medical treatment) [1997] 1 WLR 242, Oct 1996, Butler-Sloss, Waite and Roch LJJ; appeal against order of Connell J	18 months, life-threatening liver defect biliary atresia	Liver transplant operation	Local authority sought leave of court under s.100(3) CA 1989; granted; local authority neutral before judge; Guardian advocating surgery; Connell J gave declaration sought and gave leave to appeal	Appeal allowed. The judge had applied the wrong test in forming the view that the refusal of the parents was unreasonable & then considering only the unanimous medical evidence, not the reasons for the parents decision. Was well established that the role of the court is to reach an independent decision as to the best interests of the child	CA held transplant not in T's best interests; subsequently reported that parents changed their minds & T had liver transplant

(Continued)

(Continued)

Case	Age and Medical condition	Treatment	Procedure by which brought to court	Issues	Decision
Re C (a minor) (medical treatment) [1998] 1 FLR 384, Nov 1997, Sir Stephen Brown P	~6 months, spinal muscular atrophy, type 1	Remove ventilation from C to see if could breathe independently but not re-ventilate if C suffered further respiratory arrest	Application by Trust for order under inherent jurisdiction, 'to seek the court's consent in the absence of the consent of the parents'		Declaration made
Re L (Medical Treatment: Gillick Competency) [1998] 2 FLR 810, June 1998, Sir Stephen Brown P	14 years, severe burns	Administration of blood in operations necessary to ensure survived, L refused as given faith as Jehovah's Witness	Hospital authority sought leave of court to administer blood transfusions in the course of essential operative treatment		In best interests to have blood administered in surgical procedure
Re M (medical treatment: consent) [1999] 2 FLR 1097, July 1999, Johnson J	15 years, heart failure	Heart transplant	Application by hospital for authority to perform transplant	Mother consented, M did not	Best interests and lawful to perform heart transplant, although when gave judgment 6 days later no suitable heart had been found
R v Portsmouth Hospitals NHS Trust, ex parte Glass [1999] 2 FLR 905, July 1999, Woolf MR, Butler-Sloss, Robert Walker LJJ, application for permission to appeal decision of Scott Baker J	David Glass, 12 years, severe physical & mental impairments	Dispute over treatment for infection after tonsillectomy, Trust believed David was dying, would only provide palliative care in future except emergency care, Southampton would accept as a patient	Application for declaration as to the course doctors should take if admitted & disagreements arose about treatment; refused, CA heard application for permission to appeal	See *Glass v UK* [2004] EHRR 15	Judge refused relief in application for judicial review; CA refused permission to appeal

Appendix 193

(Continued)

(*Continued*)

Case	Age and Medical condition	Treatment	Procedure by which brought to court	Issues	Decision
Re C (A Child) (HIV Testing) [2000] 2 WLR 270, Sept 1999, Wilson J	4 months, test to determine HIV status	Mother HIV+, GP wanted to carry out blood test to determine C's status & appropriate medical management	Application by local authority, health professionals having sought advice, for leave to apply for SIO	CA refused permission to appeal Re C (HIV Test) [1999] 2 FLR 1004, Sept 1999, Butler-Sloss, Evans and Thorpe LJJ	SIO made. Parents had removed C from jurisdiction, tested HIV+ couple of years later when mother died, returned to jurisdiction, made a ward
Royal Wolverhampton Hospital NHS Trust v B [2000] 1 FLR 953, Sept 1999, Bodey J	5 months, multi-organ failure, respiratory failure, circulatory instability, two small holes in heart, repeated infections, bleeding into the cavities in brain	Withhold ventilation on grounds pathology cannot be reversed, would die whilst on ventilation or only permit return to current clinical state	Urgent out of hours application by Trust for directions	Counsel for Official Solicitor argued court should not make declaration sought; should be a matter for clinical judgement of the doctors; that no declaration is necessary; nor should it be granted; court cannot override 'opinions of the experts clinically responsible for the child', Bodey J thought that there might be circumstances when that was appropriate but not in urgent case where lack of trust	Lawful to withhold ventilation
Re MM (Medical Treatment) [2000] 1 FLR 224, Oct 1999, Black J	7 years, Primary immunodeficiency	Parents wished to continue with immunostimulant therapy had been administered in Russia, doctors wanted to provide immunoglobin intrevenously	Local authority application for SIO, over course of proceedings reached agreement	Parental concerns included that they would be returning to Russia in a couple of years where blood products are not as safe; concerned that the treatment would not be available or would be too expensive.	Judge accepted as appropriate the order agreed during the hearing

(*Continued*)

(Continued)

Case	Age and Medical condition	Treatment	Procedure by which brought to court	Issues	Decision
A National Health Service Trust v D [2000] 2 FLR 677, July 2000, Cazalet J	19 months, severe, chronic & irreversible lung disease, heart failure, Dandy-Walker syndrome, lissencephaly.	Withholding ventilation in the event of a respiratory or cardiac failure & provide palliative care given worsening & irreversible lung disease	Trust application for declaration in respect of ward; then for wardship to be discharged	Required ventilation shortly after birth & first 50 days; cared for at home with periods hospitalisation; application precipitated by admission to hospital with fever; parents wanted him admitted to ICU; hospital did not have ICU; 3 hospitals contacted would not admit; in event recovered with drug treatment, Referenced in GMC Guidance, *Treatment and care towards the end of life*, 2010	Declaration made & wardship discharged
Re A (Children) (Conjoined Twins: Surgical Separation) [2001] Fam 147, Sept 2000, Ward, Brooke, Robert Walker LJJ, appeal against decision of Johnson J	6 weeks, conjoined twins	Surgery to separate the twins resulting in the immediate death of one twin	Trust issued an originating summons, in the exercise of the inherent jurisdiction of the High Court and in the matter of the Children Act 1989 for a declaration	Referenced in GMC Guidance, *Treatment and care towards the end of life*, 2010; Referenced in RCPCH, *Making Decisions to Limit Treatment in Life-Limiting and Life-Threatening Conditions in Children*, 2015	Separation surgery lawful Rosie (Mary) died immediately after surgery; Gracie (Jodie) continues to do well

(Continued)

(Continued)

Case	Age and Medical condition	Treatment	Procedure by which brought to court	Issues	Decision
Donald Simms and Jonathan Simms v An NHS Trust and Secretary of State for Health; PA and JA v An NHS Trust and Secretary of State for Health [2002] EWHC 2734, Dec 2002, Butler-Sloss P	Jonathan Simms 18 & 16 year old, variant Creutzfeldt-Jakob disease, vCJD,	Innovative Pentosan Polysulphate treatment	Application by parents for declaration lawful & in best interests	PPS tested in mice, rats, dogs for treatment of other conditions; judge asked first whether there was a competent body of professional opinion which supported its administration; then whether administration was in their best interests	Declarations made as lawful and in best interests; although treating doctors were prepared to administer, clinical governance committee & drugs & therapeutic committee, neither approved; DoH assisted in finding a hospital in Northern Ireland prepared to administer, administered following court hearing in Northern Ireland Jonathan Simms lived a further 10 years
Re P (Medical Treatment: Best Interests) [2003] EWHC 2327, Aug 2003, Johnson J	16 years, hypermobility syndrome	Administration of blood against wishes as Jehovah's Witness	Application by Trust lawful to administer blood	Had suffered an acute episode; crisis passed without need for blood; issue remained as underlying cause not identified; further crisis could occur which would be life-threatening without administration of blood Referenced in GMC Guidance, 0-18 years, 2018	Lawful to administer blood in situation immediately life-threatening & if is no other form of treatment available

(Continued)

(Continued)

Case	Age and Medical condition	Treatment	Procedure by which brought to court	Issues	Decision
Glass v UK [2004] EHRR 15, ECtHR, March 2004	David Glass, by this time 18 years old, severe physical and mental disabilities,	Were the actions of the doctors in administering diamorphine without his mother's consent & placing a DNR on his notes without her knowledge a breach of their ECHR rights?	Complaint by Carol and David Glass that their ECHR Article 2, 6, 8, 13 and 14 rights had been breached	Court did not address whether his mother's Article 8 rights were interfered with; nor did the majority consider it necessary to determine whether putting a DNR on his notes without his mother's knowledge was an interference with David's Article 8 rights; Referenced in GMC, *Treatment and care towards the end of life*, 2010; Referenced in RCPCH, *Making Decisions to Limit Treatment in Life-Limiting and Life-Threatening Conditions in Children*, 2015	complaints under 2, 6, 13, 14 deemed manifestly inadmissible; administration of diamorphine to David against the continued opposition of his mother an interference with his right to respect for private life, specifically his right to physical integrity, doing so without seeking consent from the court was not necessary in a democratic & amounted to a breach of David's Article 8 right.
Portsmouth NHS Trust v Wyatt & Wyatt, Southampton NHS Trust Intervening [2004] EWHC 2247, Oct 2004, Hedley J	Charlotte Wyatt, 1 year, chronic respiratory & kidney problems, profound & irreversible brain damage	Whether lawful to withhold ventilation if required to sustain life due to lung damage or due to an infection	Application by Trust for court to exercise inherent jurisdiction	Referenced in RCPCH, *Making Decisions to Limit Treatment in Life-Limiting and Life-Threatening Conditions in Children*, 2015	Lawful to withhold ventilation, ask treating doctors to give further consideration to tracheostomy

(Continued)

(Continued)

Case	Age and Medical condition	Treatment	Procedure by which brought to court	Issues	Decision
Re L (Medical Treatment: Benefit) [2004] EWHC 2713, Oct 2004, Butler-Sloss P	9 months, Edwards' Syndrome/trisomy 18	Mechanical ventilation & cardiac massage	Application by Trust for declarations in the exercise of inherent jurisdiction	Risks of ventilation causing cardiac arrest or becoming ventilator dependent depriving him of contact with mother Referenced in RCPCH, *Making Decisions to Limit Treatment in Life-Limiting and Life-Threatening Conditions in Children*, 2015	Lawful not to provide ventilation, no order made on cardiac massage which should only be withheld after careful assessment but ultimately a matter of clinical judgement although consider carefully within context of weight attached to prolonging life and in knowledge judge and guardian uneasy about excluding it
Portsmouth Hospitals NHS Trust v Wyatt and others [2005] EWHC 117, Jan 2005, Hedley J	Charlotte Wyatt, observed improvements, reduced oxygen levels, primarily good days & not requiring pain relief	Application by parents to stay orders pending court hearing as to whether orders should be discharged	Application by parents to stay orders		Declined to stay orders in absence of further evidence & given declarations did not affect duty of doctors to treat in best interests

(*Continued*)

(Continued)

Case	Age and Medical condition	Treatment	Procedure by which brought to court	Issues	Decision
Wyatt v Portsmouth NHS Trust and Wyatt (By her Guardian) (No 3) [2005] EWHC 693, April 2005, Hedley J	Charlotte Wyatt, reduced oxygen dependency although still too high to be discharged, some responsiveness to human interaction, no change in underlying condition	Evidence that underlying condition had not improved, ventilation would in all probability not prevent death from respiratory infection but death whilst receiving aggressive treatment in ICU	Application by parents to discharge orders		Declined to discharge orders
Re Wyatt (a child) (medical treatment: continuation of order) [2005] EWCA Civ 1181, Oct 2005, Wall, Laws, Lloyd LJJ, appeal against decision of Hedley J	Charlotte Wyatt	Appeal against declarations that it was in Charlotte's best interests not to be ventilated, that decision of the court should be made once issue arose	Application by parents for permission to appeal against Hedley decision of April 2005 on 'best interests' and on 'timing' question; hearing appeal latter	Referenced in GMC, *Treatment and care towards the end of life*, 2010; Referenced in RCPCH, *Making Decisions to Limit Treatment in Life-Limiting and Life-Threatening Conditions in Children*, 2015	Permission to appeal the best interests question refused; appeal on the timing question dismissed; review of the continuation of the declarations to be accelerated
Re Wyatt [2005] EWHC 2293, Oct 2005, Hedley J	Charlotte Wyatt	Review of declarations in light of medical evidence of improvement in Charlotte's condition	Application of parents for orders to be discharged	Hedley J set out the duties of clinicians to their child patient	Declaration discharged; declaratory relief not required at that time

(Continued)

(Continued)

Case	Age and Medical condition	Treatment	Procedure by which brought to court	Issues	Decision
R (on the application of Axon) v Secretary of State for Health & Another [2006] EWHC 37, Jan 2006, Silber J		Whether Department of Health Guidance on provision of advice & treatment to under 16's on contraception, sexual & reproductive health lawful	Application by Sue Axon for declarations that DoH guidance unlawful	Duty of confidentiality where sufficiently mature to make a decision; argument that the applicant's Article 8 rights were infringed dismissed Referenced in GMC Guidance, *0-18 years*, 2018	Not entitled to the relief claimed, bound by *Gillick* [1985], guidance not unlawful
Re Wyatt [2006] EWHC 319, Feb 2006, Hedley J	Charlotte Wyatt	Significant deterioration in condition believed to be due to a viral condition	Application by Trust declarations lawful to withhold intubation & ventilation; otherwise provide life-saving treatment	Litigation surrounding Charlotte's medical treatment & together with MB decided a couple of weeks later, marks a turning point in circumstances before Trusts will seek declaration on withdrawing or withholding treatment	Declarations granted, If continued to deteriorate only option would be ventilation in 24–36 hours, paediatrician considered that futile, Charlotte discharged from hospital in Dec 2006 into foster care

(*Continued*)

(Continued)

Case	Age and Medical condition	Treatment	Procedure by which brought to court	Issues	Decision
Re MB [2006] EWHC 507, March 2006, Holman J	18 months, Spinal Muscular Atrophy, caused loss of use of voluntary muscles, so dependent on ventilation	Withdraw ventilation & provide palliative care, if removed would result in immediate death	Application by Trust for declaration in exercise inherent jurisdiction lawful to withdraw ventilation & provide palliative care	Unusual as declined to make declaration sought by Trust, emphasis upon relationship with family, pleasure and experience Referenced in GMC, *Treatment and care towards the end of life*, 2010; Referenced in RCPCH, *Making Decisions to Limit Treatment in Life-Limiting and Life-Threatening Conditions in Children*, 2015	Lawful to withhold some treatments, broadly to continue current management but not escalate; did not make declaration requested that it was lawful to withdraw ventilation but could not make declaration that was in best interests to continue with continuous pressure ventilation
K (a minor) [2006] EWHC 1007, May 2006, Sir Mark Potter P	5 months, congenital myotonica Dystrophy, neuromuscular disorder causing chronic muscle weakness & learning difficulties	Withdraw artificial nutrition & hydration & provide palliative care due to recurrent septicaemia of central venous lines	At birth in care under ICO, local authority shared parental responsibility with the parents; application by Trust for declarations	All agreed withdrawal in best interests	Declaration lawful to withdraw nutrition & hydration & move to palliative care

(Continued)

(Continued)

Case	Age and Medical condition	Treatment	Procedure by which brought to court	Issues	Decision
An NHS Trust v A [2007] EWHC 1696, July 2007, Holman J	7 months, Haemophagocytic lymphohistiocytosis	Bone marrow transplant which had to be performed whilst condition not active, only hope of cure	Trust applied for orders in the exercise of court's inherent jurisdiction	Child at home; condition being managed with drugs; Holman J said could only perform bone marrow transplant if parents took her to hospital no suggestion court should order them or she should be removed from their care	In best interests & lawful to have bone marrow transplant. End of judgment noted that A had died at home about two weeks later before receiving any further treatment
Re B [2008] EWHC 1996, June 2008, Coleridge J	22 months, profound mental & physical disabilities possibly result of an inherited metabolic condition	Withhold ventilation & cardio-pulmonary resuscitation if condition worsens due to deteriorating illness or severely unwell	In foster care under care order; local authority share parental responsibility, local authority asked Trust to make application; Trust applied for declarations	Likely to deteriorate within next few years so that resuscitation necessary; Guardian supported application; local authority adopted a neutral stance; mother 15 years and had learning difficulties, guided by medical team, mother	Declaration lawful, included should consult with foster parents, joint expert report attached to order to assist doctor new to child in a critical situation

(Continued)

(Continued)

Case	Age and Medical condition	Treatment	Procedure by which brought to court	Issues	Decision
Re OT [2009] EWHC 633, March 2009, Parker J	9 months, mitochondrial condition of genetic origin, ventilator dependent from 3 weeks old	Not to escalate treatment & withdraw ventilation when OT was believed to have an infection thought to be due to the central line	Application by Trust for declarations; Judge made declaration permitting non-escalation; hearing & judgment focused on whether lawful to withdraw ventilation	Crisis during hearing meant required high pressure ventilation for which needed sedation, could not be continued long term as causes damage to lungs; condition deteriorated so severely brain damaged including to brain stem & dependent upon ventilation, nothing could do to improve condition *T and another v An NHS Trust and another* [2009] EWCA Civ 409, March 2009, Ward, Wilson LJJ; permission to appeal on grounds had been a serious procedural flaw in the judge's conduct of the hearing which infringed OT's Article 8 rights, refused; noted OT died following morning Referenced in RCPCH, *Making Decisions to Limit Treatment in Life-Limiting and Life-Threatening Conditions in Children*, 2015	Declaration lawful not to escalate treatment but adjourned the hearing in respect of withdrawal of ventilation; lawful to withdraw ventilation; refused permission to appeal
Re RB [2010] 1 FLR 946, Nov 2009, McFarlane J	13 months, congenital myasthenic syndrome, ventilated from birth	Withdrawal ventilation	Application by Trust	All 3 known drugs trialled with no effect; at start of proceedings mother agreed withdrawal of ventilation whilst father wanted home ventilation but changed his mind during proceedings	Judgment endorsed decision to withdraw ventilation agreed by clinical team & parents

(Continued)

(Continued)

Case	Age and Medical condition	Treatment	Procedure by which brought to court	Issues	Decision
LA v SB & AB & MB [2010] EWHC 1744, July 2010, Sir Nicholas Wall	6 years rare, progressive, brain disease, Rasmussen's encephalitis	Surgery to address worsening epilepsy	Application by local authority under s.100 for leave to invoke inherent jurisdiction; application for leave to apply for a SIO		Applications denied, had invited hospital to intervene or issue summons, which declined; no issue for the court to determine as was for parents & hospital; neither asked judge to determine question
NHS Trust v Baby X and others [2012] EWHC 2188, July 2012, Hedley J	1 year, accident at home, severe irreversible brain damage, requiring ventilation & naso-gastric feeding, no consciousness or awareness of self or surroundings	Withdrawal of ventilation	Application by Trust for orders in exercise of inherent jurisdiction	Treatment serves no purpose in terms of improvement; is persistent, intense, invasive; will require ever more intervention to sustain	Declaration lawful to withdraw ventilation & provide palliative care
An NHS Trust v KH [2013] 1 F.L.R. 1471, Oct 2012, Peter Jackson J	3 years, Herpes Virus Infection caused viral encephalitis resulting in severe brain damage	Advanced care plan permitting non escalation of treatment	Application by NHS Trust for declarations; approval of a treatment plan for KH; KH in foster care under ICO; care proceedings ongoing; parents lacked capacity to make decisions	Mother did not agree to all aspects of the care plan	Declarations made on treatment issues that need to be determined & not likely to change over time

(Continued)

(Continued)

Case	Age and Medical condition	Treatment	Procedure by which brought to court	Issues	Decision
An NHS Trust v SR [2012] EWHC 3842, Dec 2012, Bodey J	7 years, Neon Roberts, malignant brain tumour medullablastoma	Chemotherapy & radiotherapy, mother wanted him to have alternative & complementary therapy following surgery to remove brain tumour	Application by Trust for declaration under inherent jurisdiction; ICO made to facilitate return of Neon to care of father when mother missing with him	Judge noted that the Trust could have provided treatment on basis of his father's consent but understood application given the serious nature of the treatment	In best interests & lawful to be administered with chemotherapy & radiotherapy
Re TM [2013] EWHC 4103, Dec 2013, Holman J	7 years, developmental issues, fed by nasogastric tube	Gastronomy, gastrojejunal tube, which would enable removal of the PICC	Application by Trust for orders in the exercise of inherent jurisdiction, although during proceedings moved to consensus on procedure	Previous hearing declaration in best interests for PICC catheter to be fitted in heart to assist with feeding after removal due to infection	Declarations made; Father by this point giving consent; mother consent to procedures but did not want the doctor who had been caring for TM to perform the procedure; not an acceptable stipulation

(*Continued*)

Appendix 205

Appendix

(Continued)

Case	Age and Medical condition	Treatment	Procedure by which brought to court	Issues	Decision
An NHS Foundation Trust v R and Mr and Mrs R [2013] EWHC 2340, Dec 2013, Peter Jackson J	Reyhan, 14 months, mitochondrial myopathy, ventilation, admitted to PICU shortly after birth, remained, minimal awareness	Withdrawal artificial ventilation	Application from Trust for declaration permitting withdrawal of ventilation	Parents wanted him home ventilated, ventilation keeping him alive with no prospect of improvement in his condition, although had some awareness e.g. gain comfort from family not able to appreciate or respond to environment	Hearing in July decided in best interests for ventilation to be withdrawn; made interim orders giving time to make arrangements with orders permitting reduction in treatment if condition deteriorated; before final orders parents applied to admit new evidence; hearing set for end Oct; Reyhan died a week before hearing
An NHS Foundation Trust v A and Others [2014] EWHC 920, Feb 2014, Hayden J	16 years, vomiting of no organic cause or malignant pathology, resulting in severe weight loss	Insert a nasofeeding tube, refused by A & mother	Application by NHS Trust lawful & in A's best interests to insert a nasofeeding tube for administration of fluid, liquid & medication.	Judge suspended contact with mother for two weeks given her resistance to the treatment; relationship between A, hospital & social services had become 'conflictual' & A required decisions to be made by an authority figure, invoked parens patriae jurisdiction & made A a ward of court	Declarations made; A lacked capacity to make decisions about her medical treatment although her views given much weight

(Continued)

(Continued)

Case	Age and Medical condition	Treatment	Procedure by which brought to court	Issues	Decision
Birmingham Children's NHS Trust v B and C [2014] EWHC 531, Feb 2014, Keehan J	- week, heart problems	Parents' consent to A undergoing cardiac surgery, couldn't consent to A receiving blood during surgery or subsequently should that be necessary given faith as Jehovah's Witnesses	Application by Trust for orders in exercise of inherent jurisdiction	Parents did not want to take part in hearing as did not want to make it more complex than necessary; understood court may overrule their objection & would not actively try to prevent the treatment of their son	Order lawful to undergo heart surgery & for administration of blood if required, to administer blood if situation life-threatening, in other circumstances to consult with the parents about alternatives
An NHS Trust v A, B, C and a local authority [2014] EWHC 1445, March 2014, Mostyn J	13 years, pregnant	Termination of pregnancy	Application by Trust for declaratory relief as to capacity & if lacks capacity that termination in best interests, if has required capacity declaration to that effect to put the matter beyond doubt	Had been discussions with Safeguarding Team; if A decided to continue with the pregnancy she would require considerable support	Declaration that A had sufficient understanding & intelligence & for A to decide

(Continued)

Appendix

(Continued)

Case	Age and Medical condition	Treatment	Procedure by which brought to court	Issues	Decision
In the Matter of JA (A Minor) [2014] EWHC 1135, April 2014, Baker J	14 years, test & treat for HIV	Test for HIV status. Having tested HIV+, was it lawful to treat	Application by Trust under inherent jurisdiction seeking declarations lawful to test for HIV status; further application with respect to ART, monitoring, blood tests, chest x-rays, psychotherapy & peer support.	Trust sought to secure testing & treatment; local authority made an application for a child assessment order under s.43 CA 1989; the judge made a direction for a report under s.37 CA 1989 and then an ICO. JA was briefly placed in foster care. Agreed threshold criteria under s.31 were satisfied; JA subject to a supervision order for 12 months	Test: Macur J made JA a ward & required parents to take JA for the test; after JA had been placed in foster care he agreed to take the test & tested HIV+.. Treatment: lacked *Gillick* competence to make a decision about ART; authorised in best interests; JA had capacity to make his own decisions with respect to monitoring, blood tests, chest x-rays, psychotherapy & peer support to which he was agreed
In the matter of X (A Child) [2014] EWHC 1871, June 2014, Munby P	13 years, pregnant	Termination, initially X was opposed then wanted termination	Application by Trust	Child protection issues addressed in care proceedings; whether any criminal offences had been committed were for the police to determine	Lacked capacity to decide; termination in her best interests & lawful but X needed to indicate her views through her words & actions, be compliant & accepting

(Continued)

(Continued)

Case	Age and Medical condition	Treatment	Procedure by which brought to court	Issues	Decision
M Children's Hospital NHS Foundation Trust v Mr and Mrs Y [2014] EWHC 2651, July 2014, Cobb J	13 years, immune mediated inflammatory disease of the brain, usually due to infection	Plasma exchange treatment involving blood products, mother unable to consent due to faith Jehovah's Witness	Application by Trust	Urgent application; parents did not oppose; content for court to decide; fluctuating level of consciousness so uncertain whether competent but had given thumbs up when asked about it	Authorise PEX & blood as situation life-threatening; in other circumstances consult first with parents
An NHS Foundation Trust v AB and CD and EF [2014] EWHC 1031, April 2014, Theis J	14 months, incurable neurodevelopmental disorder, never left hospital, in PICU for 13 months receiving CPAP	Parents agreed should be extubated but wanted intubation (father) or bagging (both) in 24 hours after extubation given experience that required additional support in the period immediately after extubation when had been ventilated for a long period	Application by Trust for declarations lawful to withhold further intubation & bagging after extubation	Treatment limitation in context of deteriorating condition for which no treatment.	Made declaration sought but in 24 hours after extubation lawful to bag, at discretion of treatment team, confident will continue to work together in partnership with parents; use of bagging in light of experience of parents & considered by Guardian to be in best interests
An NHS Foundation Hospital v P [2014] EWHC 1650, May 2014, Baker J	17 years, paracetamol overdose	Administration of antidote	Urgent application by Trust for declaration lawful to administer antidote & if necessary restrain her	Mother had given consent but reluctant to treat without court order; had taken first dose but concern that she would refuse subsequent doses	On evidence before court not able to conclude lacked capacity under MCA 2005; lawful & in best interests to have antidote, if necessary, restrain

(Continued)

(Continued)

Case	Age and Medical condition	Treatment	Procedure by which brought to court	Issues	Decision
An NHS Trust v Child B and Mr and Mrs B [2014] EWHC 3486, Aug 2014, Moylan J	Young child (age not specified), burns sustained in accident	Required skin graft which may need blood transfusion to which parents unable to agree due to faith as Jehovah's Witnesses	Emergency Application by Trust for orders authorising provision of blood, heard by telephone	Parents cannot agree & oppose administration of blood due to religious beliefs	Orders made
Re AA [2014] EWHC 4861, Aug 2014, King J	12 years, serious brain malformation, hydrocephalus & severe epilepsy, tube-fed, visually impaired, significant developmental delay, no useful mobility	Ethics Committee agreed nutrition could cease, question for court whether hydration could as well	Application by NHS Trust (Great Ormond Street) for declaration lawful & in best interests for artificial hydration to be withdrawn	Devoted care of mother & family meant AA had lived beyond expected weeks or months from birth; in pain such that had been screaming constantly; mother had agreed that nutrition should cease & agreed that hydration should	Declaration made; totality of the evidence continuation of treatment burdensome to AA, existing as she does in a state of unremitting pain
In the Matter of Ashya King [2014] EWHC 2964, Sept 2014, Baker J	Ashya King, 5 years, malignant brain tumour medullablastoma	Form of radiotherapy following surgery to remove brain tumour	Application by Portsmouth City Council to invoke inherent jurisdiction for Ashya be made a ward of court & for directions about his medical treatment	Parents had removed him from hospital when he required post-operative treatment; concerns he was at risk of significant harm due to reliance on nasogastric feeding; local authority informed the police who issued a European Arrest Warrant; when found his parents were arrested & remanded in custody; discharged before the wardship hearing	Order made approving parental plan Ashya received Proton Beam Therapy in Prague

(Continued)

(Continued)

Case	Age and Medical condition	Treatment	Procedure by which brought to court	Issues	Decision
King's College Hospital NHS Foundation Trust v T, V, and ZT [2014] EWHC 3315, Sept 2014, Russell J	17 months, born 28 weeks gestation, had not left hospital, at 7 months acute cardio-respiratory deterioration, develop multiple organ failure, severe irreversible brain damage including to brain stem, pronounced & progressive hydrocephalus	Withdrawal of ventilation, parents Christian beliefs meant they did not think they had the right to agree to withdrawal of life-sustaining treatment; hoped may recover to participate more fully in life.	Application by Trust (King's College) for permission to withdraw ventilation	Independent report concluded numerous failures in care by multi-disciplinary team caring for him; ventilated 10 months after determined severe brain damage with no prospect of being removed from ventilation & no prospect of recovery of brain function	Permission to withdraw ventilation
Kirklees Council v RE and Others [2014] EWHC 3182, Oct 2014, Moor J	6 months, chronic lung disease, multiple cardiac abnormalities, kidney problems	Further life sustaining treatment, provision palliative care	In care under ICO; local authority shared; parental responsibility; Kirklees Council sought declarations; application supported by Leeds Teaching Hospital NHS Trust		Declarations made

(Continued)

(Continued)

Case	Age and Medical condition	Treatment	Procedure by which brought to court	Issues	Decision
Re A (A Child) [2015] EWHC 443, Feb 2015, Hayden J	19 months, choked on piece of fruit, two tests carried out both determining was brain stem dead	Parents could not agree to removal from ventilation, had tried to secure a package of care to take A to Saudi Arabia where the family originated & where life-support would not be removed.	Application by Trust for declaration		Declaration that A was dead & to permit ventilation to be withdrawn
Re AA [2015] EWHC 1178, April 2015, Bodey J	7 years, heart stopped causing brain damage	ICD in event of further cardiac arrest, parents want wearable defibrillator	Application by Trust for declaration in exercise of inherent jurisdiction	No doctor in court prepared to fit or advise parents on device they wished to use; consultant considered discharging her without fitting an ICD to be medically negligent	Lawful to implant Implantable Cardioverter Defibrillator
King's College Hospital NHS Foundation Trust v MH [2015] EWHC 1920, June 2015, MacDonald J; King's College Hospital NHS Foundation Trust v Y ND MH [2015] EWHC 1966, July 2015, MacDonald J	7 years, Spinal Muscular Atrophy Type 1, had cardio-respiratory arrest which had caused irreversible neurological injury	Withhold invasive ventilation, CPR, resuscitation drugs, receive pain relief	Application by Trust for orders giving authority to withhold treatment, first urgent out of hours application, then final orders	Urgent application due to concern if did not receive intubation & ventilation would die; usually should not be decided in urgent out of hours telephone hearing without full welfare investigation or second opinions, was a real possibility circumstances might require ventilation to prevent death over night; couple of days later judge agreed should be updated second opinions	June: Declaration pending further hearing July 2016: final orders after second opinion, father no longer opposed but wanted judge to decide

(Continued)

(Continued)

Appendix 213

Case	Age and Medical condition	Treatment	Procedure by which brought to court	Issues	Decision
In re Jake (A Child) [2015] EWHC 2442, Aug 2015, Munby P	~0 months, genetic epileptic encephalopathy of infancy	Lawful to withhold life-sustaining treatment	Parents learning disabilities, ICO; local authority shared parental responsibility; Trust made urgent application; hearing over telephone; local authority agreed & parents did not oppose		Lawful to withhold bag & mask ventilation, endotracheal intubation, invasive or non-invasive ventilation, lawful to withhold specific treatments in response to specific events
Re JM [2015] EWHC 2832, Oct 2015, Mostyn J	10 years, rare aggressive cancer, craniofacial osteosarcoma, in right jawbone.	Surgery to remove an aggressive cancerous tumour from J's jaw & reconstruct jaw using bone from his leg	Trust applied for declarations in the exercise its inherent jurisdiction	Local authority joined as a party given the family had disappeared, believed to Poland seeking second opinion; treatment was now urgent so at risk of significant harm	Judge of view should have sought SIO; gave leave; further reflection concluded that if the Trust is seeking final binding declarations, should apply for leave for an application for a SIO combined with an application for declaratory relief in the exercise of the court's inherent jurisdiction; treatment in best interests, permission given

(Continued)

214 *Appendix*

(*Continued*)

Case	Age and Medical condition	Treatment	Procedure by which brought to court	Issues	Decision
An NHS Trust v W and X [2015] EWHC 2778, Oct 2015, Bodey J	11 years, virus leading to heart failure, deteriorated so no longer considered candidate for heart transplant	Withdrawal of medical support devices which were keeping X alive	Trust applied for a declaration lawful to withdraw devices keeping X alive; urgent hearing within four days; Bodey J refused permission to appeal; Parents applied for permission to appeal	Tried numerous procedures, no longer suitable for heart transplant due to extensive lung damage, nothing left to offer, continued use of devices prolong inevitable death, extreme pain, sedated, unable to talk due to breathing tube; *In the Matter of I (A Child)* [2015] EWCA Civ 1159, Oct 2015, Jackson, Black, King LLJ, permission to appeal refused	Declarations made
Central Manchester University Hospitals NHS Foundation Trust v A and others [2015] EWHC 2828, Oct 2015, Holman J	14 months, Identical male twins, progressive, incurable, untreatable, neuro-degenerative disorder, in hospital since 5 months	Withdraw mechanical ventilation	Application by NHS Trust for a declaration lawful to withdraw ventilation	Condition irreversible, deteriorating, merely surviving, invasive treatment prolonging life, causing discomfort but no interaction to bring pleasure or enjoyment of life	Declaration made
Bolton NHS Foundation Trust v C and LB and PT [2015] EWHC 2920, Oct 2015, Peter Jackson J	8 months, sustained hypoxic-ischaemic encephalopathy (brain injury) due to deprivation of oxygen at birth	Withdraw of mechanical ventilation, if able to breathe unaided provide non-mechanical support	Application by the Trust for a declaration that lawful to withdraw life-sustaining treatment from C; C subject to a child protection plan	Judgment records parental wish for treatment to continue but parents not engage with hospital staff or legal actors or proceedings; father extremely hostile & vitriolic in criticism of doctors, nurses, hospital	Withdrawal of respiratory support authorised

(*Continued*)

Appendix 215

(Continued)

Case	Age and Medical condition	Treatment	Procedure by which brought to court	Issues	Decision
A Local Health Board v Y, Y's father and Y's mother [2016] EWHC 206, Feb 2016, Baker J	6 months, premature, infection, meningitis, brain damage, ventilation, required CPR due to brain damage	Extubation at a time optimal to achieve breathing but if unable to breathe not to re-intubate, not to provide CPR	Urgent Telephone application by Trust due to parental disagreement; after directions hearing & view of independent expert treatment plan agreed		Order by consent
County Durham and Darlington NHS Foundation Trust v SS, FS and MS [2016] EWHC 535, March 2016, Cobb J	7 years, profoundly neurologically disabled, deteriorated following chest infection	Lawful to withhold CPR, ventilation, provide palliative care	Final hearing following urgent application by Trust for court to exercise inherent jurisdiction at which interim declaration made; local authority party to proceedings; S in care under final orders	Parents in India as had been during earlier care proceedings; participated in hearing via telephone; did not accept that S was in a life threatening condition & considered deterioration due to poor care	Declaration made
An NHS Trust v AB and others [2016] EWHC 1441, May 2016, Parker J	2 years, neuro developmental disorder believed of genetic origin	Non escalation of treatment	Application by Trust for declarations lawful for hospital move to palliative care by withholding medical treatment including all forms of resuscitation in the event that his condition deteriorated to the extent that such treatments would otherwise be necessary whilst continuing to provide nutrition and hydration and control symptoms	*An NHS Trust v AB* [2016] EWCA Civ 899, June 2016, McCombe, King LJJ, permission to appeal denied; no novel question of law Following proceedings about AB's medical treatment under IJ, care orders were made, appeal against allowed, la withdrew application, *In the Matter of AB* [2018] EWFC 3, Jan 2018, Munby P	Declarations made; condition terminal; no question of a cure

(Continued)

(Continued)

Case	Age and Medical condition	Treatment	Procedure by which brought to court	Issues	Decision
Re A (A Child) [2016] EWCA Civ 759, July 2016, King, McFarlane LLJ; appeal against declarations granted by Parker J	2 years, in RTA 8 months earlier, spinal cord injury, devastating hypoxic brain injury, unresponsive, bouts of pneumonia which would eventually mean could not be ventilated	Withdrawal of respiratory support & provide palliative care	Appeal by mother against order made by Parker J on application by the Trust	Appeal grounds; wrong finding on fact of pain; failed to carry out careful balancing exercise on best interests; failed to have regard to obligation to protect life	Appeal dismissed against declaration of Parker J lawful to extubate & not re-intubate but provide palliative care
In the Matter of E [2016] EWHC 2267, Sept 2016, Munby P	2 years, Craniectomy to relieve intracranial pressure	Cranioplasty	Application by local authority to invoke inherent jurisdiction under s. 100(3) for decisions about medical treatment; care proceedings ongoing	Question whether should decide about procedure or decision deferred for others to take in due course	No clear cut answer; decision should be left to those who take responsibility for care of E
An NHS Foundation Trust v Mrs and Mr T [2016] EWHC 2980, Nov 2016, Peter Jackson J	2 years, low blood platelet count, believed to be due to medical condition affecting production of bone marrow	Administration of blood/blood products without which serious & potentially fatal consequences to which parents could not consent as Jehovah's Witnesses	Application by Trust for orders in exercise of inherent jurisdiction	Parents unable to consent but did not oppose, wanted court to decide	Order lawful & in best interests to receive blood or blood products, only after consultation with parents & if there is no clinically appropriate alternative

(Continued)

Appendix 217

(Continued)

Case	Age and Medical condition	Treatment	Procedure by which brought to court	Issues	Decision
An NHS Trust v BK, LK & SK [2016] EWHC 2860, Nov 2016, judgment published April 2017, MacDonald J	11 years, end stage high grade recurrent osteosarcoma, metastatic lung disease	Palliative care	Application by Trust for declaration lawful to be provided with palliative care in accordance with the treatment plan formulated by the Trust	Mother did not think his condition had been diagnosed; did not accept he was dying	Treatment plan proposed for the Trust for palliative care in best interests, judgment notes SK died in Jan 2017
Re EQ [2016] EWHC 3418, Dec 2016, Francis J	13 weeks, bilateral congenital cataracts	Surgery to correct	Application by Trust, not clear whether for declarations in exercise of inherent jurisdiction or s.8 as both welfare principle and best interests mentioned	At the end of the period of time for optimum treatment	In best interests to undergo surgery
GOSH v NO& KK & MK [2017] EWHC 241, Feb 2017, Russell J	7 months, pre-natal diagnosis of hypoplastic left-heart syndrome, had first stage of surgery, but doctors of opinion that further surgery was no longer possible	Withhold invasive & aggressive treatment; provide palliative care	Trust applied for declaration lawful not to provide invasive or aggressive treatment	MK was dying; further surgery not possible; ventilation & CPR her parents wanted her to have would only delay her death by a very short time, but would limit her quality of life, be frightening, cause pain & distress	Declarations made

(Continued)

(Continued)

Case	Age and Medical condition	Treatment	Procedure by which brought to court	Issues	Decision
A Local Authority and An NHS Trust v MC & FC & C [2017] EWHC 370, Feb 2017, Russell J	13 years, multiple disabilities, malnourished making susceptible to infection	Ceiling of Care, limitation of life-sustaining treatment	Application by Trust for declaration on a 'ceiling of care', lawful to withhold life-sustaining treatment; Care proceedings ongoing, under ICO but due to deterioration fact finding hearing had not been held; local authority shared parental responsibility, agreed with Trust plan, mother did not	Subsequent care proceedings *A Local Authority v MC & FC & C* [2018] EWHC 1031, finding had been substantial improvement in health and enjoyment of life in foster care; final care orders made and contact with mother limited	Review ICO; threshold met by evidence that mother had removed feeding tube and fed C orally putting him at risk of significant harm; interim declaration made, to be reviewed after neurological assessment
Gosh v Yates & Gard [2017] EWHC 972, April 2017, Francis J	Charlie Gard, 8 months at first judgment, infantile onset encephalomyopathic mitochondrial DNA depletion syndrome, MDDS	Experimental nucleoside bypass therapy or withdraw artificial ventilation & provide palliative care	Trust applied for declaration in exercise of inherent jurisdiction & SIO	Parents wanted trial of therapy which doctors at GOSH had been prepared to try but of opinion futile given severe & irreversible damage to brain from seizures; doctor in US at this stage prepared to trial; parents had raised money to pay for transfer & treatment in US through crowdfunding	Nucleoside bypass therapy not in best interests as futile; given quality of life & prospect of further deterioration continued ventilation not in best interests

(Continued)

(Continued)

Case	Age and Medical condition	Treatment	Procedure by which brought to court	Issues	Decision
In the Matter of Charles Gard [2017] EWCA Civ 410, May 2017, leading judgment McFarlane LJ	Charlie Gard	Appeal against orders made in the FD	Application by parents for permission to appeal against declarations made by Francis J that it was lawful & in Charlie's best interests for ventilation to be withdrawn & not to be provided with nucleoside therapy; hearing of appeal	Argument that where parents were agreed that it was in their child's best interests to be administered with a viable alternative therapeutic option their decision should be respected absence significant harm; that the hospital in seeking to prevent another clinician providing treatment in the exercise of his professional judgement had exceeded its powers as a public authority & the court had acted outside its jurisdiction in supporting the hospital	Appeal dismissed; orders made by Francis J remain in full
In the matter of Charlie Gard (Permission to Appeal Hearing), 8 June 2017, https://www.supremecourt.uk/news/permission-to-appeal-hearing-in-the-matter-of-charlie-gard.html [last accessed 28/02/20], Lady Hale	Charlie Gard		Application by parents for permission to appeal to the Supreme Court; https://www.supremecourt.uk/news/permission-to-appeal-hearing-in-the-matter-of-charlie-gard.html	Hospital entitled to bring proceedings; judge required to determine; applied correct principles of law; findings of fact cannot be challenged on appeal; No arguable point of law of general public importance	Permission to appeal refused

(Continued)

Appendix 219

(Continued)

Case	Age and Medical condition	Treatment	Procedure by which brought to court	Issues	Decision
Judgment of the UK Supreme Court in the Case of Charlie Gard, 19 June 2017, https://www.supremecourt.uk/news/latest-judgment-in-the-matter-of-charlie-gard.html, [last accessed 28/02/20], Lady Hale	Charlie Gard		On 8 June 2017 SC had reserved the right to stay the declarations, which it did on the 8th and 9th to enable the ECHR to consider a request for interim remedies; hearing at request of UK government on question whether should direct further stay of declarations to enable ECHR to hear substantive application by parents https://www.supremecourt.uk/news/latest-judgment-in-the-matter-of-charlie-gard.html	Raised question about application by parents on behalf of child that his rights have been violated by decisions made in his best interests, pointing out that in the domestic proceedings Charlie was represented by the court-appointed Guardian	SC stayed declarations until midnight on the 10/11 July, to enable ECHR to hear substantive application by parents.
Charles Gard and Others v United Kingdom. Application no. 39793/17, June 2017, http://hudoc.echr.coe.int/eng#{"doc umentcollectionid2":["DEC GRANDCHAMBER"," ADMISSIBILITY","ADMI SSIBILITYCOM"],"item id":["001-175359"]} [last accessed 28/02/20]	Charlie Gard		Complaint that the parents' and Charlie's rights under Art 2 and 5 infringed and parental rights under Arts 6 and 8 infringed		All complaints manifestly unfounded

(Continued)

Appendix 221

(*Continued*)

Case	Age and Medical condition	Treatment	Procedure by which brought to court	Issues	Decision
An NHS Hospital Trust v GM, DK and HK [2017] EWHC 1710, June 2017, Baker J	3 months, seizure caused extensive brain damage leaving largely unresponsive, ventilated,	No further CT scan or neurological intervention; lawful not to escalate care	Initial application by parents for declaration under inherent jurisdiction concerned that ventilation would be withdrawn; made ward; order directing the Trust not to withdraw life support or sustaining or supporting treatment, including extubation, pending full hearing; judgment followed urgent application as a result of deterioration believed to be due to internal bleeding	Judgment ex tempore at about 11.30 pm Friday following telephone hearing; further hearing on Monday afternoon to determine whether to continue declaration pending full hearing later that week	Declarations given on withholding neurological intervention, CPR; hearing scheduled for following week on non-escalation of treatment
GOSH v Gard, Yates and Gard [2017] EWHC 1909, July 2017, Francis J	Charlie Gard		Application made by GOSH to court at request of parents on ground they had new evidence; Position statements from parents, GOSH, Guardian can be found at https://www.serjeantsinn.com/news/charlie-gard-position-statements/ [last accessed 28/02/20].	Multi-disciplinary meetings were held; scans showed extent of muscle deterioration such that parents agreed that it was by then too late for the proposed therapy to have any beneficial effect so parents withdrew opposition to declarations	Declarations in Charlie's best interests and lawful to withdraw ventilation and provide palliative care unopposed. Charlie died after ventilation was withdrawn
Plymouth Hospitals NHS Trust v YZ and ZZ [2017] EWHC 2211, July 2017, MacDonald J	14, suspected paracetamol overdose	Testing of blood to determine levels of paracetamol & administration of infusion to clear of paracetamol	Urgent application by Trust over telephone for declaration treatment lawful & lawful to restrain & detain if necessary to administer		Declarations made

(*Continued*)

222 *Appendix*

(Continued)

Case	Age and Medical condition	Treatment	Procedure by which brought to court	Issues	Decision
A NHS Trust v S & L [2017] EWHC 3169, Nov 2017, Williams J	Born 2015, fatal syndrome	Withhold CPR & ventilation	Trust application under inherent jurisdiction for declaration lawful to withhold CPR & ventilation & SIO for ceiling of care and withdrawal of current breathing assistance (although agreed would continue this until final orders)	Interim declarations whilst parents secured independent expert & Guardian prepared report; lawful not to provide CPR but provide basic intensive support & time limited ventilation; if deterioration in respiratory function irreversible lawful to withdraw ventilation	Interim declarations made, final declarations later that month by which time L's condition had improved
King's College NHS Trust v Thomas & Haastrup [2018] EWHC 127, Jan 2018, MacDonald J	Isaiah Haastrup, 11 months, sustained severe brain damage due to oxygen deprivation at birth following uterine rupture	Withdraw ventilation	Applications by Trust lawful to withdraw ventilation	Father represented himself; doctor upon whom parents sought to rely had misled doctors at King's in order to gain access to Isaiah & may have committed an offence under the Medical Act 1983 in examining him	Lawful & in best interests for invasive ventilation to be withdrawn & palliative care provided; no therapy which could improve condition
King's College NHS Trust v Thomas & Haastrup (No 2) [2018] EWHC 147, January 2018, MacDonald J	Isaiah Haastrup		Father applied for permission to appeal to CA and to stay of orders pending appeal		Permission to appeal refused as no real prospect of success; stay of orders granted for 2 days to allow an urgent application to CA
Re Isaiah Haastrup [2018] EWCA Civ 287	Isaiah Haastrup		Application by father to Court of Appeal for permission to appeal against declarations made by MacDonald J	Judgment not available from Bailii, Court of Appeal, Lexis or Westlaw	Permission to appeal refused

(Continued)

(Continued)

Case	Age and Medical condition	Treatment	Procedure by which brought to court	Issues	Decision
Haastrup v United Kingdom [2018] ECHR 092, (application no. 9865/18), https://hudoc.echr.coe.int/eng-press#{"fulltext":["Haastrup"]} [last accessed 03/03/20]	Isaiah Haastrup		Application by father	Inadmissible	Isaiah died after ventilation was withdrawn
Alder Hey Children's NHS Foundation Trust v Evans [2018] EWHC 308, Feb 2018, Hayden J	Alfie Evans, 21 months, progressive, ultimately fatal neurodegenerative condition	Ventilation & palliative care; parents wanted to transfer him to Rome for tracheostomy & PEG to provide long-term ventilation; then, if necessary, to Munich to prepare for home ventilation	Trust applied for declaration continued ventilation not in best interests & not lawful to continue	Parents represented themselves; the doctor who gave evidence that it would be safe to transport the child by air ambulance had examined him in a clandestine fashion and had fallen 'far below the standards expected of his profession'	Declarations made; lawful and in best interests to withdraw ventilation
In the Matter of E (A Child) [2018] EWCA Civ 550, March 2018, King, McFarlane, McCombe LLJ	Alfie Evans		Parents application for permission to appeal; hearing of appeal	Appeal grounds: (1) that the judge had failed properly to consider what would be an appropriate palliative care pathway; (2) had failed to assess matters relevant to best interests or weigh up the available alternatives; (3) overriding parental choice was, in the absence of significant harm, incompatible with Article 14 of the ECHR, read with Art 8	Permission to appeal on grounds (1) and (2) refused; appeal on ground (3) dismissed

(Continued)

224 *Appendix*

(Continued)

Case	Age and Medical condition	Treatment	Procedure by which brought to court	Issues	Decision
In the Matter of Alfie Evans, 20 March 2018, Baroness Hale https://www.supremecourt.uk/news/permission-to-appeal-determination-in-the-matter-of-alfie-evans.html [last accessed 03/03/20]	Alfie Evans		Application by the parents for permission to Appeal to SC	On grounds that in the enjoyment of their right to respect for their family life under Article 8 of the ECHR, the courts had discriminated against them contrary to Article 14 on the grounds that the question should first be whether their proposals for Alfie's future care would cause him to be likely to suffer "significant harm", before consideration of his best interests	No arguable point of law, permission refused
ECHR declares application by parents of Alfie Evans inadmissible, 28 March 2018, https://hudoc.echr.coe.int/eng-press#{"fulltext":["Alfie Evans"]} [last accessed 03/03/20]	Alfie Evans		Complaint by parents to the ECHR		Deemed inadmissible; no detail of the application available
Alder Hey Children's NHS Foundation Trust v Evans [2018] EWHC 818, April 2018, Hayden J	Alfie Evans		Remitted by Trust to Hayden J given the inability to agree the terms of end of life plan & date for withdrawal of ventilation; Counsel for parents sought a writ of habeas corpus to release Alfie from hospital		Endorsed care plan constructed by the Trust; writ of habeas corpus misconceived and unarguable

(Continued)

(Continued)

Case	Age and Medical condition	Treatment	Procedure by which brought to court	Issues	Decision
Evans v Alder Hey Children's NHS Foundation Trust [2018] EWCA Civ 805, April 2018, David, King, Moylan LJJ	Alfie Evans		Parental appeal against decision of Hayden J to make no order on the habeas corpus application.		Issue of habeas corpus misconceived; matter determined by best interests; to act contrary to his best interests would be to infringe Alfie's rights
In the Matter of Alfie Evans, April 2018, Lady Hale, Lords Kerr, Wilson, https://www.supremecourt.uk/news/permission-to-appeal-application-in-the-matter-of-alfie-evans.html [last accessed 03/03/20]	Alfie Evans		Application by parents for permission to appeal against the decision of the Court of Appeal	An important case but did not present an arguable point of law of general importance	Refused, all issues determined by Alfie's best interests; not in best interests for treatment to continue, not lawful to keep him in Alder Hey or elsewhere, the release he was entitled to was from the imposition of treatment that is not in is best interests
ECHR finds fresh application from family of Alfie Evans inadmissible, April 2018 https://www.echr.coe.int/Documents/Decision_Evans_v_UK.pdf [last accessed 03/03/20]	Alfie Evans		Application to ECHR	Argument that prevention of Alfie's transfer from Alder Hey Hospital constituted deprivation of liberty & a violation of Article 5 (right to liberty and security) of the European Convention on Human Rights	Manifestly unfounded

(Continued)

Appendix 225

(Continued)

Case	Age and Medical condition	Treatment	Procedure by which brought to court	Issues	Decision
Alder Hey Children's NHS Foundation Trust v Evans [2018] EWHC 953, April 2018, Hayden J	Alfie Evans		Application to permit his removal to Italy having been made an Italian citizen had been denied previous day; ventilation withdrawn; application to set aside declarations on basis had demonstrated that his condition was significantly better than doctors had assessed	Noted that father had sought to issue a Private Prosecution alleging murder against some of the doctors at Alder Hey, rejected by District Judge	Refused, decisions upheld by CA later that evening in urgent application.
Evans v Alder Hey Children's NHS Foundation Trust [2018] EWCA Civ 984, April 2018, McFarlane, King, Coulson LLJ	Alfie Evans		Application by parents for permission to appeal. By father on grounds that Alfie had survived longer than expected & this represented a change in circumstances which justified review of the decision; that he was now an Italian citizen; on behalf of mother on basis of right to free movement within EU & that the course of action being contrary to Italian Law could lead to extradition & prosecution of clinical staff involved	Noted that Hayden J had conducted 10–12 hearings concerning Alfie's care, [26]; expressed concern about the unhelpful involvement of supporters in developing the grounds for appeal presented on behalf of the mother	Application for permission refused; no reasonable grounds for success; would need medical evidence for view circumstances changed Alfie died

(Continued)

(Continued)

Case	Age and Medical condition	Treatment	Procedure by which brought to court	Issues	Decision
An NHS Trust v A & B & C [2018] EWHC 2750, Oct 2018, Russell J	2 months, severe brain abnormality identified antenatally, almost constant seizures caused by brain abnormality becoming more frequent, prolonged & with more profound effects	Withheld intubation; as he suffered numerous seizures a day which required bag or mask or CPR event would soon occur where life-sustaining treatment could be withheld	Trust application for declarations lawful to withhold intubation or mechanical ventilation; cardiac massage & bag & mask ventilation, provide palliative care	Had tried 9 anti-convulsant drugs; mother wanted trial of further but no evidence before the court would make any difference; no available treatment for underlying brain abnormality; seizures which required bagging or mask & CPR could not be controlled; no treatment for them; death inevitable; notes reluctance of doctors to inflict pain and suffering on him	Declarations made
Manchester University NHS Foundation Trust v M & OA [2019] EWHC 468, Feb 2019, Hayden J; Manchester University NHS Foundation Trust v M & OA [2019] EWHC 1244, May 2019, Hayden J	13 months, end stage renal failure	Haemodialysis or palliative care (Feb); gastronomy (May)	In care under ICO; application on issue of medical treatment by Trust; local authority represented	parents both had mental health issues and believed in power of prayer; judge previously made order authorising removal of infected catheter; in first case evidence of consultant haemodialysis was in her best interests by narrow margin; judgment addresses the circumstances in which the case would have to be brought back to court	In best interests to have haemodialysis; in the event not working and palliative care considered need to return to court; in May court told had responded positively to the dialysis, gastronomy in best interests
University Hospitals Plymouth NHS Trust v B (A Minor) [2019] EWHC 1670, June 2019, MacDonald J	16, diabetes for which refusing insulin resulting in diabetic ketoacidosis (DKA)	Administration of insulin & intravenous fluids in treatment of DKA which B was refusing	Urgent & without notice application by Trust, 2pm Friday afternoon	Lived with grandfather who agreed to administration; difficult relationship with mother who B did not want contacted; no relationship with father; no evidence B lacked capacity, understood risk of death from refusal.	Treatment in B's best interests

(Continued)

228 *Appendix*

(Continued)

Case	Age and Medical condition	Treatment	Procedure by which brought to court	Issues	Decision
Cardiff and Vale University Health Board v T and H [2019] EWHC 1671, June 2019, MacDonald J	3 weeks, cardiac failure due to congenital condition	Administration of blood to manage cardiac failure refused by mother due to faith as Jehovah's Witness	Urgent application by Trust, 4pm Friday afternoon	Mother not represented nor were her solicitors present, T not represented	In best interests to have blood transfusion; orders made but listed for further hearing following Tuesday
Z v Y [2019] EWHC 2255, Aug 2019, Gwynneth Knowles J	6 years, intractable epilepsy not relieved by medication	Brain surgery	Application by mother for SIO, father opposed to surgery	Mother represented, father litigant in person, A not represented but matter urgent	Order made for A to have surgery as a matter of urgency
Tafida Raqeeb v Barts NHS Foundation Trust [2019] EWHC 2531 *(Admin) & Barts NHS Foundation Trust v Shalina Begum and Muhamed Raqeeb & Tafida Raqeeb* [2019] EWHC 2530 (Fam), Oct 2019, MacDonald J	Tafida Raqeeb, 5 years, catastrophic brain insult, unable to sustain breathing, minimally conscious state	Parents wanted transfer to Italy for continued care; doctors considered withdrawal of ventilation in best interests	Parents sought judicial review of refusal of Trust to permit transfer to Italy for continued ventilation; Trust sought SIO and declarations under IJ that it was lawful & in best interests to withdraw ventilation	Key to decision transfer in best interests evidence that Tafida was believed to be minimally conscious state, not in pain, stable & could be maintained for 10-20 years, as other children in a similar state in UK	Trust had acted unlawfully in failing to consider Art 56 TFEU right to receive medical treatment in another MS but no remedy as would have reached same decision had they done so; declaration on withdrawal of ventilation not made
An NHS Trust v CX [2019] EWHC 3033, Oct 2019, Roberts J	14 years, lymphatic cancer for which had been treated when 3 returned in different form	Administer blood & blood products which CX was refusing due to beliefs as Jehovah's Witness in treatment plan to which otherwise agreed	Trust applied for declaration lawful to administer blood & blood products	*Gillick* competent but in best interests to receive blood; doctors would use as little as possible to respect CX's views & accommodate them within treatment plan	Declaration lawful to use blood & blood products in treatment plan

(Continued)

(Continued)

Case	Age and Medical condition	Treatment	Procedure by which brought to court	Issues	Decision
Manchester University NHS Foundation Trust v Namiq, Ali, Namiq [2020] EWHC 180, Jan 2020, Lieven J	Midrar Namiq, 4 months old, deprived of oxygen during birth, born without heartbeat or respiratory function, heartbeat resumed & ventilated ever since	Withdrawal of ventilation & ensure a dignified death	Trust applied for declaration was dead	Referred to Academy of Medical Royal Colleges, *A Code of Practice for the Diagnosis and Confirmation of Death*, 2008, does not apply to babies under 2 months, so supplemented by guidance from RCPCH, *The diagnosis of death by neurological criteria in infants less than two months old*, 2015	Question whether Midrar was brain dead, established by clinicians applying tests for Death by Neurological Criteria on 3 occasions; as was dead no best interests analysis
Re M (Declaration of Death of Child) [2020] EWCA Civ 164, Feb 2020, Farlane, Patten, King LLJ; appeal from decision Lieven J	Midrar Namiq		Application by Midrar Namiq's parents for permission to appeal		Permission to appeal refused, declaration that Midrar had died on 1 October 2019

*Does not include cases concerning mental health or deprivation of liberty, vaccination or circumcision. 30 April 2020.

Bibliography

Auckland C and Goold I, 'Parental Rights, Best Interests and Significant Harms: Who Should Have the Final Say Over a Child's Medical Care?' (2019) 78 *Cambridge Law Journal* 287.

Bainham A, 'Changing Families and Changing Concepts: Reforming the Language of Family Law' (1998) 10 *Child and Family Law Quarterly* 1.

Bainham A, 'Private and Public Children Law: An Under-Explored Relationship' (2013) 25 *Child and Family Law Quarterly* 138.

Biggs H, *Healthcare Research Ethics and Law: Regulation, Review and Responsibility* (Routledge, 2009).

Birchley G, 'The Harm Principle and the Best Interests Standard: Are Aspirational or Minimal Standards the Key?' (2018) 18 *American Journal of Bioethics* 32.

Birchley G, 'The Harm Threshold: A View from the Clinic' in Goold I, Herring J and Auckland C (eds), *Parental Rights, Best Interests and Significant Harms: Medical Decision-Making on Behalf of Children Post-Great Ormond Street Hospital v Gard* (Hart, 2019) 107.

Brazier M and Bridge C, 'Coercion or Caring: Analysing Adolescent Autonomy' (1996) 16 *Legal Studies* 84.

Brazier M and Miola J, 'Bye Bye Bolam: A Medical-Litigation Revolution?' (2000) 8 *Medical Law Review* 85.

Brazier M and Fovargue S, 'Transforming Wrong into Right: What Is "Proper Medical Treatment"?' in Fovargue S and Mullock A (eds), *The Legitimacy of Medical Treatment: What Role for the Medical Exception?* (Routledge, 2015), 12.

Brazier M and Cave E, *Medicine, Patients and the Law* (Manchester University Press, 2016).

Brazier M and Montgomery J, 'Whence and Whither "Modern Medical Law"?' (2019) 70 *Northern Ireland Legal Quarterly* 5.

Bridge C, 'Religion, Culture and Conviction – The Medical Treatment of Young Children' (1999) 11 *Child and Family Law Quarterly* 1.

Bridgeman J, 'Caring for Children with Severe Disabilities: Boundaried and Relational Rights' (2005) 13 *The International Journal of Children's Rights* 99.

Bridgeman J, 'When Systems Fail: Parents, Children and the Quality of Healthcare' in Jane Holder and Colm O'Cinneide (eds), (2005) 58 *Current Legal Problems* (OUP, 2006) 183.

Bridgeman J, *Parental Responsibility, Children and Healthcare Law* (Cambridge University Press, 2007).

Bridgeman J, 'Misunderstanding, Threats, and Fear, of the Law in Conflicts Over Children's Healthcare: *In the Matter of Ashya King* [2014] EWHC 2964' (2015) 23 *Medical Law Review* 477.

Bridgeman J, 'The Provision of Healthcare to Young and Dependent Children: The Principles, Concepts, and Utility of the Children Act 1989' (2017) 25 *Medical Law Review* 363.

Brierley J and Larcher J, 'Compassionate and Innovative Treatments in Children: A Proposal for an Ethical Framework' (2009) 94 *Archives of Disease in Childhood* 651.

Cave E and Nottingham E, 'Who Knows Best (Interests)? The Case of Charlie Gard' (2018) 26 *Medical Law Review* 500.

Cave E and Purshouse C, 'Think of the Children: Liability for Non-Disclosure of Information Post-Montgomery' (2020) 28 *Medical Law Review* 270.

Cave E, Brierley J and Archard D, 'Making Decisions for Children – Accommodating Parental Choice in Best Interests Determinations: *Barts Health NHS Trust v Raqeeb* [2019] EWHC 2530 (Fam); *Raqeeb and Barts Health NHS Trust* [2019] EWHC 2531 (Admin)' (2020) 28 *Medical Law Review* 183.

Cobley C and Lowe NV, 'The Statutory "Threshold" under Section 31 of the Children Act 1989 – Time to Take Stock' (2011) 127 *Law Quarterly Review* 396.

Cretney S, 'Defining the Limits of State Intervention: The Child and the Courts' in Freestone D (ed), *Children and the Law: Essays in Honour of HK Professor Bevan* (Hull University Press, 1990) 58.

Cretney S, 'The Children Act 1948 – Lessons for Today' (1997) 9 *Child and Family Law Quarterly* 359.

Das R, 'Populist Discourse on a British Social Media Patient-Support Community: The Case of the Charlie Gard Support Campaign on Facebook' (2018) 24 *Discourse, Context & Media* 76.

Davies M, 'Selective Non-Treatment of the Newborn: In Whose Best Interests – In Whose Judgement' (1998) 49 *Northern Ireland Legal Quarterly* 82.

De Cruz SP, 'Parents, Doctors and Children: The Gillick Case and Beyond' (1987) 9 *Journal of Social Welfare and Family Law* 93.

Dingwall R, Eekelaar JM and Murray T, 'Childhood as a Social Problem: A Survey of the History of Legal Regulation' (1984) 11 *Journal of Law and Society* 207.

Douglas G, 'Family Law under the Thatcher Government' (1990) 17 *Journal of Law and Society* 411.

Douglas G, 'The Retreat from *Gillick*' (1992) 55 *Modern Law Review* 569.

Downie R and Macnaughton J, 'In Defence of Professional Judgement' (2013) 15 *Advances in Psychiatric Treatment* 322.

Dressler G and Kelly SA, 'Ethical Implications of Medical Crowdfunding: The Case of Charlie Gard' (2018) 44 *Journal of Medical Ethics* 453.

Dyer C, 'Sterilisation of Mentally Handicapped Women' (1987) 294 *British Medical Journal* 825.

Editorial, 'The Right to Live or the Right to Die' (1981) 283 *British Medical Journal* 569.

Eekelaar J, 'Parental Responsibility: State of Nature or Nature of the State?' (1991) 13 *Journal of Social Welfare and Family Law* 37.

Eekelaar J, 'Beyond the Welfare Principle' (2002) 14 *Child and Family Law Quarterly* 237.

Eekelaar J, *Family Law and Personal Life* (OUP, 2007).

Eekelaar J and Dingwall R, 'The Role of the Courts under the Children Bill' (1989) 139 *New Law Journal* 217.

Eekelaar J and Maclean M (eds), *A Reader on Family Law* (OUP, 1994).

Elias-Jones AC and Samanta J, 'The Implications of the David Glass Case for Future Clinical Practice in the UK' (2005) 90 *Archives of Disease in Childhood* 822.

Elliston S, *The Best Interests of the Child in Healthcare* (Routledge, 2007).

Entwistle V, Watt I, Bradbury R and Pehl L, 'Media Coverage of the Child B Case' (1996) 312 *British Medical Journal* 1587.

Ferguson PR and Laurie GT (eds), *Inspiring a Medico-Legal Revolution: Essays in Honour of Sheila McLean* (Routledge, 2015).

Forbat L, Teuten B and Barclay S, 'Conflict Escalation in Paediatric Services: Findings from a Qualitative Study' (2015) 100 *Archives of Disease in Childhood* 769.

Forbat L and Others, 'Conflict in a Paediatric Hospital: A Prospective Mixed-Method Study' (2016) 101 *Archives of Disease in Childhood* 23.

Foster C and Miola J, 'Who's in Charge? The Relationship Between Medical Law, Medical Ethics and Medical Morality' (2015) 23 *Medical Law Review* 505.

Fovargue S, 'The (Ab)use of Those with No Other Hope? Ethical and Legal Safeguards for Recipients of Experimental Procedures' (2013) 22 *Cambridge Quarterly of Healthcare Ethics* 181.

Fovargue S, 'Preserving the Therapeutic Alliance: Court Intervention and Experimental Treatment Requests' in Goold I, Herring J and Auckland C (eds), *Parental Rights, Best Interests and Significant Harms: Medical Decision-Making on Behalf of Children Post-Great Ormond Street Hospital v Gard*, (Hart, 2019) 153.

Fovargue S, McGuinness S, Mullock A and Smith S (eds), 'Conscience and Proper Medical Treatment' Special Issue (2015) 23 *Medical Law Review* 173–320.

Fovargue S and Neal M, '"In Good Conscience": Conscience-Based Exemptions and Proper Medical Treatment' (2015) 23 *Medical Law Review* 221.

Fox M and McHale J, 'In Whose Best Interests?' (1997) 60 *Modern Law Review* 700.

Fox M and Thomson M, 'Bodily Integrity, Embodiment, and the Regulation of Parental Choice' (2017) 44 *Journal of Law and Society* 501.

Freeman M, *The Rights and Wrongs of Children* (Frances Pinter, 1983).

Freeman M, 'Freedom and the Welfare State: Child-Rearing, Parental Autonomy and State Intervention' (1983) 5 *Journal of Social Welfare and Family Law* 70.

Freeman M, 'Sterilising the Mentally Handicapped' in Freeman M (ed), *Medicine, Ethics and the Law* (Stevens & Sons, 1988) 55.

Freeman M, 'Care After 1991' in Freestone D (ed), *Children and the Law: Essays in Honour of HK Professor Bevan* (Hull University Press, 1990) 130.

Freeman M, 'Taking Children's Rights More Seriously' (1992) 6 *International Journal of Law, Policy and the Family* 52.

Freeman M, 'Can We Leave the Best Interests of Very Sick Children to Their Parents?' in Freeman M (ed), *Law and Medicine, Current Legal Issues 2000* (OUP, 2000) 257.

George R, 'The Legal Basis of the Court's Jurisdiction to Authorise Medical Treatment of Children' in Goold I, Herring J and Auckland C (eds), *Parental Rights, Best Interests and Significant Harms: Medical Decision-Making on Behalf of Children Post-Great Ormond Street Hospital v Gard* (Hart, 2019) 67.

Gilmore S, 'The Nature, Scope and Use of the Specific Issue Order' (2004) 16 *Child and Family Law Quarterly* 367.

Gilmore S, 'The Limits of Parental Responsibility' in Probert R, Gilmore S and Herring J (eds), *Responsible Parents and Parental Responsibility* (Hart, 2009) 63.

Gilmore S and Herring J, '"No" is the Hardest Word: Consent and Children's Autonomy' (2011) 23 *Child and Family Law Quarterly* 3.

Grubb A, 'Treatment Decisions: Keeping it in the Family' in Grubb A (ed), *Choices and Decisions in Health Care* (John Wiley & Sons, 1993) 37.

Grubb A, 'Medical Treatment (Child): Parental Refusal and the Role of the Court' (1996) 4 *Medical Law Review* 315.

Hale B, 'In Defence of the Children Act' (2000) 83 *Archives of Disease in Childhood* 463.

Hallett C, 'The Children Act 1989 and Community Care: Comparisons and Contrasts' (1991) 19 *Policy and Politics* 283.

Ham C and Pickard S, *Tragic Choices in Health Care: The case of Child B* (King's Fund, 1998).

Harrington J, 'Deciding Best Interests: Medical Progress, Clinical Judgment and the "Good Family"' (2003) 3 *Web Journal of Current Legal Issues* https://www.bailii.org/uk/other/journals/WebJCLI/2003/issue3/harrington3.html.

Herring J, 'The Human Rights Act and the Welfare Principle in Family Law – Conflicting or Complementary?' (1999) 11 *Child and Family Law Quarterly* 223.

Herring J, 'Farewell Welfare?' (2005) 27 *Journal of Social Welfare and Family Law* 159.

Herring J, '*Re B (A Minor) (Wardship: Medical Treatment)*; 'The Child Must Live': Disability, Parents and the Law' in Herring J and Wall J (eds), *Landmark Cases in Medical Law* (Hart, 2015) 63.

Herring J, *Family Law* (Pearson, 2019).

Heywood R, 'Mature Teenagers and Medical Intervention Revisited: A Right to Consent, a Wrong to Refuse' (2008) 37 *Common Law World Review* 191.

Heywood R and Miola J, 'The Changing Face of Pre-operative Medical Disclosure: Placing the Patient at the Heart of the Matter' (2017) 133 *Law Quarterly Review* 296.

Hewson B, 'When Maternal Instinct Outweighs Medical Opinion' (2004) 154 *New Law Journal* 522.

Hoggett B, 'The Children Bill: The Aim' (1989) *Family Law* 217.

Hoggett B, *Parents and Children: The Law of Parental Responsibility* (Sweet & Maxwell, 1993).

Hoggett B, 'Joint Parenting Systems: The English Experiment' (1994) 6 *Tolley's Journal of Child Law* 8.

Jackson L and Huxtable R, 'The Doctor-Parent Relationship: as Fragile As Glass?' (2005) 27 *Journal of Social Welfare and Family Law* 369.

Kennedy I, 'Response to the Critics' (1981) 7 *Journal of Medical Ethics* 202–2.

Kennedy I, *The Unmasking of Medicine* (Granada, 1981, revised 1983).

Kennedy I (ed), *Treat Me Right: Essays in Medical Law and Ethics* (Clarendon Press, 1988a reprinted 2001).

Kennedy I, 'Emerging Problems of Medicine, Technology, and the Law' in Kennedy I (ed), *Treat Me Right: Essays in Medical Law and Ethics* (Clarendon Press, 1988b, reprinted 2001) 1.

Kennedy I, 'Patients, Doctors and Human Rights' in Kennedy I, *Treat Me Rights: Essays in Medical Law and Ethics* (Clarendon Press, 1988c, reprinted 2001) 1385.

Kennedy I, '*R v Arthur, Re B*, and the Severely Disabled Newborn Baby' in Kennedy I, *Treat Me Rights: Essays in Medical Law and Ethics* (Clarendon Press, 1988c, reprinted 2001) 154.

Kennedy I, 'The Doctor, the Pill, the 15-Year-old Girl' in Kennedy I, *Treat Me Right: Essays in Medical Law and Ethics* (Clarendon Press, 1988d, reprinted 2001) 52.

Kennedy I, 'What is a Medical Decision?' in Kennedy I, *Treat Me Rights: Essays in Medical Law and Ethics* (Clarendon Press, 1988e, reprinted 2001) 19.

Keywood K, 'Sterilising the Woman with Learning Difficulties – In Her Best Interests?' in Bridgeman J and Milllns S (eds), *Law and Body Politics: Regulating the Female Body* (Dartmouth, 1995) 125.

Keywood K, '"I'd Rather Keep Him Chaste": Retelling the Story of Sterilisation, Learning Difficulty and (Non)sexed Embodiment' (2001) 9 *Feminist Legal Studies* 185.

Keywood K, '*Re* B (A Minor) (Wardship: Sterilisation) [1988]: "People Like Us Don't Have Babies"' in Herring J and Wall J (eds), *Landmark Cases in Medical Law* (Hart, 2015) 39.

Kmietowicz Z, 'Down's Children Received "Less Favourable" Hospital Treatment' (2001) 322 *British Medical Journal* 815.

Kuhse H and Singer P, *Should the Baby Live? The Problem of Handicapped Infants* (Oxford University Press, 1985).

Laing J, 'Delivering Informed Consent Post-Montgomery: Implications for Medical Practice and Professionalism' (2017) 2 *Professional Negligence* 128.

Larcher V, Turnham H and Brierley J, 'Medical Innovation in a Children's Hospital: "Diseases Desperate Grown by Desperate Appliance Are Relieved, or Not at All"' (2018) 32 *Bioethics* 36.

Lee R and Morgan D, 'Sterilisation and Mental Handicap: Sapping the Strength of the State?' (1988) 15 *Journal of Law and Society* 229.

Lewis J, '"It All Really Starts in the Family...." Community Care in the 1980s' (1989) 16 *Journal of Law and Society* 83.

Lewis J and Cannell F, 'The Politics of Motherhood in the 1980s: Warnock, Gillick and Feminists' (1986) 13 *Journal of Law and Society* 321.

Mackay, Lord, 'Joseph Jackson Memorial Lecture – Perceptions of the Children Bill and Beyond' (1989) 139 *New Law Journal* 505.

Maclean A, 'Keyholders and Flak Jackets: The Method in the Madness of Mixed Metaphors' (2008) 3 *Clinical Ethics* 121.

Martin N, '*Re* B (A Child)' (1987) 9 *Journal of Social Welfare Law* 369.

Masson J, 'The Climbié Inquiry – Context and Critique' (2006) 33 *Journal of Law and Society* 221.

McLean S, *Old Law, New Medicine: Medical Ethics and Human Rights* (Pandora, 1999).

McLean S (ed), *First Do No Harm: Law, Ethics and Healthcare* (Ashgate, 2006).

Meller S and Barclay S, 'Mediation: An Approach to Intractable Disputes Between Parents and Paediatricians' (2011) 96 *Archives of Disease in Childhood* 619.

Michalowki S, 'Is it in the Best Interests of a Child to Have a Life-Saving Liver Transplantation?' (1997) 9 *Child and Family Law Quarterly* 179.

Miola J, 'Bye-Bye Bolitho? The Curious Case of the Medical Innovation Bill' (2015) 15 *Medical Law International* 124.

Miola J, 'Postscript to the Medical Innovation Bill: Clearing Up Loose Ends' (2019) 11 *Law, Innovation and Technology* 17.

Montgomery J, 'Children as Property?' (1988) 51 *Modern Law Review* 323.

Montgomery J, 'Consent to Health Care for Children' (1993) 5 *Tolley's Journal of Child Law* 117.

Montgomery J, 'Time for a Paradigm Shift? Medical Law in Transition' (2000) 53 *Current Legal Problems* 363.

Montgomery J, 'Law and the Demoralisation of Medicine' (2006) 26 *Legal Studies* 185.

Montgomery J, 'Conscientious Objection: Personal and Professional Ethics in the Public Square' (2015) 23 *Medical Law Review* 200.

Montgomery J, 'Patient No longer? What Next in Healthcare Law?' (2017) 70 *Current Legal Problems* 73.

Montgomery J, 'The 'Tragedy' of Charlie Gard: A Case Study for Regulation of Innovation?' (2019) 11 *Law, Innovation and Technology* 155.

Montgomery J and Montgomery E, 'Montgomery on Informed Consent: An Inexpert Decision' (2016) 42 *Journal of Medical Ethics* 89–94.

Morris A, 'Selective Treatment of Irreversibly Impaired Infants: Decision-Making at the Threshold' (2009) 17 *Medical Law Review* 347.

Neal M and Fovargue S, 'Conscience and Agent-Integrity: A Defence of Conscience-Based Exemptions in the Health Care Context' (2016) 24 *Medical Law Review* 544.

Oliver D, 'Challenging Local Authority Decisions in Relation to Children in Care – Part 1' (1988) 1 *Journal of Child Law* 26.

Oswin M, 'An Historical Perspective' in Robinson C and Stalker K (eds), *Growing Up with Disability* (J Kingsley, 1998) 29.

Packman J and Jordan B, 'The Children Act: Looking Forward, Looking Back' (1991) 21 *British Journal of Social Work* 315.

Parry M, 'The Children Act 1989: Local Authorities, Wardship and the Revival of the Inherent Jurisdiction' (1992) 14 *Journal of Social Welfare and Family Law* 212.

Parton N, *Governing the Family: Child Care, Child Protection and the State* (Macmillan, 1991).

Parton N, "The Changing Politics and Practice of Child Protection and Safeguarding in England' in Wagg S and Pilcher J (eds), *Thatcher's Grandchildren? Politics and Childhood in the Twenty-First Century* (Palgrave Macmillan, 2014) 45.

Read J and Clements L, 'Demonstrably Awful: The Right to Life and the Selective Non-Treatment of Disabled Babies and Young Children' (2004) 31 *Journal of Law and Society* 482.

Reece H, 'The Paramountcy Principle: Consensus or Construct?' (1996) 49 *Current Legal Problems* 267.

Ryan J and Thomas F, *The Politics of Mental Handicap* (Free Association Books, 1987).

Scroggie F, 'Why Do Parents Want Their Children Sterilised – A Broader Approach to Sterilisation Requests' (1990) 2 *Journal of Child Law* 35.

Smith C, 'Disabling Autonomy: The Role of Government, the Law and the Family' (1997) 24 *Journal of Law and Society* 421.

Smith P, 'Disabled Children and the Children Act 1989' (2010) 5 *Journal of Children's Services* 61.

Smith R, 'Child Care: Welfare, Protection or Rights?' (1991) 13 *Journal of Social Welfare & Family Law* 469.

Smith S, 'A Bridge too Far: Individualised Claims of Conscience' (2015) 23 *Medical Law Review* 283.

Smith SW, Coggon J, Hobson C, Huxtable R, McGuinness S, Miola J, and Neal M (eds), *Ethical Judgments: Re-Writing Medical Law* (Hart, 2017).

Smith SW, 'Catherine Stanton, Sarah Devaney, Anne-Maree Farrell, Alexandra Mullock (eds), *Pioneering Healthcare Law: Essays in Honour of Margaret Brazier*, and Pamela R Ferguson, Graeme T Laurie (eds), *Inspiring a Medico-Legal Revolution: Essays in Honour of Sheila McLean*' (2017) 25 *Medical Law Review* 165.

Smith SW, 'Individualised Claims of Conscience, Clinical Judgement and Best Interests' (2018) 26 *Health Care Analysis* 81.

Stansfield AJ, Holland AJ, Clare IH, 'The Sterilisation of People with Intellectual Disabilities in England and Wales During the Period 1988 to 1999' (2007) 51 *Journal of Intellectual Disability Research* 569.

Taylor R, 'Parental Decisions and Court Jurisdiction: Best Interests or Significant Harm?' in Goold I, Herring J and Auckland C(eds), *Parental Rights, Best Interests and Significant Harms: Medical Decision-Making on Behalf of Children Post-Great Ormond Street Hospital v Gard* (Hart, 2019), 49.

Tunstill J, Aldgate J and Thoburn J, 'Promoting and Safeguarding the Welfare of Children: A Bridge too Far?' (2010) 5 *Journal of Children's Services* 14.

Van Leuwen B, 'Free Movement of Life? The Interaction Between the Best Interests Test and the Right to Freely Receive Services in Tafida Raqeeb' (2020) *Public Law* 398.

Veitch K, *The Jurisdiction of Medical Law* (Ashgate, 2007).

Wilkinson D, 'In Defence of a Conditional Harm Threshold Test for Paediatric Decision-Making' in Goold I, Herring J and Auckland C(eds), *Parental Rights, Best Interests and Significant Harms: Medical Decision-Making on Behalf of Children Post-Great Ormond Street Hospital v Gard* (Hart, 2019), 85.

Wilkinson D and Others, 'Death in the Neonatal Intensive Care Unit: Changing Patterns of End of Life Treatment Over Two Decades' (2006) 91 *Archives of Disease in Childhood, Fetal and Neonatal Edition* F268.

Reports and Consultations

Bristol Royal Infirmary Interim Report, *Removal and Retention of Human Material*, (May 2000).

Butler-Sloss LJ, *Report of the Inquiry into Child Abuse in Cleveland* (Cm 412, 1988).

Department of Health, *Mitochondrial Donation: A Consultation on Draft Regulations to Permit the Use of New Treatment Techniques to Prevent the Transmission of a Serious Mitochondrial Disease from Mother to Child* (2014).

Department for Health and Social Security, *Report of the Committee of Enquiry into the Allegations of Ill-Treatment and Other Irregularities at Ely Hospital, Cardiff* (Cmnd 3785, 1969).

Department for Health and Social Security, *Better Services for the Mentally Handicapped* (Cmnd 4683, 1971).

Department for Health and Social Security, *Review of Child Care Law. Report to Ministers of an Interdepartmental Working Party* (HMSO, 1985).

Evans R (Chair), *Report of the Independent Inquiries into Paediatric Cardiac Services at the Royal Brompton Hospital and Harefield Hospital* (April 2001).

Grey E and Kennedy I, *Independent Review of Children's Cardiac Services in Bristol Report* (2016) https://www.thebristolreview.co.uk/ accessed 26 March 2020.

House of Commons Social Services Committee, *Children in Care* (HC 360, 1984).

Kennedy I (Chair), *Report of the Public Inquiry into Children's Heart Surgery at the Bristol Royal Infirmary 1984–1995: Learning from Bristol*, CM5207(I) (July 2001) http://webarchive.nationalarchives.gov.uk/20090811143745/http://www.bristol-inquiry.org.uk (accessed 26 March 2020).
Law Commission, *Family Law: Illegitimacy* (Law Com No. 118, 1982).
Law Commission, *Review of Child Law: Guardianship* (Law Com No. 91, 1985).
Law Commission, *Review of Child Law: Custody* (Law Com No. 96, 1986).
Law Commission, *Review of Child Law: Care, Supervision and Interim Orders in Custody Proceedings* (Law Com No. 100, 1987).
Law Commission, *Review of Child Law: Wards of Court* (Law Com No. 101, 1987).
Law Commission, *Review of Child Law: Guardianship and Custody* (Law Com No. 172, 1988).
London Borough of Brent, *A Child in Trust* (1985).
London Borough of Lambeth, *Whose Child?* (1987).
London Borough of Greenwich, *A Child in Mind* (1987).
Nuffield Council on Bioethics, *Critical Care Decisions in Fetal and Neonatal Medicine: Ethical Issues* (2006).
Nuffield Council on Bioethics, *Children and Clinical Research: Ethical Issues* (2014).
Nuffield Council on Bioethics, *Disagreements in the Care of Critically Ill Children: Emerging Issues in a Changing Landscape* (2018).
Nuffield Council on Bioethics, *UK Processes for Resolution of Disagreements about the Care of Critically Ill Children* (2018).
Nuffield Council on Bioethics, *Bioethics Briefing Note: Disagreements in the Care of Critically Ill Children* (2019).
Redfern, M, *Royal Liverpool Children's Inquiry: Report* (January 2001).
White Paper, *The Law on Child Care and Family Services* (Cm 62, 1987).

Professional and Clinical Guidance

BMA, *Children and Young People Toolkit* (last updated 2019) https://www.bma.org.uk/advice/employment/ethics/children-and-young-people/children-and-young-peoples-ethics-tool-kit/introduction (accessed 16 April 2020).
Court of Protection, *Practice Guidance 9E: Applications Relating to Medical Treatment* (2020) EWCOP 2.
Department of Constitutional Affairs, *Mental Capacity Act Code of Practice* (2007 last updated 2016) https://www.gov.uk/government/publications/mental-capacity-act-code-of-practice (accessed 27 March 2020 (under review)). 170.
GMC, *Protecting Children and Young People: The Responsibilities of All Doctors* (2012) https://www.gmc-uk.org/ethical-guidance/ethical-guidance-for-doctors/protecting-children-and-young-people (accessed 29 February 2020).
GMC, *Good Practice in Prescribing and Managing Medicines and Devices* (2013) file:///D:/Research%202018%20Book/materials%20read/GMC%20prescribing.pdf (accessed 8 March 2020).
GMC, *0–18 Years: Guidance for All Doctors* (2018) https://www.gmc-uk.org/ethical-guidance/ethical-guidance-for-doctors/0-18-years (accessed 16 April 2020).
GMC, *Good Medical Practice*, https://www.gmc-uk.org/ethical-guidance/ethical-guidance-for-doctors/good-medical-practice, last updated April 2014 (accessed 16 April 2020).

Bibliography

GMC, *Treatment and Care Towards the End of Life: Good Practice in Decision-Making* (2010) https://www.gmc-uk.org/ethical-guidance/ethical-guidance-for-doctors/treatment-and-care-towards-the-end-of-life (accessed 16 April 2020).

HM Government, *Working Together to Safeguard Children: A Guide to Inter-Agency Working to Safeguard and Promote the Welfare of Children* (2018) https://assets.publishing.service.gov.uk/government/uploads/system/uploads/attachment_data/file/779401/Working_Together_to_Safeguard-Children.pdf (accessed 24 February 2020).

Medicines and Healthcare Products Regulatory Agency, *Off-Label or Unlicensed Use of Medicines: Prescribers' Responsibilities* (2014) https://www.gov.uk/drug-safety-update/off-label-or-unlicensed-use-of-medicines-prescribers-responsibilities (accessed 8 March 2020).

Medicines and Healthcare Products Regulatory Agency, *The Supply of Unlicensed Medicinal Products ('specials') Guidance Note 14* (2014) https://www.gov.uk/government/publications/supply-unlicensed-medicinal-products-specials (accessed 8 March 2020).

National Specialised Commissioning Team, *Guidance for the Referral of Patients Abroad for NHS Proton Treatment* (2011) http://www.england.nhs.uk/commissioning/spec-services/npc-crg/group-b/b01/ (accessed 19 January 2015).

NHS England, *Clinical Commissioning Policy: Proton Beam Therapy for Children, Teenagers and Young Adults in the Treatment of Malignant and Non-malignant Tumours* (2018) https://www.england.nhs.uk/commissioning/wp-content/uploads/sites/12/2019/07/Interim-Policy-PBT-for-CTYA-for-malignant-and-non-malignant-tumours.pdf (accessed 24 February 2020).

NICE, *End of Life Care for Infants, Children and Young People with Life-Limiting Conditions: Planning and Management* (2016) https://www.nice.org.uk/guidance/ng61 (accessed 16 April 2020).

NICE, *COVID-19 Rapid Guideline: Critical Care in Adults* (2020) https://www.nice.org.uk/guidance/ng159 (accessed 29 April 2020).

RCPCH, *Achieving Consensus Advice for Paediatricians and Other Health Professionals: On Prevention, Recognition and Management of Conflict in Paediatric Practice* (2019) https://www.rcpch.ac.uk/resources/achieving-consensus (accessed 16 April 2020).

RCPCH, *Making Decisions to Limit Treatment in Life-Limiting and Life-Threatening Conditions in Children: A Framework for Practice* (2015) https://adc.bmj.com/content/100/Suppl_2/s1.full.pdf+html (accessed 16 April 2020).

UK Government, *Explanatory Memorandum to the Human Medicines Regulations 2012, No. 1916* (2012), http://www.legislation.gov.uk/uksi/2012/1916/pdfs/uksiem_20121916_en.pdf (accessed 8 March 2020).

World Medical Association, *Declaration of Helsinki – Ethical Principles for Medical Research Involving Human Subjects* (2013) https://www.wma.net/policies-post/wma-declaration-of-helsinki-ethical-principles-for-medical-research-involving-human-subjects/ (accessed 8 March 2020).

News Items

BBC News, 'Alfie Evans Parents 'Feared' They Would Resent New Baby' (3 September 2018) https://www.bbc.co.uk/news/uk-england-merseyside-45402094 (accessed 24 February 2020).

BBC News, 'Isaiah Haastrup: Parents Make Appeal to European Court' (2 March 2018) http://www.bbc.co.uk/news/uk-england-london-43245813 (accessed 5 March 2018).
Boseley S, 'NHS to Pay for Ashya King's Proton Therapy Treatment' *The Guardian* (26 September 2014) 8.
Editorial, 'Sterilization – The Need for Safeguards' *The Times* (22 July 1975).
Editorial, 'A Wise and Compassionate Decision' *The Times* (18 September 1975).
Editorial, 'Heart Baby Challenge', *The Guardian* (7 December 1987).
Editorial, 'Rational Rationing' *The Times* (27 October 1995).
Fernand D, 'A baby Waiting for His Turn to Live - Which Sick Child Will be Given a Vital Heart Operation?' *Sunday Times* (31 January 1988).
Hoyland P and Wintour P, 'Hole-in-Heart Child Loses Fight for Life' *The Guardian* (21 February 1988).
Huckerby M, 'High Court Forbids Sterilization of Handicapped Girl Aged 11' *The Times* (18 September 1975).
Osman A, 'Conscience Is Clear, Murder Case Doctor Says' *The Times* (3 April 1981).
Payne S, 'Christmas with Foster Parents for Right-to-Life Charlotte' *Daily Telegraph* (21 December 2006).
'Sky News, Parents of Tafida Raqeeb: Our Victory Shows Need for Law Change' (5 October 2019) https://www.youtube.com/watch?v=FNOykm02IV4 (accessed 26 March 2020).
Symons X, 'Charlie Gard Amendment Introduced into British Parliament' *Bioedge* (15 September 2018) https://www.bioedge.org/bioethics/charlie-gard-amendment-introduced-into-british-parliament/12811 accessed 31 January 2020.
Woolfe S, 'The Alfie Evans Case Has Proven that We Need to Change the Law in Favour of Parents' *The Independent* (27 April 2020).

Resources relating to individual children

Alfie Evans: Website: http://www.savealfieevans.com/; Facebook: https://www.facebook.com/groups/alfiesarmy/; Twitter: @Alfiesarmy16; Instagram: alfiesarmy16.
Ashya King: Naveed King, 'Real Story of Ashya King', https://www.youtube.com/watch?v=F93RjILFOXk, posted 30 August 2014 (accessed 19 April 2020); BBC 1, *Ashya – The Untold Story*.
Charlie Gard: Website: http://www.charliesfight.org; Facebook: Charlie Gard Public Group; Twitter: @Fight4Charlie; Instagram: #charliesfight; Charlie Gard Foundation, https://www.thecharliegardfoundation.org/charlies-law/ (accessed 26 March 2020).
David Glass, http://www.angelfire.com/ex/davidglass1/ (accessed 19 April 2020).
Jaymee Bowen: Panorama, *The Story of Child B* (26 October 1995); Barclay S, *Jaymee; The Story of Child B* (Viking, 1996).
Neon Roberts: *Against All Odds: The Sally Roberts Story*, https://sallyrobertsourstory.wordpress.com/sally-roberts-story/ (accessed 19 April 2020); Channel 4, *You're Killing My Son: The Mum Who Went on the Run* (2013); Alliance for Natural Health International, 'Sally Roberts in Her Own Words' (2013) https://www.anhinternational.org/2013/08/21/anh-exclusive-sally-roberts-in-her-own-words/ (accessed 19 April 2020).
Charlotte Wyatt, http://charlottewyatt.blogspot.com (no longer accessible).

Other

HC Deb 26 October 1989, vol 158, col 1075.

HL Deb 6 December 1988, vol 502, col 488, 493.

Ministry of Justice, *Practice Direction 12D – Inherent Jurisdiction (including Wardship) Proceedings*, https://www.justice.gov.uk/courts/procedure-rules/family/practice_directions/pd_part_12d (accessed 28 March 2020).

NHS England, Proton Beam Therapy, https://www.england.nhs.uk/commissioning/spec-services/highly-spec-services/pbt/ (accessed 24 February 2020).

Cases Index

A v Liverpool City Council [1982] AC 363 34
Aintree University Hospital NHS Foundation Trust v James [2013] UKSC 67 66, 85
Airedale NHS Trust v Bland [1993] 2 WLR 316 19n95, 57
Alder Hey Children's NHS Foundation Trust v Evans [2018] EWHC 308 142–143
Axon [2006] EWHC 37 13, 80

Barnet London Borough Council v AL and others [2017] EWHC 125 171
Barts NHS Foundation Trust v Shalina Begum & Tafida Raqeeb [2019] EWHC 2531; [2019] EWHC 2530 11–12, 17, 41, 70–71, 82, 144–145
Birmingham Children's NHS Trust v B and C [2014] EWHC 531 78
Bolam v Friern Hospital Management Committee [1957] 1 WLR 582 4, 19, 57, 75, 105, 129, 155–156, 163
Bolitho v City & Hackney HA [1998] AC 232 18n84, 75–76, 156
Bolton NHS Foundation Trust v C and LB and PT [2015] EWHC 2920 76n20

Cardiff and Vale University Health Board v T and H [2019] EWHC 1671 79
Central Manchester University Hospitals NHS Foundation Trust v A and others [2015] EWHC 2828 136n106
Charles Gard and Others v United Kingdom (2017) 65, 141, 163, 172
Chester v Afshar [2004] UKHL 41 19

County Durham and Darlington NHS Foundation Trust v SS, FS and MS [2016] EWHC 535 76n20, 138n117

Darnley v Croydon Health Services NHS Trust [2018] UKSC 50 75
Donald Simms and Jonathan Simms v An NHS Trust and Secretary of State for Health, PA and JA v An NHS Trust and Secretary of State for Health [2002] EWHC 2734 155–156, 159

ECHR declares application by parents of Alfie Evans inadmissible, 28 March 2018 174
Evans v Alder Hey Children's NHS Foundation Trust [2018] EWCA Civ 805 13–14

Gillick v West Norfolk and Wisbech Area Health Authority and another [1986] AC 112 10, 12, 30, 31, 46, 49, 50–51, 64, 80–81, 99, 104
Glass [1999] 2 FLR 905 22n107, 69–70
Glass v UK [2004] EHRR 15 22n107, 59–63, 173
Gloucestershire County Council v Re K [2017] EWHC 1083 55
Gorringe v Calderdale Metropolitan Borough Council [2004] UKHL 15 16
GOSH v Gard, Yates and Gard [2017] EWHC 1909 163
GOSH v NO & KK & MK [2017] EWHC 241 84n60
Gosh v Yates & Gard [2017] EWHC 927 10, 139–140, 159

An Hospital Trust v GM, DK, HK [2017] EWHC 1710 133–134

In re Jake [2015] EWHC 2442 110–111
In the Matter of Alfie Evans (2018) 71, 167, 173
In the Matter of Ashya King (2014) 10, 29, 39n97, 152–154, 169n13, 170
In the Matter of Charles Gard [2017] EWCA Civ 410 37, 65, 76, 82, 140
In the Matter of Charlie Gard (Permission to Appeal Hearing), 8 June 2017 38, 65, 172
In the Matter of E [2016] EWHC 2267 30
In the Matter of E [2018] EWCA Civ 550 112–113, 143, 173
In the Matter of JA [2014] EWHC 1135 76n25, 80n39

J v C [1970] AC 668 14n68, 64
Judgment of the UK Supreme Court in the Case of Charlie Gard (2017) 139–141

King's College Hospital NHS Foundation Trust v MH [2015] EWHC 1920 132, 135
King's College Hospital NHS Foundation Trust v T, V, and ZT Foundation Trust v T, V, and ZT 135n104
King's College NHS Trust v Thomas & Haastrup [2018] EWHC 127 76, 82, 141–142, 143
Kirklees Council v RE and Others [2014] EWHC 3182 108–109

LA v SB & AB & MB [2010] EWHC 1744 39n94
A Local Authority and An NHS Trust v MC & FC & C [2017] EWHC 370 113–114
A Local Authority v J, S and R [2018] EWFC 28 114

Mabon v Mabon [2005] 3 WLR 460 13
Manchester University NHS Foundation Trust v Namiq, Ali, Namiq [2020] EWHC 180 146–147
Maynard v West Midlands Regional Health Authority [1984] 1 WLR 634 75

Montgomery v Lanarkshire Health Board [2015] UKSC 11 19–21, 57, 77n30, 139, 158
Ms B v An NHS Hospital Trust [2002] EWHC 429 85n65

A National Health Service Trust v D [2000] 2 FLR 677 125
An NHS Foundation Hospital v P [2014] EWHC 1650 80n39
An NHS Trust v A [2007] EWHC 1696 66, 148–149
An NHS Foundation Trust v A and Others [2014] EWHC 920 80n39, 81
An NHS Trust v AB [2016] EWCA Civ 899 62, 137
NHS Foundation Trust v Mrs and Mr T [2016] EWHC 2980 78n34
NHS Trust v A & B & C [2018] EWHC 2750 134, 135, 137
NHS Trust v Baby X and others [2012] EWHC 2188 136n105, 139n120
An NHS Trust v CX [2019] EWHC 3033 80n39, 99n24
An NHS Trust v MB [2006] EWHC 507 65, 66, 117, 125, 129–132, 146
An NHS Trust v SR [2012] EWHC 3842 22, 76n25, 151–152
An NHS Trust v W and X [2015] EWHC 2778 134–135

Plymouth Hospitals NHS Trust v YZ and ZZ [2017] EWHC 2211 80n39, 81
Portsmouth NHS Trust v Wyatt & Wyatt, Southampton NHS Trust Intervening [2004] EWHC 2247 55, 65, 126–127, 146
Portsmouth Hospitals NHS Trust v Wyatt and others [2005] EWHC 117 127

R (G) v Barnet London Borough Council [2003] UKHL 57 123n28
R v Arthur [1981] 12 BMLR 1 2, 11, 47–49, 119, 176, 184
R v Cambridge District Health Authority, ex parte B [1981] 12 BMLR 1 9, 68–69, 149–151
R v Central Birmingham Health Authority ex parte Collier (1988) 54n43, 67–68
R v Central Birmingham Health Authority ex parte Walker [1987] BMLR 32 54n43, 67–68

Cases Index

R v Reed [1982] Crim LR 819 2
Re A [2001] Fam 147 5, 32n41, 106
Re A [2000] 1 FLR 549 66, 106
Re A (A Child) [2015] EWHC 443 146n157
Re A (A Child) [2016] EWCA Civ 759 137n112, 135
Re AA [2014] EWHC 4861 132
Re AA [2015] EWHC 1178 76
Re B [1981] 1 WLR 1421 2, 46–49, 54, 95–96, 118–119, 123
Re B [1988] AC 199 42, 54, 64, 95
Re B [1991] 2 FLR 426 54
Re B [2008] EWHC 1996 109
Re C [1990] Fam 26 52, 54, 95, 120–121
Re C [1996] 2 FLR 43 124
Re C [1997] 2 FLR 180 39
Re C [1998] 1 FLR 384 124 131
Re C [2016] EWCA Civ 374 171
Re D [1976] Fam 185 42, 45, 54, 58, 63–64, 95, 101–102
Re E [1991] 2 FLR. 585 100n30, 104
Re E [1993] 1 FLR 386 42, 54–55, 58, 80n39
Re F [1990] 2 AC 1 19n95, 57, 102n41
Re G [2012] EWCA Civ 1233 14
Re G-U [1984] FLR 811 42, 54
Re HG [1993] 1 FLR 587 100n30, 104–105
Re J [1991] Fam 33 52–54, 65–66, 77, 79, 83, 95, 121, 134, 145
Re J Re J [1993] Fam 15 53–54, 65, 77, 79, 82–83, 121–124
Re JM [2015] EWHC 2832 55–56, 66
Re K [2011] EWHC 4031 113
Re K, W and H [1993] 1 FLR 854 55n58, 80n41, 98n22
Re L [1998] 2 FLR 810 80n41, 81
Re L [2004] EWHC 2713 84n61
Re M [1988] 2 FLR 497 100n30

Re M [1999] 2 FLR 1097 80n41
Re M [2020] EWCA Civ 164 147n159
Re MM [2000] 1 FLR 224 55n58
Re O [1993] 2 FLR 149 55, 97
Re OT [2009] EWHC 633 136n108
Re P [1986] 1 FLR 272 42, 54, 95
Re P [2003] EWHC 2327 80n39
Re R [1992] 1 FLR 190 54, 63, 80, 94, 97–98, 122n22
Re R [1993] 2 FLR 757 55, 97
Re S [1993] 1 FLR 376 78
Re S [1994] 2 FLR 1065 80n41, 81
Re S [2000] 2 FLR 389 19n95
Re SL [2000] 2 FLR 452 106
Re T [1997] 1 WLR 242 18, 59–60, 66n112, 148, 168–169
Re W [1993] Fam 64 64, 80n40, 94, 98–100
Re Wyatt [2005] EWHC 2293 74, 77, 83, 84–85, 128–129
Re Wyatt [2005] EWCA Civ 1181 49, 65, 128, 132, 146
Re Wyatt [2006] EWHC 319 129
Royal Wolverhampton Hospital NHS Trust v B [2000] 1 FLR 953 59, 124

Sidaway v Board of Governors of the Bethlem Royal Hospital [1985] 2 WLR 480 19–20, 57

University Hospitals Plymouth NHS Trust v B [2019] EWHC 1670 80n39, 99n24

Westminster City Council v M and F and H [2017] EWHC 518 111n89
Wyatt v Portsmouth NHS Trust and Wyatt [2005] EWCA Civ 1181 199
Wyatt v Portsmouth NHS Trust and Wyatt (No 3) [2005] EWHC 693 127–128

Index

0-18 years, GMC (General Medical Council) 89–90

abortion 42
Abortion Act 1967 85
Access to Medical Treatments (Innovation) Act 2016 157n41
Access to Palliative Care and Treatment of Children Bill 177–178
Alder Hey 8, 112, 142
Alfie Evans 13, 24, 71, 117, 139, 145, 174, 177
allocation decisions 70
alternative therapies 159
appropriate treatment 76; limiting life-sustaining treatment 144–146
Armstrong, Grant 162
Arthur, Dr. 47
Auckland, Cressida 13, 174–175
Austin, Louise 178
authorities, support for parents (Children Act 1989) 33–34

Bainham, Andrew 33n46, 171n23
Barclay, Sarah 70
Beckford, Jasmine 28
bed-blocker 70
best interests of children 17–18, 91; duty of doctors 77–80; guidance on 89–92; judicial determination of 63–67
blood, administration of 78–79, 97
BMA (British Medical Association): *Children and Young People Ethics Toolkit* 88, 90, 106
Bolam test 57, 155–156
Brazier, Margaret 100
Bridge, Caroline 100
Brierley, Joe 154–155, 158

Bristol Inquiry 7–8

Cambridge Health Authority 22
cardiac services 7
care for sick infants 47–48
care proceedings 38
Carlile, Kimberley 28
Cave, Emma 164
ceiling of care 114
Charlie Gard 13, 24, 71, 117, 139, 145, 174, 177
Charlie's Law 177
Charlotte Wyatt 22, 74, 84, 117, 125–129
Child Abuse scandal 28
Childhood Cancer Leukaemia Group 150–151
Children Act 1989 11, 15, 16, 26–30, 90, 178; disabled children 123; inherent jurisdiction 37–38; medical treatment 41–43; new orders 35–38; parental responsibility 30–32; public law 38–41; public responsibilities 93; responsibility to support parents 33–34; wardship 34–38; welfare principle 32–33
Children Act 2004 16
Children and Young Persons Act 1933 31
children's healthcare services 6–10
children's rights 12–13
Christie NHS Proton Beam Therapy Centre 152n18
Clatterbridge Cancer Centre NHS Foundation Trust 152n18
Clements, Luke 48, 101, 105, 118–119, 123
clinical ethics committees 158
clinical frailty scale 146n156

Code of Practice 3
Community Care legislation 28
conflict between parents and professionals 9–10
conscience, professional judgement and 83–85
consumerism 18–23
contraception, *Gillick* 49–51
courts, decision-making 57–63
Cretney, Stephen 44
criminal liability, parental authority and 46–49
Critical care decision in fetal and neonatal medicine 131–132
crowdfunding 23

David Glass 22, 59–62, 69
decision-making: by the court 57–63; duty of doctors 80–81
differences of medical opinion 62, 75, 177–178
Disability Discrimination Act 1995 133n82
disabled babies 116–119
disabled people 118, 123
disagreements 84
doctor/adult patient relationship 18–20
doctors: decision-making 80–81; duty of care to child 75–77; duty to act in best interests of the child 77–80; *Good Medical Practice* 87–92; legal duties of 73–75; professional judgement and conscience 83–85
Douglas, Gillian 28, 44
Downie, Robin 74
Down's Syndrome 47, 49

ECtHR (European Court of Human Rights 59, 163n77; *Gard* 61n79, 172; Glass, David 61–62
Eekelaar, John 14, 15, 31
Elliston, Sara 174
Emergency Protection Order (EPO) 96
Equality Act 2010 71, 133n82
ethical precepts 3
European Convention on Human Rights 28
European Court of Human Rights (ECtHR) 59
Every Child Matters agenda 28, 93
experimental medicine, parental pursuit of innovative therapy 149–154

failure to seek treatment 39
Family Law Reform Act 1969 64
Finlay, Baroness 177–178
Forbat, Liz 8
Foster, Charles 87
Fovargue, Sara 155n29
Fox, Marie 107
Freeman, Michael 12, 42, 47, 48

Gard, Chris 177
Gaslini Paediatric Hospital (Genoa, Italy) 144
George, Rob 56n62
Gillick competent 97–98
Gillick, Victoria 50
Gilmore, Stephen 51
GMC (General Medical Council) 87, 89, 92; 0-18 years 89–90; *Protecting Children and Young People: the responsibilities of all doctors* 94
Goldman, Professor 150
Good Medical Practice 74, 87–92, 94
Goold, Imogen 13, 174–175
Gravett, Dr 150
Great Ormond Street Hospital (GOSH) 89, 139, 172n29; *Gard* 29n26, 159–165
Grubb, Andrew 167–168
guidance: on best interests 89–92; *Good Medical Practice* 87–92

Hale, Brenda 34
Hallett, Dr. 61
Ham, Chris 150
Harrington, John 156
Henry, Tyra 28
Herring, Jonathan 179–180
Hewson, Barbara 63
Hirano, Professor 160, 163
Hoggett, Brenda 11–12, 21, 30
hospital trusts 16
Howe, Geoffrey 27
Human Fertilisation and Embryology Act 1990 85
Human Medicines Regulations 2012 157n42
Human Rights Act 1998 13, 16
Huxtable, Richard 129

information, duty of doctors 80–81
inherent jurisdiction 57; Children Act 1989 37–38

innovative therapy 154–159; *Gard* 159–165; parental pursuit of 149–154
interests of the child 12–13; limiting life-sustaining treatment 132–139
Interim Care Order (ICO) 96
Isaiah Haastrup 13, 71, 117, 139, 143

Jackson, Louise 129
Jordan, Bill 27
judicial determination of best interests 63–67
judicial review 67–71
jurisdiction argument, *Gard* (2018) 174

Kennedy, Ian 1–3, 6, 17, 48–49; *Gillick* 51; open-heart surgery 7
Keywood, Kirsty 104, 105, 106
Kuhse, Helga 119

lack of guidance 52–57
Larcher, Vic 154, 155, 158
learning disabilities, sterilisation 100–107
leave of the court, Children Act 1989 36–37
Lee, Robert 100
legal duties of doctors 73–75; conscience 83–85; duty of care to child 75–77; duty to act in best interests of the child 77–80; Good Medical Practice 87–92; *Wyatt* 74
legislative reform 176–181
leukaemia treatment 58, 68–69, 149–151
Limitation of Treatment Bill 176
limiting life-sustaining treatment 107–111, 116–117, 132–139; appropriate treatment 144–146; changing practices 125–132; interests of the child 132–139; lack of guidance 52–57; *An NHS Trust v MB* 125, 129–132; partnerships in care 120–125; professional judgement 146–147; *R (G) v Barnet London Borough Council* (2003) 123n28; *Re B* 123; *Re C* (1990) 120–121; *Re C* (1996) 124; *Re C* (1998) 124; *Re J* (1991) 121; *Re J* (1993) 121–124; unsuccessful appeals 139–144; *Wyatt* 125–129
local authority care: limiting life-sustaining treatment 107–111; public responsibilities 95–96; vulnerable young women 97–100

Mackay, Lord 27, 29, 35, 42
Maclean, Mavis 15
Macnaughton, Jane 74
Macpherson J 67
Making Decisions to Limit Treatment in Life-Limiting and Life-Threatening Conditions in Children: A Framework for Practice 88
Martin, Norma 103
Mason, Ken 3
Masson, Judith 34, 39, 123n28
McLean, Sheila 3
medical law, nature of 1–6
medical paternalism, moving to consumerism 18–23
medical treatment, Children Act 1989 41–43
medically preferable 158
medical-technical decisions 1–2
Medicines and Healthcare Products Regulatory Agency 157
medulloblastoma 153
Mellor, Simon 70
Mental Capacity Act 2005 90, 92, 106; amendments 177
Miola, José 87
mitochondrial DNA depletion syndrome (MDDS) 139–140, 160
Montgomery, Jonathan 4–5, 18–21, 42–43, 76
Morgan, Derek 100
Morris, Anne 131n74

National Health Service Act 2006 70
National Health Service (NHS) 6–7
National Institute for Health and Care Excellence (NICE) 88
National Specialist Commissioning Team 153
nature of medical law 1–6
neonatal intensive care units, limiting life-sustaining treatment 116
Neon Roberts 22, 151, 165
new orders, Children Act 1989 35–38
NHS Trusts 37
NICE (National Institute for Health and Care Excellence) 88
non-therapeutic sterilisation 58
Nottingham, Emma 164

Index

nucleoside bypass therapy, *Gard* 160–161
Nuffield Council on Bioethics 17; *Critical care decision in fetal and neonatal medicine* 131–132

open-heart surgery 7
organ retention 8

Packman, Jean 27
parental authority: potential criminal liability and 46–49; significant harm and 174–176
parental opposition, unsuccessful appeals 139–144
parental pursuit of innovative therapy 149–154
parental responsibility 11, 77, 94; Children Act 1989 30–32
parental rights 10–11, 13–14
parental support, Children Act 1989 33–34
parental trust 7–10
parental views 66
parent/child relationships, changes in 10–15
parent/professional relationship 18
participation, duty of doctors 80–81
partnerships: Children Act 1989 34; limiting life-sustaining treatment 120–125
Parton, Nigel 15, 28, 43
paternalism, moving to consumerism 18–23
patient autonomy 19
Pearson, John 47
Permanent Standing Advisory Committee 3
permissive order 63
Perry, Martin 34
Pickard, Susan 150
Plank, David 118
Portsmouth Hospitals NHS Trust 69
potential criminal liability, parental authority and 46–49
Practice Guidance 106
procedure 155n29
professional conscience 84–85
professional judgement: conscience and 83–85; limiting life-sustaining treatment 146–147
Prohibited Steps Order (PSO) 35–36
Protecting Children and Young People: the responsibilities of all doctors 94
Proton Beam Therapy 152–153, 159, 170

public interrogation 48
public law, Children Act 1989 38–41
public responsibilities 93–95, 181; early case law 95–97; life-sustaining treatment, withholding or withdrawing 107–111; parental care that puts children at risk of harm 111–114

quality of life 120–121; limiting life-sustaining treatment 134

rationing 69
Read, Janet 48, 101, 105, 118–119, 123
reasonable bias 84
reasonable body of opinion 76
reasonable care 75
reasonableness 167–169
Regulation 167 of the Human Medicines Regulations 2012 157
relationships: doctor/adult patient relationship 18–20; parent/professional relationship 18
responsibilities for children's medical treatment 17–18; parental responsibility 11, 77, 94
retention of organs 8
rights of the child 13–14
Roberts, Neon 22
role of State in protecting children 15–17
Royal College of Paediatrics and Child Health (RCPCH) 88–89, 91–92; Framework for Good Practice 175; limiting life-sustaining treatment 109, 138; *Withholding or Withdrawing Life Saving Treatment in Children, a Framework for Practice* 125

s.8 order 56
Scroggie, Felicity 106
second opinions 82
significant harm 39; parental authority and 174–176
Singer, Peter 119
Smith, Peter 123
Smith, Roger 12
Smith, Stephen 85–86
social movements 22–23
social services 95
Specific Issue Order (SIO) 33, 35–36, 55–56, 96
spina bifida 2
standard of care 75

Standing Advisory Committee 17
Stansfield, AJ 100
State, role in protecting children 15–17
sterilisation 42, 95–96, 100–107; non-therapeutic sterilisation 58
The Story of Child B 22
support for parents, Children Act 1989 33–34

Tafida Raqeeb 17, 70–71, 117, 144–145, 177
Thomson, Michael 107
threshold of significant harm 169–176
Treatment and care towards the end of life: good practice in decision-making 88
treatment decisions of older children, *Gillick* 80–81
trust, parental trust 7–10
Turnham, Helen 158

United Kingdom Children's Cancer Study Group 150–151
United Nations Convention on the Rights of Persons with Disabilities (2007) 132
United Nations Convention on the Rights of the Child 13
unproven interventions in clinical practice 157–158

unsuccessful appeals, limiting life-sustaining treatment 139–144

variant Creutzfeldt-Jakob disease (vCJD) 155–156
Veitch, Kenneth 5–6, 20, 21
vulnerable young women, in local authority care 97–100

wards of the court, life-sustaining treatment 53–55
wardship 96: Children Act 1989 34–38; *Re D* (1976) 58; *see also* local authority care
welfare principle, Children Act 1989 32–33
Wilkinson, Dominic 116, 174n40
wise parent 65
withholding or withdrawing life-sustaining treatment 116–117; changing practices 125–132
Withholding or Withdrawing Life Saving Treatment in Children: A Framework for Practice 88, 125
World Medical Association 157n41

Yates, Connie 177
young women in local authority care 97–100